THE STORY OF THE EUROPEAN-ATLANTIC GROUP

Justin Glass

Copyright © Justin Glass 2024

No part of this publication may be reproduced, stored in a retrieval system, or transmitted in any form or by any means, electronic, mechanical, photocopying, recording, scanning, or otherwise, without the prior written permission of the author.

Table of Contents

1. SUMMARY of the period 1987 to 2012 9
2. PENSÉES AND THINKING IN THE E-AG 43
3. BEHIND THE SCENES 78
4. THE EUROPEAN-ATLANTIC GROUP JOURNALS 113
5. THE EARLY DAYS OF THE EUROPEAN-ATLANTIC GROUP 131
6. ADDENDUM 175
   President's Report of 1958 175
   Brochure For Nato Banquet 2009 181
   A Preamble from Catherine Glass 216
   The European Atlantic Group Brochure 241
   Index 246

Dedication

To the late Maria Guissipina Gussago, whose sheltering arms and advice sustained the author throughout the period of his part in this history and his wife, Catherine Glass, his greatly supportive assistant – a tribute from her appears in the Addendum.

Foreword

A FOREWORD BY THE DIRECTOR-GENERAL OF THE GROUP

In the Autumn of 1987, I was introduced to the European Atlantic Group and was a regular attendee until early noughties, by which time I was living in Somerset. I was struck at once by the passion of one of the founders, Elma Dangerfield, matched by the never tiring Director, Justin Glass, who staged thought provoking, stimulating events with speakers one rarely got to hear. Politicians, Ambassadors, Business Leaders, and others of academic and international renown. I recall a sell-out event when the America Ambassador spoke which included people eating in the gallery at the St Ermin Hotel, then the home of the EAG.

I appreciated not only the quality of speaker but also the mix of other guests from all walks of life and nationalities. It was also special because it had no political bias. Politicians from all sides of the House came together as officer holders of the EAG. I was saddened to see that after Elma's death in 2006 and Justin stepping down 15 years later after 25 years of service, that it then began to drift and by 2020 was barely functioning. It was then that Justin asked me to take on the role of Director General, which I did with some trepidation. In the years since the heyday of the EAG a plethora of discussion groups have sprouted and the market is very crowded. But never one to duck a challenge, I agreed and although a shadow of the dizzy days of last half of the last century we are today a smaller group but still attracting a high quality of speaker with a varied and interesting membership. Many groups have morphed into online Zoom events mainly or only, but for me a major part of the magic of the EAG was the human interaction with interesting people. As any business leader will tell you, the ability to adapt to changing markets is crucial to survival and we have done that in the EAG. Dinners are less formal and as the fad for doing everything remotely evaporates whilst we may never return to regular attendances of hundreds, we will be well placed to accommodate larger audiences.

David Selves

May 2024

The E-AG was a 'laboratory of ideas' with international high flyers of varied hues invariably facing a Brain's Trust of delegates with questioning acutely put. It was brain-storming valuable to those at the political coalface. From a historical perspective, it is a pity that debates were often off-the-record but the speeches on the E-AG website yield insight into the diplomacy of those times. I was glad, first as Chairman then as President, to lead this group from the front.

Sir Geoffrey Clifton Brown

June 2024

Lest we forget

Society is indeed a contract. It becomes a partnership between not only those who are living but between those who are living, those who are dead, and those who are not yet born.

- Edmund Burke (quoted in 'Politics Tomorrow', a Journal of the European-Atlantic Group)

History can be a stimulus or a burden to those who wrestle with the problems of the present. History is a good friend but a bad mistress.

- The Rt. Hon. Douglas Hurd CBE MP, Secretary of State for Northern Ireland, addressing the E-AG at the House of Commons on 24th January 1985

The E-AG tie and cuff links

THE EUROPEAN-ATLANTIC GROUP

1. SUMMARY of the period 1987 to 2012

A retrospective by B. Justin Glass, Director of the E-AG 1988 – 2012

Introduction

Those hoping for an E-AG history that delves into international politics should head straight to the cache of the speeches delivered at the E-AG and the Book Reviews. *This history is of the E-AG as seen when looking up at, and down from, its summits.*

Millennial: this paragraph has you in mind. Hard to convey now in a changed world what the E-AG accomplished from 1954 till when you were born; social media, diminishing reverence for 'august' personages, your sense of entitlement to pass judgement on greybeards, instant access to the Great of the political stage – if indeed such a mantle is merited when you can see so clearly their feet of clay – via media and demos and so forth contribute to a misunderstanding of what that aspect of 'Life At the Top' was then like at the E-AG. There are many different elites in society and the E-AG was a passport for those angling for an upward path in its own métier.

Experts and the well-informed on topics discussed at the E-AG could, in relative privacy, glean what was going on from, and voice views to, the decision-takers. They were on the podium or floor or the Top Table at dinner, where guests were graded according to protocol and ranked according to social pre-eminence – tears could be shed if a guest felt unduly downgraded – and for their potential for mutual congeniality. The delegates felt empowered to make some difference, usually an imperceptible one, to the thinking processes that ebb and flow in the circles of high politics. It allowed those at the political summit from abroad or at home to meet counterparts on a relatively informal stage and engage in friendly, verbal spats; and to hobnob with Mr Joseph Public without hoopla. In those days there was much adulation of most of the Presidents, Royalty or the grandees who graced the E-AG speaker roster and audiences. The Group began *inter alia* as a meeting ground secluded from prying eyes for visiting Senators and Congressmen and Council of Europe representatives to cosy up to one another. Its remit grew early on to encompass in subject any controversy in any area of the globe where European and American interests were at stake. Its directing brain and sinews, those of Mrs Elma Dangerfield, extrapolated from this first principle that the world, even the cosmos – given meetings on the Space race – was its oyster.

It was the biggest Group of its kind in London, possibly barring the 'Pilgrims' which focussed more on the American community, and it was the best-known. Some 150 delegates on average came monthly to a Committee Room in Parliament, frequently followed by dinner-discussions, rechristened dinner-debates in the 1990s, at a nearby hotel, usually St. Ermin's, and, in the 2000s, premier London clubs. It meant that speakers often sang twice for their supper. Grand titles, a few with dubious middle-European provenance, and guests with impressive thumbnail CVs, adorned the E-AG Guest Lists. Such was the pervasive atmosphere of swank that a Corporate Member, Hugh Stewart, recalls '…Lady Stewart asking me which branch of the family I was! I said "I don't think I'm from a direct Royal line".'

The speakers were second to none. The press came, as well as Generals, specialists, and diplomats by the score; a typical line-up at an event included several Ambassadors who, though asked to pay for their dinners might nevertheless attend, so bemused or amused were they at so brazen a request. Industrialists and academics came, though not in profusion. The time frame at a double-header event amounted to three hours' worth of discussion, not counting receptions. It was too long for catchy slogans and sound bites to bamboozle the Brains Trust of which the E-AG gallery invariably was comprised. Delegates 'had a go at' what the Speakers were on about; they in turn tended to give as good as they got.

There was a yesteryear feel, not altogether illusory, of elegance in High Places in the talk about what mattered in 'the realm'. English virtues were on display, politeness a watchword. It could seem, while rubbing shoulders with Milords galore, that guests were savouring the last exhalations of the Raj along with some of the old boys who had run the Empire. They were cut from the same mould as their predecessors, and so would cause The Hun to have second thoughts about tangling with them, but at the E-AG their human side was on display. Few cared if the ghost of 'meat and two veg' returned to haunt E-AG dinners. Justin Glass, when new to the team, was button-holed by Colonel Crawley whose name inadvertently had been omitted from the Guest List. The Colonel's mock-plaintive plea, 'But I only want a sandwich!' was not a comment on the very basic food served. The buzz of conversation about the latest international controversies was part of a mix that lulled politicos into unbending from their more public *persona*. As former Congresswoman Sue Kelly put it, '...you gentlemen want to loosen your ties, ladies kick off your shoes.' Neil Kinnock, having abbreviated in his diary the name of venue – The Jolly Group St Ermins Hotel – to Jolly Group was anything but disappointed. It was quite some 'Last Hurrah'.

Lt-Colonel James Crawley OBE, Lt-Colonel Mike Lowry MBE MC[1], Patrick Emek

The impressive details concerning those who came to the E-AG are in the monthly Delegate lists. The attention to detail fed guests the notion that the Group was professional and efficient. 'Tribal' information about publications and so forth was carried in those lists that were available to all comers and it surely played no small part in the popularity of the Group. As the Argentine Ambassador, H.E. Dr Mario Campora, wrote in 1993: 'I have been regularly attending... the E-AG. I am well acquainted with the high standards both of the speakers and of the audience'. Sir Oliver Wright wrote in 1994: 'The way subjects are important and topical, and the speakers distinguished. The way things are going in Europe and America, the Group is ever more relevant and necessary'. Sir Eldon Griffiths wrote in 2002: 'The stresses and strains in the trans-Atlantic partnership make your work at the E-AG all the more important.' There is a digest

---

[1] *The European-Atlantic Group is listed among Mr Lowry's Associations in his obituary (d.9.10.2008) in 'The Telegraph' which details some of his wartime exploits in India, Burma and Malaya as described in his book, 'Fighting Through to Kohima'.*
Neil Kinnock, former leader of the Labour party, spoke to the E-AG on February 18th 2002.

of over 30 pages of such quotes to Mr Glass. Some people dug into their pockets or those of their charities in support. Meg Allen who donated sums in excess of six figures over the years wrote in 2003 that the E-AG 'has enormous potential to enable balanced, constructive debate on world events.'

Those interested in the political history of those times should visit the E-AG cache of speech transcripts, European-Atlantic Journals or hear tape recordings of E-AG events. They say much about how we have got to where we are in international relations.

Reception

Mr Robert Tuttle, Ambassador of the United States of America, held a discussion on "The Special Relationship: The Way Forward" at the Boothroyd Room, Portcullis House, and a dinner debate at St Ermins Hotel, Caxton Street, SW1, on Friday 2 February. Chairman of House of Commons meeting was Geoffrey Clifton Brown, MP, and chairman of dinner debate was the the Baroness Hooper.

The delegates included: Lord Dykes, chairman, E-AG, foreign affairs policy team, Liberal Democrats; Mrs Maria Tuttle; Mr Dalrain Davaasambuu, Ambassador of Mongolia*; Mr Michael Eng Cheng Teo, High Commissioner for Singapore; Mr Erian Idrissov, Ambassador of Kazakhstan; Mr Jean-Louis Wolfield, Ambassador of Luxembourg*; Mr Josip Paro, Ambassador of Croatia; Dr Vahe Gabrielyan, Ambassador of Armenia; Mr Federico Mirré, Ambassador of Argentina; Mr Ricardo Varela, Ambassador of Uruguay; Mr Iztok Mirošič, Ambassador of Slovenia; Mr Jaakko Laavara, Ambassador of Finland; Mrs Mariana Durlesteanu, Ambassador of Moldova; Mr Anibal De Castro, Ambassador of the Dominican Republic; Mr Jan Winkler, Ambassador of the Czech Republic*; Dr Vladimoro P. Villata, Ambassador of El Salvador; Prince Mohammed Bin Nawaf, Ambassador of Saudi Arabia*; Mr Edmundo Urrutia, Ambassador of Guatemala*; Mr Aleksandr Mikhnevich, Ambassador of Belarus*; Mrs Pilar Sabario, Ambassador of Costa Rica*; Ms Borbála Czakó, Ambassador of Hungary; Lady Armstrong of Ilminster; Princess Helena Gagarin-Moustafian, trustee, E-AG, patron, Commonwealth Countries League; Sheikha Shenda Khazal-Amery, Middle East advisory panel, E-AG; Jacqueline, Lady Killearn; Professor Alan Lee Williams, Executive Committee, director, Atlantic Council of the UK; Sir John Osborn, executive committee, E-AG, formerly UK delegation to WEU; Lady Osborn, member of E-AG; Professor Sir Bryan Thwaites, vice-president, E-AG, formerly principal, Westfield College, University of London and Wessex Regional Health Authority*; Mr Anthony Westnedge, committee, E-AG, director, Anthony Westnedge Associates Ltd, governor, English Speaking Union, formerly chairman, Canning House; Sir Ronald Arculus, Member of E-AG, formerly Ambassador to Italy; Lady Arculus, member of E-AG; Sir Stephen Barrett, formerly Ambassador to Czechoslovakia and Poland, formerly Head British Interests Section, Iran; Professor Peter Barta, member of E-AG, author, lecturer; Professor John M. Belohlavek, London Study Centre, Florida State University*; Mr Clive Betts, MP, Labour, Sheffield and Attercliffe, Committee on the Office of the Deputy Prime Minister, Finance and Services Committee; Sir Clive Bossom, Bt, member of E-AG, formerly MP, president, Anglo-Belgium Union and Anglo-Netherlands Society, chairman, Europe Assistance Ltd; Lady Barbara Bossom, member of E-AG; Mr Graham Brady, MP, Conservative, Altrincham and Sale West, Shadow Minister for Europe; Nick Brown, MP, Minister for Work*; Mr David Chaytor, MP, Labour, Bury North, Education and Skills Select Committee, Environmental Audit Select Committee, chairman of All-Party Group for Intelligent Energy, secretary, Globe UK, the British branch of the international network of environmentalist parliamentarians*; Mr Christopher MP, Conservative, Christchurch, chairman, Conservative, Way Forward*; Ms Ann Clwyd, MP, Labour, Cynon Valley; member of the Privy Council*; Professor James Coveney, member of E-AG, Emeritus Professor of French, Bath University, formerly Nato secretariat*; The Countess Of Dartmouth, member of E-AG; Countess De Bessenyey, Member of E-AG; Mr Greg Hands, MP, Conservative, Hammersmith and Fulham, treasurer, All-Party Russia Group*; Mr Mark Hendrick, MP, Labour, Preston, secretary, All-Party Group on Romania*; Ms Sharon Hodgson, MP, Labour, Gateshead East and Washington West, Regulatory Reform Committee, Home Office*; Lady Hylton, member of E-AG; Mr Brian Jenkins, MP, Labour, Tamworth, Public Accounts Select Committee, Broadcasting Select Committee; Sir Peter Jennings, CVO, member of E-AG, formerly Serjeant-at-Arms, House of Commons; Lady Jennings, member of E-AG; Prince Mohsin Ali Khan of Hyderabad; Sir Christopher Laidlaw, member of E-AG, formerly director, Amerada Hess Corporation, director, Daimler Benz (UK), former chairman ICI, deputy chairman BP, director, Barclays, Dalgety, Redland; Mr Ralph Land, Member of E-AG, chairman, Russo-British Chamber of Commerce; Professor Sidney Mayer, Member of E-AG; Mr Steve McCabe, MP, Labour, Birmingham Hall Green, Assistant Government Whip, Home Affairs Committee; Ms Anne McIntosh, MP, Conservative, Vale of York, Shadow Minister for Children Young People and families*; Sir Michael Palliser, member of E-AG, European Movement, formerly PUS, Foreign and Commonwealth Office and head of the Diplomatic Service*; David Ruffley, MP, Conservative, Bury St Edmunds, Shadow Minister for Work and Pensions*; Mr Mark Simmonds, MP, Conservative, Boston and Skegness, Shadow Minister for International Development*; Mr Richard Spring, MP, Conservative, West Suffolk, vice-chairman, business Conservative Party*; Sir Sigmund Sternberg, member of E-AG, Mr Fred Tuckman, member of E-AG, formerly MEP; Mrs Pat Tuckman,member of E-AG; Mr Andrew Tyrie, MP, Conservative, chairman of All Parliamentary Group on Extraordinary Rendition*.

* = only attending Portcullis House meeting

Social Column in 'The Times' of February 5th 2007

The Group earned its spurs in its bid to 'inform', as per the Charity Commission's brief. Months before the first shot was fired in the Iraq War of 2003, twenty-two former U.S. Congressmen led by the Hon. Lou Frey from Florida spoke for a total of four hours. The event was chaired by Geoffrey Clifton Brown MP, and at the subsequent dinner by the Earl of Limerick, Sir Michael Burton giving the Vote of Thanks. The St Ermin's hotel catering staff was tethered to their posts until 11.30pm. The Americans spoke in accents ranging from Southern drawl to clipped East Coast precision about Saddam Hussein's iniquities, the throwing of his *bêtes noirs* to the lions and so forth, waxing almost biblical in their determination to wage war on him. Their British cousins were exhorted to do likewise. Public opinion was ill-prepared for it – a reservation shared by some, though not all, of the E-AG Top Brass, as relevant letters on file show. *The American*, 'The only newspaper published in Britain for all Americans' ran a headline article about the event:

'...it was a clear and feisty exchange between people close to the government in America and people close to the government in the UK – on particularly the controversies regarding the war on terror.'

The Group also featured in *The European*[2]. Behind the public face of the Group, books and papers followed up the range of subjects discussed. The E-AG was not a lobby group. It was independent, apolitical, and non-partisan, accountable only to its members, its record and reputation, and to no one else including the government of the day. Mr Glass once caught sight of a report by an ambassador's assistant describing the profile of the Council – a touch inaccurately – as 'like the front bench of the Conservative party in the House of Lords'. As one result, and physically on bended knee, he invited the

---

[2] *See article in later section on event in the Banqueting House with Otto von Habsberg.*

Labour MP Frank Cook onto the Committee. Frank accepted and did manful E-AG work. The formula of 'speaking truth to power!' permeated its thinking. This 'truth' was an individual, not a collegiate, totem. There were almost a thousand members, a few with personal agendas or, to be candid, bees in their bonnets. There were the eccentrics, usually amusing, who imbued the Q&A sessions with an aura of quintessential British idiosyncrasy. Dr John MacRae,  *doppelgänger* of Karl Marx with ancient, long, flowing white locks, broad forehead and animated expression, once rose majestically, magisterially, to his feet to spear a Chinese Ambassador with the shaft that, judging him by his looks, was to be epoch-changing. It transpired to be: 'WHAT DO YOU THINK OF PEACE?' His Excellency took this as pertinent, not impertinence, so gave close attention to the implied proposition. It was deducible after various circumlocutions that, taken in the round, he was, on the whole, peaceable.[3] In this, he and Michael Shrimpton, author and barrister, were not peas out of a pod: British diplomats were more scandalised even than the French Ambassador to hear of the UK's forthcoming unilateral Declaration of War on France! As for Lady Snow! No topic in her presence escaped her angst-laden if obscure slant on a fate befalling white elephants. It came to seem global, whatever it was. If speakers from far afield struggled to damp down her concern, none added fuel to her fire with more sanguinity about where their greyer mammal cousins might go to die. Such exceptions stood out among

---

[3] *Perhaps the question was not as wide of the acceptable mark as originally thought. Abba Eban, former Israeli Foreign Minister, speaking to the Group put a not dissimilar rhetorical question: '...you promise Israel a just and durable peace. ...If you are not careful you get into a philosophical argument about what is peace'. Dr MacRae was the Doctor present at the birth of Elma's daughter and lived a fairly isolated life in Scotland's Western Isles.*

the interrogative questioning, *pace* elephant (white) lovers and grim Little Englanders. Tom Curtin, Head of Corporate Communications at UK Nirex – responsible for safe disposal of radioactive nuclear waste – made no reference to such Old Faithfuls when he wrote of Sir Richard Morris' presentation to the E-AG on 22nd May 1995: 'All at Nirex were very pleased (at) such a high-level audience and we were most impressed with the depth of understanding and the level of questioning.'

The experience of seeing at close quarters those who made the news was part of this charmed circle. The Group was a setting in which observant people could learn about the characters who sometimes changed the course of history. Lord Rippon accompanied the Prime Minister, Edward Heath, when the instrument of accession to the Common Market was signed in 1972. Geoffrey Rippon's luminous, all-round intelligence, his incisive way of slicing through dross, seemed nothing if not rational. He was chairing a committee with his customary gravitas when the topic of Europe came up. His remarks flowed in consistent patterns of tone and speech. It was only when sitting close to him that the pupils of his eyes could be seen dilating as soon as his pet beliefs were touched upon. He switched in a trice from logician mode to one more akin to that of a visionary without the slightest of change of vocal inflexion.

Left: **Lord Sherfield**, **Hon Royce Frith QC**, *High Commissioner for Canada addressed the E-AG on 27.4.1995 in the St Ermins Hotel; on his right are* **Viscount Montgomery of Alamein CMG CBE** *(Chairman, E-AG) and the Ambassador of Spain. Elma Dangerfield is facing them. See Speech below and anecdote at the foot of Page 27. Photographer:* **Krishan Dutt LRPS**

Right: **Rt Hon Lord Hamilton of Epsom** *(Trustee & Chairman, E-AG),* **Sir Eldon Griffiths**, **Justin Glass**, **Sir Philip Goodhart** *(Trustee, E-AG) &* **Julia Couchman** *at the East India Club.* **Sir Eldon** *was a long-standing committee member perfectly attuned to the needs of the E-AG. He was formerly an MP who immigrated to the USA, where he ran the World Affairs Council in Orange County. He had the ear of U.S. Presidents. He spoke to the Group in the East India Club on 6.4.2011*

A student of the history of that era can get a snapshot of the big issues by casting their eyes over topics explored in the E-AG. A contemporary went one better; he had advance notice, as if the knowhow behind the programme foresaw the burning topics about to set the world by its ears. It was not just guests who derived pleasure and profit from meetings. As Neil Kinnock, the leader of the Opposition, wrote in 2002: 'Many thanks for the warm welcome which I received from the EAG people. It was, of course, a delight to meet some old friends and (I think) to make some new ones.' It was called 'the E-AG's Jeremiah streak'. A Yugoslav Ambassador was invited to speak at the Group weeks before the first shot was fired in anger in a war few knew was to engulf his country. This Cassandra-like record of the Group looked set to be marred when a French Ambassador held forth at the E-AG podium, exuding goodwill about rosy bi-lateral relations. Thorny issues were all but resolved. Nothing was going to go wrong. The debate was squib rather than fireworks. Jeremiah, no quitter, unlatched the back door to let in Cassandra. It transpired that, while speaking to the E-AG, the Ambassador's house burnt down!

President Kaunda of Zambia[4], a father of modern Africa, was hugely jovial as well as being highly educated by his missionary parents. One hardly expected to see him in a Music Hall, much less in London's Naval and Military club, treating the audience to a sing-song-along even if he was once captured on TV dancing with Mrs Thatcher.

---

[4] *President Kaunda founded the Zambian African National Congress and was the first President of independent Zambia.in 1973. He spoke to the Group on 8.6.2008.*

European-Atlantic Group Newsletter, *Page 1* – May 2009 edition

European-Atlantic Group

Volume 1, Issue 3

May 2009

Newsletter

Former President of Zambia at the E-AG

H.E. Dr Kenneth Kaunda

H.E. Dr. KENNETH KAUNDA will address the Group. A consummate player on the world stage, one no stranger to constructive controversy, this is a treat in store.

Dr Kaunda works in concert with former heads of states such as Nelson Mandela, and luminaries such as Desmond Tutu, in an official grouping that 'offers leadership and the sharing of wisdom on a range of developmental challenges facing the African continent.'. Dr Kaunda's huge efforts are concentrated *inter alia* on SOUTH AFRICA, ZIMBABWE and HIV.

Dr Kaunda's greatest achievements include founding and running the African National Congress, which as leader of the Frontline States was - with his links to Lady Thatcher and Lord Carrington - critical in ensuring white minority rule in Rhodesia and South Africa peacefully ended.

Dr Kaunda's credentials augment this tale: he was imprisoned for nationalist activities, led the militant United National Independence Party, served as a Minister in the last colonial administration of Zambia, was the country's first Prime Minister under black governance, was President of the Pan African Freedom Movement, Chairman of the Organisation of African Unity (OAU), and he finally stood down from government in Zambia after eventual multiparty elections.

Dr Kaunda has adamantly opposed any form of racial discrimination, a principle he encouraged the Liberation Movements to follow. His economic vision for Zambia and Africa is anchored in hard work, acquisition of skills, education for all and educational opportunities for women and enterprise in business development, transparent economic and political accountability allied with cooperative global trading relations with the USA, the EU, China, Russia, India, South America and Inter African Trade.

A colossal figure in his homelands, Dr Kaunda has earned the venerated Swahili Title of 'Mzee', literally 'Old Man' but its intrinsic meaning is: 'Fount of Wisdom and Knowledge, Sage of Our Future and our Shield'.

The E-AG is privileged to hear Dr. Kaunda's insider views and his stories -- he is writing his autobiography -- and to do so in the opulent setting of the Naval and Military Club.

CHANGES to Dates for your diary

18 May
Dele Ogun

8 June
Dr Kenneth Kaunda

9 November
60th Anniversary Banquet to celebrate the founding of NATO

CONTINUING THE THEME OF AFRICA....

In DELE OGUN the sights of the E-AG turn towards a rising sun. Mr Ogun is a man with a bright future in Nigeria so far as anyone can judge of these things. His plans no less than his assessments and his oratorical delivery — characterised here as penetrating, if with a fire brand at its core — will unveil pointers in the constantly shifting African political scene. *Ex Africa semper aliquid novi...* The invitation notices provide in brief his biographical credentials but the interest value of this E-AG House of Commons event promises to be more than 'Out of Africa, always something new'. Dele Ogun is one whose mission concerns all friends of Africa and the wider world.

Top: **President Kaunda** with **Sir Geoffrey Clifton Brown MP** at the Army and Navy Club with **Dr Martin Kazuka** and his granddaughter in the background.
Bottom: E-AG Chairmen and then Presidents: **Sir Ralph (later Lord) Dahrendorf, KBE, FBA** speaking on 'The New Europe' on 11.7.1991 in St. Ermin's Hotel. On his right is **The Rt. Hon. Lord Rippon of Hexham QC, PC**

In a letter of 8th June 2009, Julia Couchman, an assistant to the E-AG, wrote privately to Everett Hoffman, the author and artist, in the USA:

'…Justin insists that I entertain Dr Kenneth Kaunda – "the father of Africa", his High Commissioner and his entourage as he waits away from the guests in the Library of the IN & OUT, Nancy Astor's former home in St James's Square. "Hasn't changed much" comments Jacqueline, Lady Killearn to Justin. She stayed in the house way back then. I start with a handshake, warmly reciprocated, his hand travels up my wrist, pulls back to half mast and we share a massive squeeze.

'…The High Commissioner had been educated in Zambia and then moved to Florida University…I asked him how big the Muslim population is "Very small, very small…the main problem for Zambia is that the mines are closing." I ask him "What about the Chinese?" He's pleased with them as they have built a hospital and Zambian staff is not a problem as lots of Zambians have trained and worked in the UK.

'Dr Kaunda's talk is designed as a Conversation with Geoffrey (Now Sir Geoffrey) Clifton Brown MP leading with questions and Dr Kaunda replying. Towards the end Clifton Brown raised the problem of Aids in Africa, a very personal item for KK as his son died of Aids. After a couple of minutes, he broke into Clifton Brown's cautious beginning and tells us his wife isn't here but that he always sings a song to her wherever he goes. So we have a marvellous rendition of a love song, which peaks the scales at the end. Whow! The choir boy voice, the solid knowledge of the Bible. 'Love thy neighbour' was his text and he perambulated through that idea as a way to encourage tribal cohesion that could be rolled out as an example to all the world. Then, and he was speaking as someone who the UK placed in prison for ten years, if Independence isn't granted as in the case of Ian Smith in Rhodesia and Vorster in South Africa you have to fight, so Zambia sent arms to

Rhodesia and South Africa. In other words, he portrayed himself, not a terrorist leader, but a freedom fighter.'

At the time there was a furore over the enforced repossession of Rhodesian land by Robert Mugabe – a hate figure in the West – from their owners, white farmers whose methods brought employment and prosperity to the country. Kaunda in his answer to a question pointed out that this was simply a case of stolen land being reclaimed.

President Vytautas Landsbergis[5], revered throughout Lithuania and across the globe as the man of iron who withstood the real threat of invasion by President Gorbachev, thus paving the way for the fall of the Iron Curtain and the independence of his country, came across at the E-AG as a thinking academic, one who made his fateful choices calmly, with volatile crowds on the streets and Russian troops ready to attack, much as a lecturer ruminating on delicate questions of alternative options.[6]

The President was not at the E-AG to retell of past glories, but to warn the members, including MPS and Peers, of the dangers currently lurking on his country's borders. Did all the vim and occasional venom make any real difference to the country at large? A tall order that. No one can say for sure whether a chance, though seminal, remark or new acquaintanceship can affect the thinking that leads to action. The rivers of historical happenstance are fed by innumerable tributaries. Players in the field of international diplomacy like Lieutenant A.L Taylor, of the Royal Navy at Northwood after hearing Sir John

---

[5] *President Vytautas Landesbergis spoke three times to the Group, twice in the Houses of Parliament and once at the Oxford and Cambridge Club on 3.6.2009. See speech on the website of the Group with hard copies in the office records.*
[6] *King Hussein went one better, his delivery on 20.7.1989 so hushed that delegates strained to hear every word. His speech, and that of Prince Hassan, occasioned much debate and are on the website of the Group with hard copies in the office records.*

Goulden, KCMG, UK Permanent Representative on the North Atlantic Council, wrote in March 1998: 'For those of us so closely involved with actuality of turning policy into practice, it was a fascinating insight into future possible directions.' Or as Luc Bourgan, Defence Attaché at the French Embassy, wrote in 2000: 'The presentation given by Sir Brian Unwin on 'A View from the Heart of Europe' proved extremely constructive and informative.' Seating plans affect every guest's experience at every event as the hubbub of a hundred conversations constricts meaningful dialogue to within the range of immediate neighbours.

Mr Glass has this to say to anyone asking why make a song and dance about all this sound and fury. He was enjoying a pub dinner with some friends, and the Lithuanian barmaid, hearing that he had met Landsbergis, gave all of them meals on the house!

Vytautą Landsbergį su labai geraį pavykusia paskaita sveikina EAG grupės direktorius Justin Glass. Už jų stovi seras Dallas Bernard.
Dariaus Furmonavičiaus ir **Vygaudo Ušacko** nuotraukos

President Landsbergis, Neil College and Justin Glass at the E-AG meeting at the Oxford and Cambridge Club in 2009 in an article appearing in the Lithuanian newspaper 'Draugas'

The mantra at the E-AG was always: 'What is the way forward?' Speakers were asked to slant their discourse towards this perspective. Q&A sessions could bring this out more clearly, but three speakers at least wanted a reset of political systems in their countries.[7]

Speeches at the E-AG were mainly given by the people involved in taking the decisions. Transcripts went the rounds of institutes and think tanks. They were consulted, and included, in specialist publications. They played a part in shaping opinion, including in press reports and journals. Keen, off the record questioning at the E-AG may have prompted reconsideration of decisions. We can never know.

Oliver Young, GATT Secretary-General, spoke at the E-AG in 1978, co-panellists being Sir Geoffrey de Freitas MP, Mr Eldon Griffiths MP, Lord Layton and Mr Russell Johnstone MP. It was blandly put in the Annual Record that Mr Young 'replied most frankly to the many questions raised by Members and Guests'. Weasel words those – 'replied most frankly'! Similar understatement characterised the E-AG record when his successor at GATT, Arthur Dunkel, addressed the Group in 1991. The E-AG reportage was lofty, judicial, if in the sense of being diplomatic, prone to camouflage spiky questions and tough positions of speakers. It papered over the gap between what was said and …what was really thought. Newshounds however could throw such constraint to the winds, as in the example below:

---

[7] *Chief Ajmal Khan (Afghanistan), Bo Aung Din (Burma), and Dele Ogun (Nigeria).*

Dunkel deplores war of words

'Dialogue of deaf' at Gatt

By COLIN NARBROUGH
ECONOMICS CORRESPONDENT

IN A departure from his usual diplomatic approach, Arthur Dunkel, the head of the General Agreement on Tariffs and Trade, has launched a ferocious attack on the European Community and America for holding up trade talks that promise the world an era of dynamic growth.

Mr Dunkel, Gatt's Swiss director-general, accused Brussels and Washington of engaging in a "dialogue of the deaf" while the rest of the world stands helplessly by as the chance of economic benefit slips away.

In a speech to the European Atlantic Group at the House of Commons, Mr Dunkel urged both parties to the transatlantic dispute to put their money where their mouth was over commitments to liberalised world trade.

He said: "Let us be in no doubt, the days of passing the buck all round the globe as a means of avoiding the crucial political challenges in trade

Dunkel: ferocious attack

policies are long gone." The focus was now clearly on Washington, Brussels and the other capitals of Europe.

Gatt's ambitious Uruguay Round of talks, originally due for completion at the end of last year after four years of negotiation, have been kept alive at a technical level, thanks largely to the efforts of Mr Dunkel.

Noting that trade officials at the Gatt talks in Geneva and many of the 108 member governments were anxious to start the final phase of the Uruguay Round, Mr Dunkel said he saw no reason why there should not be "significant progress" at the technical and political levels by the summer.

Recalling Gatt reports on the Community and America, he said trade relations across the Atlantic were "bedevilled by accusations, self-righteousness, mutual misunderstanding and the inability to distinguish special-interest pleading for the general public good".

Mr Dunkel stressed the political responsibility the Community and America shared over freer trade. He said the Uruguay Round was about growth that would allow world economic improvement, protection of the environment, economic reinforcement and political reform in the emerging democracies of eastern Europe.

America, while holding up the Gatt talks, has been pressing other leading economies to give priority to faster growth and less attention to reducing inflation.

Article in 'The Times' of 16th May 1991 on the address by Arthur Dunkel to the Group in the St Ermins Hotel [8]

It neither fell to that nor this E-AG record to hash over the thorny issues. Transcripts do that job. William Burger, European Editor of *Newsweek*, spoke at the E-AG in 1993 about the EU: 'Americans are great believers in grassroots democracy and political accountability. It still looks to us that a lot of power has been placed in the hands of

---

[8] *Transcripts of the speeches by Arthur Dunkel and William Burger are on the website of the Group with hard copies in the office records.*

17 unelected officials...' Howls of execration might greet his arguments, or cheers. It would hugely protract the length of this account if it descended into that soup, or others. The E-AG objective was that all sides of all cases be put well.

The books published by 'European-Atlantic Publications Ltd' conveyed a more historical aspect of the international scene. *'My Flying Circus'*[9] by Richard Leven was a gripping account by the pilot who flew the record number of WW2 daylight bombing missions, and whose additional claim to uniqueness was that he went on to enjoy a successful career as a circus ringmaster. So far so good, but the historical relevance lay in the light shed by this Englishman who studied at the *Schule Schloss Salem*, founded by Kurt Hahn. After being forced to leave Germany, Hahn founded in 1935 the UK school of Gordonstoun. The book has a fresh perspective on a period which, in Germany particularly, still seems a source of breast-beating.

A more far-reaching revision of historical record was aired in *'Hitler and the King'*[10] by John Hall-Spencer. It depicted the part played by King Boris of Bulgaria in saving the lives of thousands of Jews by hoodwinking Hitler. Churchill's put-down of the King as a 'weak and vacillating cipher' had been the received wisdom but the E-AG helped to corroborate the views of Herr Herman Goering, Hitler's WW2 Luftwaffe chief, in his more accurate depiction of the King as 'a cunning fox'. Boris's son Simeon, King and subsequently Prime Minister of Bulgaria, expressed gratitude to the E-AG for helping expose to the light of day the truth about what went on in the drama of those days.

---

[9] *'My Flying Circus'* has since been republished by Andrew Lownie and can be ordered on Amazon.
[10] A podcast inspired by *'Hitler and the King'* came out in 2024 under the title of *'The Butterfly King'* produced by Blanchard House.

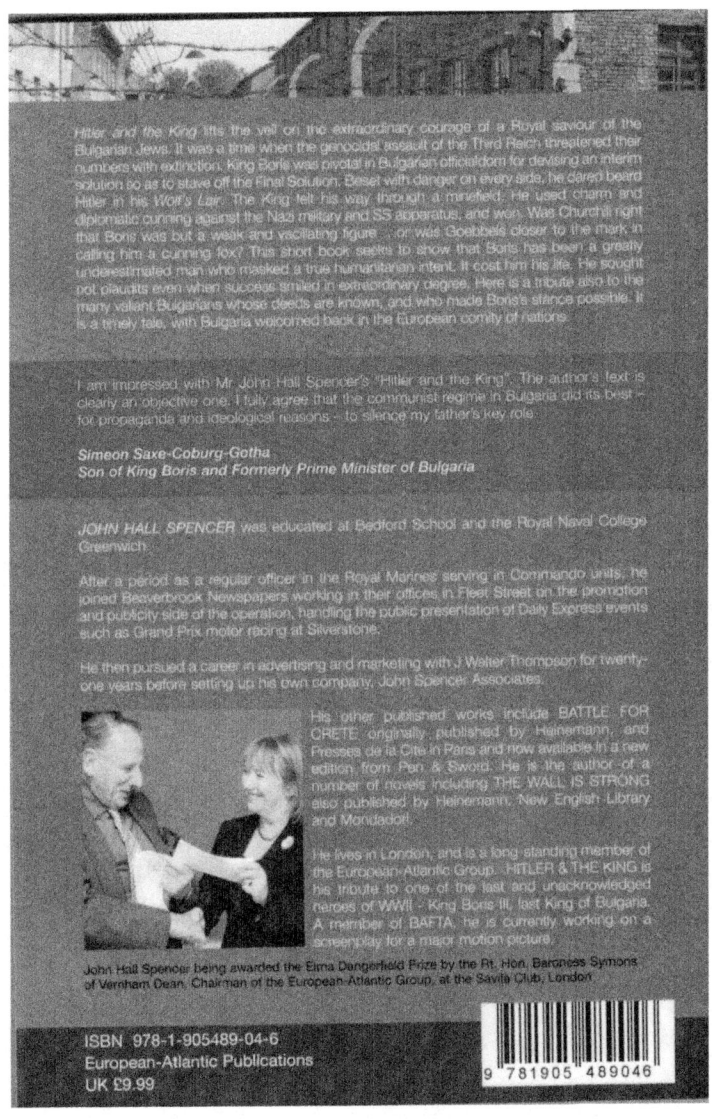

Back cover of 'Hitler and the King' by John Hall-Spencer.

The photograph (bottom left of book jacket) depicts Lady Symons, E-AG Chairman, presenting a cheque to John Hall-Spencer for winning the Elma Dangerfield Prize for literature. Political capital was made in the book's blurb: *'In a year when Bulgaria has acceded to the European Union, it is a timely reminder of the value of reintegrating these latest members of the European comity of nations.'*.

20/20 vision is a wonderful thing, but a look back at the long list of E-AG events does not convey the heat of the moment, the nature of cutting-edge controversies, at least not without the help of imagination though, true, a sense of it all is conveyed by the E-AG transcripts and Journals. Conversely, words spoken at the E-AG could come back to haunt speakers. Robert Maxwell's chief of Staff, Peter Jay, in 1987, quoted the novelist Trollope in decrying a deficiency of British culture, exemplified by the lady who 'always had the utmost difficulty in distinguishing between commerce and fraud'.[11] Sir David Gore-Booth[12] quoted the observation of a Vice-Chancellor of Hull University, Professor David Dilks – 'If we imagine that we can foresee even the broad outline of affairs five or ten years ahead we delude ourselves.' H.E. Don Felipe De La Morena, the Spanish Ambassador, was even more cautious at the E-AG in 1992: 'A diplomat must never give predictions, not even about what happened yesterday!'

---

[11] *The career of 'Captain Bob' Maxwell MC, a former MP and billionaire media mogul who bankrolled the E-AG Journal, ended in ignominy when a massive fraud was uncovered in his business dealings.*
[12] *Sir David spoke to the Group on October 25th 1999.*

Top: **HRH Prince Hassan of Jordan** addressing the Group in June 1995 at the St Ermins Hotel with **Baroness Hooper CMG**, Chairman of the Group. (See transcript of the speech and debate in the E-AG Journal, 'Politics Tomorrow' in 'Speeches' section)
Bottom: **Sir Anthony Buck** giving the Vote of Thanks in the House of Commons in January 1990 to **Peter Unwin CMG**, Deputy Secretary General (Economic) of the Commonwealth. On the right is **The Earl of Bessborough** who chaired the meeting.

The Directors knew when to use their own names, or those of others, in issuing invitations. Shenda Amery on the E-AG Ladies Committee sculpted Prince Hassan. No prizes for guessing who invited a speaker pictured above.

Prince Hassan addressed the Group twice. In a letter of 21 November 2003, Julia Couchman wrote privately to her friend Everett in the USA:

'Prince Hassan came across as a statesman. He had the overview and leadership qualities. He is not a man to fear death. That was refreshing. He was impressive. His attitude was that countries should allow themselves to be led by their majorities who were responsible and Liberal in the wider sense. The Israeli wall was also separating Liberal from Liberal. Arms would never win. Efforts had to be made to make people's countries attractive to live in.

'By chance I had the chance to walk from our meeting place, Committee Room 14, down the stairs and into St Stephen's Hall with him chatting to him on my own. I said I was glad to be with the United States. Imagine being aligned to Russia that we agreed was falling apart or China. I told him that I had walked past Winston Churchill lying in State and he said he had been there representing his country…He wasn't a tall man but his suit was superbly cut.

'(*At the dinner that took place afterwards*) Prince Hasssan must have spoken and answered questions for about two and a half hours. His range of topic was vast. He said he must have been one of the few people to have stood up to Saddam Hussein and disagreed with him to his face. He said we would be amazed if he named the people from the West who sat there allowing Saddam to say outrageous things without a contradiction. Also all states in the region owned biological weapons but only a few were prepared to admit it. He said it was a world of double standards. This was a worldwide situation not just an

Arab one. The books exposing the private affairs of the Saudi family were being avidly read by Westerners – he'd seen it in their homes. He talked of a sign he'd seen outside a Christian church: "We are all hypocrites here". He made a little light-hearted joke to the effect that "There is always room for one more". In a worst-case scenario, the Arabs would blow up the Israelis and the Israelis would blow up the Arabs and when we opened our eyes, we would find ourselves in Pakistan! His talk was leavened with humour and the British like that. The whole evening was unusual in that no one adversely criticised him afterwards. I think that is because he is a man of courage. (Behind the scenes, the Palace, the Prince's office and Scotland Yard had been trying to stop him from coming to us – our argument was that if he didn't turn up, he would weaken his viewpoint and his case.) What a day!'

The shape of things to come, however, could be descried on a good night at the European-Atlantic Group. The press article below is an instance of the E-AG being put on notice of developments in train. The 'Rapid Reaction Force' is part of the toolbox of the international community, but t'was not ever thus.[13]

---

[13] *Mr de Cuellar's speech is on the website of the Group with hard copies in the office records, as is Dr Segell's article referring to the Rapid Reaction Force.*

JANES DEFENCE WEEKLY - 26ᵗʰ February 1994

Call for reaction force

UNITED NATIONS

The United Nations should have a Rapid Reaction Force of peacemakers on instant readiness, former UN Secretary-General Javier Perez de Cuellar *(above)* said last week.

"In time of crisis, the sooner the UN intervenes, the easier it will be to avert a crisis," he told the European-Atlantic Group in London.

Ambassador Perez de Cuellar cited Bosnia and Somalia as examples of where the UN should have been mandated to react immediately. He said it was unrealistic for troops to undertake peacekeeping when "the seeds of renewed conflict are present.

"We have already seen the move from simply monitoring towards peace enforcement," he said. "It started in Cambodia, was successful, and now is needed in Bosnia.

"But there is no just solution to that war (Bosnia) and no solution will be long lasting. In any case, I do not want to see UNPROFOR troops becoming forces of repression."

Many a speaker was glad of the chance of an E-AG rostrum when singled out for preferment by a Group with so august a letterhead. A look at the E-AG letterhead instilled the notion into those asked to speak at the E-AG and those invited to attend events that this was a special invitation. Elma knew about Brand Image long before the term was fashionable. An entire column on the left-hand side of Group notepaper and its masthead were replete with names that bespoke power in the land. Once ensconced on that imposing paper, the halt or lame, the retired or even the deceased rarely defied Elma's wishes that they remain *in situ*. Lord Montgomery grumbled that the *nomenklatura* was proof even against the sting of death. This was not quite fair. Vice-Presidents were asked annually for their consent to stay put and, if there was demurral or silence from the grave, then delay in re-printing the letterhead played its loyal part in keeping ermined shoulders to the public weal of the E-AG.

THE EUROPEAN-ATLANTIC GROUP

6, GERTRUDE STREET, CHELSEA, LONDON SW10 0JN
WWW.EAG.ORG.UK
Tel and fax: 020-7352-1226
E-Mail: info@eag.org.uk

COUNCIL
President
THE EARL OF LIMERICK KBE

Vice-Presidents

The Rt. Hon. Sir Frederic Bennett DL
President, Anglo-Turkish Society
Baron Steven Bentinck
President, Adolphe Bentinck Prize
The Rt. Hon. Lord Carrington KG GCMG CH MC
The Rt. Hon. Lord Chalfont OBE MC
President, House of Lords Defence Group
David Colvin CMG
Chairman, British-Italian Society
The Lord Dahrendorf KBE FBA
Sir Timothy Daunt KCMG
Chairman, Anglo-Turkish Society
Hugh Dykes
Vice President, London Europe Society
The Lord Ezra MBE
Sir Patrick Fairweather KCMG
Sir John Fretwell GCMG
Chairman, Franco-British Society
Sir Eldon Griffiths
Chairman, World Affairs Councils of America
The Rt. Hon. Earl Jellicoe KBE DSO MC FRS
Lord Judd
Sir David Miers KBE CMG
Chairman, Anglo-Hellenic League
The Viscount Montgomery of Alamein CMG CBE
President, Anglo-Belgian Society
David Pownall
Derek Prag
President, London Europe Society
The Rt. Hon. Lord Slynn of Hadley
President, Atlantic 2000
President, Luxembourg Society
Sir Roger Tomkys KCMG
The Lord Watson of Richmond CBE
President, British-German Association
Chairman, English Speaking Union
Roger Westbrook CMG
Chairman, Anglo-Portuguese Society
Alan Lee Williams OBE
President, Atlantic Treaty Association
Sir Andrew Wood GCMG
Chairman, Britain Russia Centre
Professor Robert M. Worcester
Chairman, The Pilgrims

* Founder Members

Registered Charity No 274898

COMMITTEE
Chairman
SIR MICHAEL BURTON KCVO CMG

Vice-Chairmen

Geoffrey Clifton Brown MP
The Rt. Hon. Menzies Campbell CBE QC MP
The Rt Hon Lord Radice

Committee

*The Lord Abinger
Colin Baker
The Rt. Hon. Lord Blaker KCMG
Frank Cook MP
Sir Robin Fearn KCMG
David Griffiths TD
Dr Uwe Kitzinger CBE
Sir Peter Marshall KCMG
Mrs Valerie Mitchell OBE

Robert Newell LVO
Sir John Osborn
Admiral of the Fleet Sir
Julian Oswald GCB
Hon Edward Streator
Christopher Robson
Sir Neville Trotter
Lord Temple-Morris

Hon Treasurers

The Lord Layton
Harold Sands

Geoffrey Smith FCCA

Directors

*Mrs Elma Dangerfield CBE
Hon Director

Justin Glass
Financial Director

THE OBJECTIVES AND ACTIVITIES OF THE GROUP

The European-Atlantic Group was founded in London in 1954 by the late Lord Layton (then Vice-President of the Council of Europe) together with other Members of both Houses of Parliament, Industrialists, Bankers, Economists and Journalists. Its main object is to promote closer relations between European and Atlantic countries by providing a regular forum in Britain for informed discussion of their problems and possibilities for better economic, strategic and political co-operation with each other and with the rest of the world.

The Purpose of the Founders was to disseminate authoritative information concerning the work of International Organisations such as the Council of Europe, the North Atlantic Treaty Organisation, the Organisation for Economic Co-operation and Development, the European Union, the World Trade Organisation, and the Organisation for European Security and Co-operation. It has been addressed by leading Representatives of all these Organisations.

In addition to holding monthly Dinners and Meetings in London, the Group has sent many Delegations abroad to study at first hand the European and NATO institutions in Brussels, Paris, Luxembourg, as well as visiting Germany, Italy, Turkey and Greece as the Guests of Governments and International Organisations. Group Representatives have also visited the United States, Russia and Central European countries with the object of improving relations between the West and East.

The Group has also held Discussions on European-Atlantic relations with the rest of the world, including the Middle and Far East, Africa and Latin America, with distinguished Speakers from many countries.

It may be deemed strange by aficionados of the E-AG that this account of its history has reached this point without closer attention to the founder, Elma Dangerfield CBE, 'the most formidable lady in London' according to the financier, Peter Oppenheimer.

Peter Oppenheimer speaking to the Group on 21st November 1988.

Elma Dangerfield CBE

Elma Dangerfield did not spring into the group 'fully formed' without already having chalked up major achievements[14]. She stood as a Liberal for Parliament but had more success in running the political magazine 'Whitehall News'. She was largely responsible though without due international recognition with the Red Duchess for alerting the world to the Katyn massacre of Polish officers by the Russians. The UK Foreign Office had wanted to keep wraps over the story in the interests of not tarnishing the reputation of Britain's wartime allies.

Elma Dangerfield could put the fear of damnation into the heart of man a foot and a half taller than her, and a great many were. Called a 'Pocket Thatcher', a comment on her personality not her politics, which were Liberal, Elma was a force of nature. To know how the British Empire with so few people, relatively speaking, controlled a third of the globe, one could do worse that to behold her in action. This was a quintessential English memsahib, born to command, and who refined that breeding throughout her life. Not a moment to waste, Elma had a toilet bowl installed in her bedroom. Not a moment to waste in front of the mirror, Elma heaped coals on the head of the Duchess of Argyll who, if Elma was to be believed, bestowed on mirrors rather more than a modicum of scrutiny. It was 'Do this!' imperiously, and 'Do that!' to friends and especially foes. At the age of 92 Elma was still spending every night on the tiles in town. Utterly determined, tough as old rope, totally self-assured, certain of her place at the centre of the E-AG and of its central place in the world, Elma let fly her brickbats in all directions. Little imagination would be required to envisage Jove himself ducking such a missile had she

---

[14] *Aspects of the biography of Elma Dangerfield prior to her E-AG days are on the Group website. This includes correspondence with her Royal connections and extracts from 'MI6: FIFTY YEARS OF SPECIAL OPERATIONS' by Stephen Dorril (published by 4th Estate; ISBN1-85702-093-6) which goes into the above story.*

blasted one in his direction! They came, they took it on the chin, and they fawned (the vast majority, that is, though Mrs Dangerfield would have couched it differently). "DON'T put it in brackets! If you have something to say, say it!"

The following story is not merely apocryphal. Sheikh Yamani, the Saudi who controlled OPEC, the oil cartel, and effectively silted up European roads with queues at garages in the early 1970s with his oil price hike, had real power. He was invited to speak to the Group, a favour conferred on him by Mrs Dangerfield. Elma was doubtless upset with OPEC because it threatened to curtail her scurrying about town, notwithstanding the words of Her Majesty's leader of the Opposition, the Rt. Hon. Michael Foot, that 'Elma is the most lethal driver in England!'[15] The date was set, the notices sent, and all awaited in awe the arrival of the mighty man. Except Mrs Dangerfield. This did not mean that our diva set little store by the invitation, as Yamani soon discovered. He telephoned to cancel the engagement with sincere apologies. That, at least, was his intention at the start of the diatribe that threatened to perforate his eardrum:

'YOU WILL COME TO THE GROUP.... IF YOU DO NOT COME IT WILL BE AN INSULT TO THIS COUNTRY!' The register of Elma's tone descended to the sepulchral when she reached the climax with her deadly point: 'And the Palace will have to be told!'

No fool, Sheikh Yamani; he came, and he fawned. His impudence was forgiven, but not forgotten. Elma's regal demeanour was tempered with graciousness. It was evident that the Duke of

---

[15] *This may be seen as an illustration of Randolph Churchill's dictum: 'All Great Men make mistakes.' Was Michael Foot right in his assessment? Olivia Forrest-Miquel, a biology lecturer who enjoyed the world of the E-AG, once remarked to Catherine Glass, the wife of the Director: "Until I'd been in a car as a passenger of yours, I'd never really known Fear!"*

Edinburgh, when asked who qualified to be in the enclosure at the top of the dais, understood the E-AG pecking order. He replied, 'You have to know Mrs Dangerfield!'

The past mattered not, it was the present that counted, and how to shape it into its proper design, that is to say in her image. The envelope of every letter from her was marked 'Personal! First Class! Urgent!'; her assistant, Rosemary, was despatched to the post office several times a day. Lord Judd, a former Labour Minister, never forgot being summoned to the telephone from a ski slope while on holiday in Switzerland, only to be asked by Elma about a seating position on the top table for an event the following week. Elma always knew better than everyone, and everyone nearly always knew better than to disagree. Elma got things done. Elma went out to bat for her people. It was part of the order of things. Wary cronies, deeply respectful Parliamentarians, cowed traffic wardens, it was all the same. Elma would descend on country houses to visit friends like the Earl of Bessborough or Lady Killearn, often with her cat Poppety-Pooh in tow. And a host of weekend guests would be called from their recreations to hunt for Poppety when she disappeared into the long grass.

Poppety P. Dangerfield with **Elma** in a rare sculpture pose.

Always ready with a purposive question at E-AG meetings in Parliament and often at the St Ermin's hotel *(see photo below)*, Elma's words were invariably heeded, not least because of the sharply plum accent in which they were couched.

Elma's spirit infused the Group even after her active period was over. Her mid-nineties finally saw her retire to her bed, from which she hardly moved for about two years, her encyclicals dwindling to a faint trickle until the end came almost on the very day that her bank balance reached 'nul points'. Her successor, Justin Glass, whose 26 years as Director included the decade following her demise, quaffed deep her lessons, her example and her formulas. The letterhead was continuously replenished by Properly Placed People in whose names and to whose contacts, and subsequently also to his own, invitations went forth. Former Presidents came, each seeing he was among coevals.

There was only one person throughout the decades who Justin recalls declining an invitation to speak to the E-AG: Kenneth Clarke, the Chancellor of the Exchequer. He did host the Byron Society, Elma's other society, at 11 Downing Street. Justin remarked to him there that the refurbished Locarno Room looked magnificent and he replied, "All we need now is an Empire to go with it!"

Above: **Maureen O'Connor**, Secretary then Director after Elma of the Byron Society; **Christine Symeonides**, widow of Simon, proprietor of 'The Byron Taverna'; **Alexander Bryett**, 'the Maestro' of 'Opera Italiana'; **Patricia Ellison**, whose late husband was Astronomer Royal and who lived in a Grace & Favour house in Buckingham Palace – her daughter, **Rose**, was the violinist at the 30th Anniversary celebration of the E-AG – and **Mary Melville**, Elma's assistant and the daughter of a former Solicitor-General.

Each month, without exception during Elma's hospitalisation at the grand old age of 98, followed by her funeral in 2006, the procession of speakers continued unabated: David Blunkett, former Home Secretary, the Earl of Onslow, Sir Ronald Cohen who built a shopping mall in Gaza that was blown up by terrorists, the French Ambassador,

Cardinal Murphy O'Connor, Lord Radice and so on, as if by decree of Elma from beyond the grave. Justin's determination to uphold the principles deeply instilled in him during his years at the feet of this most imperious of Mistresses once culminated in an awful moment after Manfred Wörner, the Secretary-General of NATO, accepted an invitation to address the E-AG's celebration of the Fiftieth Anniversary of the founding of NATO. Over 500 prominent guests had booked to come to Guildhall when Herr Wörner, the man who was to hold the line of Europe against an attack by the Russians, rang the E-AG to apologise that he was unable to come. He could not be the Guest of Honour when Germany was just about to opt out of NATO. It was child's play for him to fob off a European-Atlantic Group Director and no amount of larding with a perfunctory regret at this 11th hour withdrawal from the event could mask a crisis staring the Group in the face. '*Hamlet* – without the King' was a doddle in comparison. There followed a Pavlovian moment as Mr Glass's training kicked in:

'But you HAVE to come! …If you do not come, it will be seen as an insult to this country! And …Oh my goodness! The Palace must be told!'

The formula worked its black magic. English manhood was given no cause to blush. Buckingham Palace escaped by a whisker the convulsion that must have ensued at Herr Wörner's snub. The NATO Secretary-General came to Guildhall and, in the event, hardly a British grandee, save Prince Philip, would so much as speak to him.

Above: **HRH the Duke of Edinburgh**, the **Secretary-General of NATO**, **Justin Glass**, and the **Earl of Bessborough**

© Copyright April 2020 All Rights Reserved – J. Glass. justinglass2020@gmail.com

2. *PENSÉES* AND THINKING IN THE E-AG

With a soupçon of drama and a sprinkling of humour

A French Ambassador, Daniel Bernard, cautioned the Group in June 2002 that: 'We run two risks when we talk about Euro-Atlantic relations: that of wallowing in platitudes, or luxuriating in grandiloquence.' This point might have been made of the European-Atlantic Group story. Old-style reportage of the early days teeters on the brink of the former trap; incomers of later decades were sucked into the latter. A less deferential social order might cock a snook at it but, then, one either went along with it and in good part, or left. This boat was not for rocking.

Sir Patrick Mayhew, Secretary of State for Northern Ireland, defined the main purpose of the Group on 10th March 1994 as being 'to promote closer relations between the European and Atlantic counties especially by providing a regular forum for informed discussion of problems and possibilities for better co-operation'....

All so true but running the organisation was '98% perspiration, 2% immersion in the subject'. A comparable gum, though more poisonous, constricted Congressmen during the global financial 'meltdown' to go by the fact that their representatives spent most of the time allotted for discussion at the E-AG in reviewing their office's backstabbing.

A reader wanted detail on Afghanistan: 'Countless lives and 7 trillion dollars lost'; and on Sir Frank Roberts[16]*, who was 'instrumental in the*

---

[16] *A Review by Sir Curtis Keeble of Sir Frank Roberts's book, 'Dealing with Dictators', is in on the website of the Group with hard copies in the office records*

mindset reconstruction of post-War Germany': Assessments – in this tale of the Group – can be controversial; brief phrases however true also are often inadequate. The E-AG project on Afghanistan is in the Speeches section. Sir Frank in his book 'Dealing with Dictators' told the story of Khrushchev saying 'I am a bear!' when bodily picking up a British Ambassador. Sir Curtis Keeble said that the book 'offers the condiment that brings out the flavour of history'. It is an approach taken in these pages.

A facet of the successes of the E-AG was that it was social, fun even; politicians felt at ease. After a gala, personal memories remain. This story is of how it all was got together and what was learned at its events. Penseés are everywhere to be found in speeches and extempore comments at the E-AG. Some actuating ideas of Speakers and their philosophy filters through their anecdotes, observations and personalities. It serves to remind that it is human beings who take the key decisions. Quarrying for such insight into Affairs of State is a subjective exercise but there is reward according to taste in essaying such a Lucky Dip…

***

By way of a 'PS', a 'postscript' that is more 'pre-scriptum', this is what the Countess of Munster, an eminent rheumatologist, wrote on seeing a draft of this E-AG history:

'…I read your manuscript with great interest and affection. It is very well written and I have learned a lot about the early days of the E-AG …I would welcome mention of the Polish Ambassador, the late Stanislaw Komorowski, who gave a very good speech to E-AG. He

---

& Book Reviews section, as are book reviews by Sir Frank Roberts, and one of his speeches to the E-AG.

was a distinguished academic, who joined the diplomatic service as an ambassador at the time of Poland's accession to NATO and then to EU in 2004. (Also) Would Jas Pomian, the loyal secretary to Joseph Retinger, be worth mentioning?...'

All so true! The Ambassador's words to the E-AG are included in the Speeches section. Of Mr Pomian, be it said that Mrs Dangerfield had a soft spot for the quick-minded and warm-hearted 'Pom', a renaissance man whose cultivation embraced the arts world as well as politics and who was at one time canvassed as a possible E-AG Director. Pom wrote the biography of Joseph Retinger, an Eminence Grise – a footnote in history whereas his true contribution may well merit a greater weight. Such is the fate of many movers and shakers in the shadows. If this can be said of the E-AG, its job will have been well done.

***

A loud crash sufficient to 'throw' Michael Portillo[17] when reaching a climactic point in his speech occurred when the gentleman taking round the microphone, actor and screenwriter Michael Wade, accidently dislodged a painting from the wall. Portillo, quick as a flash, hit his oratorical peak with cod sympathy for Mr Wade:[18] 'I never liked

---

[17] *The Rt. Hon. Michael Portillo, Secretary of State for Defence, speaking to the E-AG on 21.11.1996.*

[18] *Michael Wade is the editor of this E-AG History as well as of books and screenplays. In his lecture to the English Speaking Union on the English language, he referred to one of his '...Great Displeasures (as the lecture was) ...a lament or, if you prefer, a light-hearted rant about the grievous assault on English grammar and syntax that pervades our airwaves.' Among many other credits his hour-long recitation, 'Cardinal Newman: The Second Spring', was given at the Vatican, Westminster Cathedral and the Brompton Oratory. (mikewade416@hotmail.com)*

that picture!' Cue laughter! Leon Brittan[19], told of the Chatham House rule banning quotes being attributed to them in the Off-the-Record section, approved this caution: 'I prefer it that way. What I say is more sure of being reported!' Cue laughter! On occasion absence of quicksilver *repartee* was a bolt that shot home. The wife of the Director, Catherine Glass, her arm in a plaster cast, would constantly tell of a minor accident that had caused it, an account that staled by repetition. "Can't you vary that story!" Justin admonished, 'Say anything, even being bitten by a crocodile would be better!' So Catherine knew what to tell President Kaunda on his asking her, 'Oh my dear, how did it happen?' Duly informed of the reptilian munch by a dutiful wife, Kaunda palpably relaxed, and his po-faced comment, 'Ah, yes!' was as if to say: 'Ten a penny, crocs in downtown Lusaka!'

Carolyn Chamberlain, who recalls being downgraded from Table C to Table F on Elma telling her that 'the wife of the Ukrainian Ambassador has unexpectedly come and of course we can't have her on Table F' more fondly remembers Sir Julian Oswald talking of King George VI and the Queen visiting a coastal town in WW2 knocking at the door of the one house left standing in a bombed out street to offer royal sympathies and being told by a girl of about six squinting at his Admiralty uniform and regalia: 'Mum's out but she said that if a sailor and his girlfriend come, tell them it's sixpence in the back room for half an hour!'

---

[19] *The Rt. Hon. Sir Leon Brittan, PC, QC, Vice-President, Commission of the European Communities, spoke to the Group at a Luncheon Discussion on 6.11.1992. His apparently cavalier attitude to reportage did not extend to inaccuracies; his office wrote on 16.11.1992 to correct a quotation in a Reuters note submitted to the E-AG for checking, Sir Leon not having said that "John Major is wrong and Martin Bangeman is right." but the reverse.*

Of course, it tended to be more serious than that. Abba Eban[20] regaled the E-AG with his exchange when Foreign Minister of Israel and the Russian Ambassador saw him in Tel Aviv to break off diplomatic relations: 'But Mr Ambassador, there is trouble between our two countries. That is when our being able to talk matters most. If all is rosy, there is just the usual round of diplomatic cocktail parties!'

The Russian reaction said it all:

'What you say, Mr Foreign Minister, is perfectly logical. But I have not come here to be logical. I have come here to break off diplomatic relations!'

Many a true word in what was not jest. The exchange was worthy of a thought of Sir Bryan Cartledge[21]:

'They (the Russians) have no tradition of debate and their idea of winning an argument is to shatter their opponent beyond the capacity to respond.'

Sir Bryan spoke approvingly of a way of life, now seemingly under threat that typified British attitudes. It was a guiding line for the E-AG:

'We need able people who know how to live with an opponent. Certainly not people who, whether in defence of left or right positions, crave at least to crush an opponent, to drive him from the platform.'

---

[20] *Abba Eban, Former Foreign Minister of Israel, spoke to the Group on 4.3.1985. His speech is in the Speeches section.*
[21] *Sir Bryan Cartledge KCMG, Ambassador to the Soviet Union, spoke at the E-AG on 20,2,1989. His speech is on the website of the Group with hard copies in the office records, as is that of Daniel Bernard, mentioned at the start of this Section, and that of Mr Peres.*

Shimon Peres[22] explained how he dealt with an opposing party in a confrontation:

'The art of negotiation is that of making partners.'

There arguably is a natural fellowship among notables. Shimon Peres recounted to the Group his first greeting to the Prime Minister of Indonesia, a country with more than 700 languages: 'How are you getting on in your Tower of Babel?'[23] Group Captain John Constable, of the Central Criminal Court, wrote in 1997: 'Your meticulous arrangements ensured that Shimon Peres had a superb platform for his magisterial address. It was a very inspiring evening and I sensed that everyone rose to him and to the occasion.'

Chief Anyaoko, the Commonwealth Secretary-General, went one better in 1993 than the *pensèes* or aphorisms to which the E-AG was regularly treated. He may have coined the term 'Intermestic issues': domestic incidents – like fratricidal murders in Ireland or secessionist uprisings in Russia – that acquire international ramifications.

This history would be longer than all the transcripts were it to encapsulate them so a few examples must suffice.

Lord Dykes, E-AG Chairman, introduced General Sir Mike Jackson[24] by reference to events of 1999 in Bosnia:

'General Sir Mike Jackson refused to block the Russian-occupied (airport) runway. as British troops (could) have come into armed

---

[22] *The Hon. Shimon Peres MK, former Prime Minister of Israel, speaking to the E-AG on 2.12.1997.*
[23] *In Genesis, dwellers in a tower to Heaven babbled in so many tongues they did not understand each other.*
[24] *General Sir Michael Jackson GCB CBE DSO ADC spoke to the Group at the Naval and Military Club on 26.2.2008.*

conflict with them. ...Defying orders from the Commander, Wesley Clarke...could have led to his dismissal...and...the beginning of World War 111. We say thanks...to him for (his) wisdom...'

Clearly, this was no gentleman of ordinary human clay about to address the E-AG. General Sir Mike began by making political capital out of the 'unusually decisive actions' taken by the 1000 military fielded by the British in Sierra Leone in 2000.

'Whether we like it or not, it was not until 1996 and the eventual decision by the United States to apply its political will backed up by its military power, that we got an end to the Bosnian war ... the UN force of 17,500 soldiers seemed incapable of stopping the obscene brutality.'

Events were made both graphic and explicable by Sir Mike's illustrations. Authentic breath from between Stiff Upper Lips was exhaled. His time-honoured Brit attitude sheds light on how much can depend on the man on the ground. The E-AG was told how his son, Captain Mark Jackson, comported himself when detailed to check on the safety of the British High Commissioner:

Mark went to the home of the British High Commission to ensure that the great man was well. 'Leave it to me boss', said his demolitions expert, 'I'll get that door down, ten seconds and I'm done.'

'Well perhaps it wouldn't be quite smart to blow down the door at the British High Commission!' replied Mark. 'Why don't you give it a push?'

The door simply swung open. It was the prelude to an exchange worthy of the pages of G.A. Henty:

'Captain Mark Jackson, Sir, here, of the British Army, to make sure you're okay.'

'My dear boy, I knew you'd make it. Would you like a drink?'

'Well, I would!'

Lady Symons took up Sir Mike's story in recounting her conversation with a squaddie at the time about the regulation rifle:

'It's really good, really, really, really good. It's got really good aim. We never miss. When we use this rifle and have the target in sight, I shall never miss!'

'I thought "This is great. Completely different from what everyone else is saying."'

A formidable weapon – unless it was used, as the soldier explained:

'Only trouble, Ma'am, fucking trigger falls off!'

General Sir Mike had interceded with 'I am appalled, Sir!' but confessed to the E-AG it was 'the use of the vernacular that had thrown me', not the speaking of truth to power, of which he approved. It is by such minutiae that light is shed on political as well as military goings-on. People of flesh and blood take real decisions in the heat of the moment when in the heat of the kitchen. It was a leitmotif of the E-AG to show how situations looked from the perspective of those who were taking the decisions. Sir Stephen Wall KCMG LVO[25] put this almost in so many words at the E-AG:

---

[25] *Sir Stephen Wall KCMG LVO UK, Permanent Representative to the EU, speaking to the Group on 12.2.1998. His speech is on the website of the Group with hard copies in the office records.*

'It must be a salutary exercise for any politician, as it is for any bureaucrat, to ask oneself the question: "What would I have done if it had been my responsibility to decide or to advise?" on any of the great issues of the day.'

The Director was pulled up short when, his heart prompting his head, he put to Douglas Hurd, the Foreign Secretary of the day, the concern about the hardship faced by the Vietnamese Boat People; Her Majesty's Government was cracking down on helping them. Mr Hurd had been affability itself till the moment of the question but then turned on his heel abruptly signalling the end of the conversation. In the light of the subsequent issue about boats of immigrants illegally crossing the channel it becomes easier to see what was forcing Mr Hurd's hand. He referred in the course of the evening to the many little worries that beset the mind of a Minister every day at the periphery of what needed to be done; one had little option but to keep them out of the clear focus.

High-ranking former soldiers like Lord Chalfont, a leading E-AG light for many years, or General Lord Richards[26], whose eulogy of Chief Ajmal Khan alas is debarred from quoting because of the Chatham House rule (*pace* Leon Brittan), were penetrating. Sir David Richards, as he then was, regretted the passing of the class once common of 'soldier-diplomats'. Asked from the floor if it would ever be possible to eradicate terrorism, General Lord Guthrie replied:

'The realistic goal is less to eradicate terrorism than to drive it down!'

---

[26] *Sir David, now Lord, Richards spoke to E-AG in February 2009; his speech is on the website of the Group with hard copies in the office records, which includes a paper put out by the Group.*

A thought from J.M.A.H. Luns writing in the European-Atlantic Review (see below) in 1959 was as relevant to the E-AG of 40 years later as when penned:[27]

'The human mind has the unfortunate but natural tendency little by little to relax and to become less aware of dangers that have been threatening for a long time without materializing. If NATO is to remain strong and effective it cannot afford the luxury to draw, as it were, a cheque on the alluring era of peace and prosperity which our technical achievements seem to make possible.'

Philosophical reflection was imparted at the E-AG as well as political thinking.

President Trump's alleged volatility may have its uses? His critics may care to remember General Galvin, Supreme Allied Commander, speaking on the Cold War (the following quote being from memory):

'It may be thought that the US is too docile in the face of Russian belligerence. But when you have two sides in a stand-off both of which are volatile and unreasonable, the result can be combustion. When one side has that approach, the other side has to be more than reasonable.'

The Supreme Allied commander at the E-AG quoted (of all sources!) the cartoon character, Yogi Bear: 'A thing ain't over until it's over!' To be fair, he also cited Napoleon: 'In the battle the will to win is to everything else as three to one.'

---

[27] *J.M.A.H. Luns, Foreign Minister of the Netherlands and President of the North Atlantic Council.*

How true today is the concern aired by Lord Carrington KG CH KCMG MC when Secretary-General of NATO and speaking to the Group about NATO in 1985[28]:

'I never fail to be struck how quickly the issues change…it projects an image of the Alliance as sixteen nations in search of a crisis…senior decision-making bodies of the Alliance, spend too much time handling the problem of the present, and too little on the questions which may be of the greatest significance for the longer term. And by that I mean not only the issues of tomorrow; but also some of the issues of yesterday, which do not lose their importance as quickly as they seem to lose their fashionability.'

In the same year at the E-AG, Klaus Sahlgren, the Executive Secretary of the UN Economic Commission for Europe, saw fit to quote a *pensée* of Myrdal[29] from 1947:

'I suggest that the message holds true even today…Confidence does not as a rule trickle down from the mountain-tops of theory. It must start at the bottom – in the realm of practical things.'

Luddites can take note that Klaus Sahlgen pointed out that 'There is much evidence to show that technological change is not the cause of long-run unemployment. Indeed, there is much evidence to the contrary, especially if we look at what has happened in the electronics and computer fields.' *Plus ça change!*

President Tan Mathathir of Malaysia, with energised intelligence that seemed to pulsate from his immaculate and slight person, talked casually of the pressure that his country had been under from the

---

[28] *His speech is in the Speeches section.*
[29] *Karl Gunnar Myrdal was a Swedish economist and sociologist. In 1974, he received the Nobel Memorial Prize in Economic Sciences with Friedrich Hayek.*

World Bank demanding austerity in order to service Malaysia's crippling debts:

'I was sitting round the table with my Cabinet and we thought about it and we said "No! We are just not going to do that. We are going to spend our way out of this."'

The guts it took to think this, say it, and then go on to implement it!

The former President, often credited with the turn-around of Malaysia from the Sick Man of Asia to a Tiger Economy, was quizzed about his human rights record. With a disarming smile, the President spoke of the strong-arm men in his cabinet:

'When a man comes up to you with a gun, it is difficult to say "No"'.[30]

Above: **President Tan Mathathir** at the E-AG in the Grand Committee Room in 2010 with the **Director**

It comes down to a perspective; what for instance would former hippies make of this 'tough guy'? At the fag end of the Hippy Trail, south East Asia was known as a land of lovely girls whose easy virtue, acquiescence to whims of Westerners, and appetite for their dollars,

---

[30] *The former Malaysian President was introduced by Kevin Cahill, author of 'Who Owns What in the UK'.*

was fabled. Tan Mathatir recollected how unattainable, he felt, was any nubile girl of his salad days. He had to pluck up all his courage even to speak to one of them. A man of flesh and iron!

Time and again, the question came up of whether the image in the press fitted that of the man at the podium. The beam suffusing President Nyerere's face as he handed out gold medals from his Foundation seemed to give the lie to a view of some critics that *au fond* a ruthless streak actuated him. Time and again, the best orators were the entertainers. American speakers were genial, even fun, taking people into their confidence, softening them, rather than 'softening them up'. Raymond Seitz[31] described his meal at an English pub, lured in by a sign that read, 'Eat Here – Have a Pie and a Friendly Word'. Served up the pie-of-the-house in a surly manner he drew the attention of the landlord to how service fell short of expectation, to be told with a more ingratiating grin: 'If I were you, I'd watch out for what's in that pie!' His humour contrasted with his serious points and bubbled below the surface. Voters at that time did not pronounce so much on concerns of leaders but, depicting a dearth of interest on the part of the general public in the controversy then moving the political world about the Maastricht Treaty, he had his own his way of suggesting a 'Project Stealth' whereby Europhiles in power were quietly getting their own way:

'If I asked anyone where I live what they think about "The Maastricht Treaty", the bemused reaction I'd get would be "I haven't seen the movie!"'

---

[31] *H.E. the Hon Raymond Seitz, the US Ambassador, spoke to the Group on 26.3.1992.*

General John Galvin[32], also began his speech with a gag:

'I am reminded of the story of the boy who said to his father: "Dad, I have a question!" His father replied: "I am busy, ask your mother!" The son rejoined, "But, Dad, I don't want to know that much about it!" The E-AG audience was in the palm of his hand when he had a real point, political and philosophical, to make:

'I remind you of the words of the Greek philosopher, Heraclites: "An invisible bond is stronger than a visible one". For a formal bond such as a treaty alliance (NATO in this instance) to be really strong it should be the tangible expression of bonds and feelings of belonging together.'

The E-AG's niche was not grounded in the groves of Academe or the Profit of Big Business. The idea was more to 'Get opposing sides in international relations to confront each other in front of the thinking public.'

The Canadian High Commissioner and Spanish Ambassador squaring up to each other over the 'Cod war' prompted a journalist out for 'copy' to ask the Director what would happen if they came actually to blows, to be met by the retort of: 'Lord Montgomery is sitting between them and he is nothing if not burly!'[33] Why visit the theatre when there was the alternative of the E-AG?

---

[32] *General John Galvin Supreme Allied Commander, spoke to the Group at Guildhall at the Group Commemoration of the 40th Anniversary of NATO on 24.4.1989, and on 23.11.1987. See his speech.*
[33] *The Hon Royce Frith QC, High Commissioner for Canada, and H.E. Don Alberto Aza Arias, Ambassador of Spain, spoke to the Group on 27.4.1995. See transcript of Royce Frith's speech on the website of the Group with hard copies in the office records, also for photograph of the occasion on Page 17*

Two hundred plus delegates in the Grand Committee Room[34] heard another Russian Ambassador[35], physically imposing though a thinker, hymning the achievements of his Communist Government. The memories and prejudices of George Ben who was in the audience were poles apart from those of the speaker. George said in private, 'We always got drunk at parties; so when the KGB came round the following morning to ask who had said what, we could reply "Too drunk to remember!"' He fled Russia with the KGB on his tail. Perhaps the secret police had not thought him as drunk as all that? The moment chance offered in the Q&A session, George let fly vituperation at the Ambassador but was stalled when the Russian got to his feet from the podium, one hand on his breast and the other outstretched to George:

'You and I, we are both Russians. Speak to me, Comrade, in our language!'

George fell into it. His furious diatribe was reduced to Russian which virtually no one there understood. The Russian Ambassador then stood up: 'I will translate that into English.' His translation had George leaping to his feet again, fury uncontainable, in a pitch almost a scream. It was too much for the Ambassador, who stood up slowly, threateningly, turned to the Earl of Bessborough, the Chairman, and demanded in a voice to out-foghorn George:

'Have the audience come here to listen to him… or To **ME**!'

---

[34] *This was before a horseshoe seating arrangement limited numbers in the Grand Committee Room.*
[35] *H.E. Mr Leonid Zemyatin, Ambassador of the USSR to the UK, spoke to the Group on 26.4.1990. A copy of which is on the website of the Group with hard copies in the office records.*

The proverbial pin could be heard to drop. Silence! The two protagonists on their feet glared at each other. All looked to Eric Bessborough. He pondered. He was not quite decided. Moments passed. His wrestle with the poser, awaited with baited breath, crystallised at last in the ruling:

'Er… We-ll…!'

It was telling. George and the Ambassador sat down, shaken. Passion so inflamed, was doused. The debate continued on in majestic way. A True Blue British way of dealing with foreign dissension had been put to the test and it was fit for purpose. It turned out that the Ambassador had mistranslated what George said but hardly a soul there knew it. … and that Eric Bessborough might have been slightly senile. [36]

---

[36] *Apart from giving participants a fair hearing, traditionally British and in the 'E-AG Debating Conventions, the E-AG gave price of place to descendants of illustrious figures of English history, such as Lady Olga Maitland, Lord Onslow, the Duke of Somerset, David Gladstone, and David Montagu Corry (descendant of Disraeli's Secretary), to name but some, as well as to those bearing great names of the past, such as Lady Londonderry.; and, from abroad: Christopher Dreyfuss and Count Bernstorff. The list is long.*

*Above: **The Ambassador, the Chairman, and the Awkward Squad**, in photographs taken on happier occasions*

It never came to fisticuffs at the E-AG though it came close. George Galloway MP had a meeting due to start at 7.30pm in the Grand Committee Room and at 7.25pm was about to enter it bullishly and demand that some 200 E-AG guests immediately vacate it. This incursion was prevented by dint of an unseemly scuffle. The Director got as far once as tightening his hands round the jugular of a delegate, the Rev John Papworth, and forcing him bodily back into his seat as the only means putting an end to his bellows of 'STOP THE BOMBING'[37] distracting 500 guests at Guildhall for the 1999 NATO thrash, there to hear, rather, what HRH the Duke of York had to say. [38]

---

[37] *In the Bosnia War.*
[38] *As Jan Bolting wrote: '...the distinguished guests made very good speeches, especially General Sir Charles Guthrie but it was sad that a certain gentleman felt it necessary to shout out about the bombing. I could see though that you had him well in line.' Letter to Mr Glass from Jan Bolting 20. 5.1999.*

E-AG NATO Banquet 2009 in St James's Palace. Left: **The Rt. Hon. Lord Carrington KG CH GCMG MC,** *a former NATO Secretary-General and a vice-President of the E-AG,* **The Viscount Montgomery** *of Alamein CMG CBE former Chairman of the E-G; and* **General Sir Mike Jackson GCB CBE DSO ADC.** [39] *Right:* **HRH Prince Andrew with Jan Boulting**, *a generous E-AG Sponsor*

HRH Prince Andrew's office wrote after the NATO banquet at St James's Palace in 2009 and the speeches which deserve inclusion here (along with a hundred others):

'The evening went well (apart from the fire alarm interruption)[40]...I am grateful for the assistance you gave in making sure that the

---

[39] *See the website of the Group with hard copies in the office records for speeches to the E-AG by Lord Carrington and summary of Sir Mike's talk.*
[40] *Was there a coded reference to the fact that HRH Prince Andrew, as he then was, according to his staff had said that he would be a platform speaker only if he was to be the only one? By that stage, five other speakers had accepted to speak from the podium. The Director, in a bind over this request from the Palace, which had not applied in the proceeding NATO celebration with Prince Andrew, said their contributions could be relayed to guests from tape recordings. The Palace then intervened to say that, in that case, all the previous commitments to speak in person should be honoured.*

Household's wishes were taken into account in organising the evening.'[41]

The 'Fire Alarm interruption' might sound *en passant* when considered against the weighty speeches delivered that night but it had threatened to upend the entire proceedings. Guests including the 27 Ambassadors were heading for the exit, and a freezing November night, disbelieving the siren was but a practice drill on so august an occasion. The ensuing scramble was upending the military precision of the ordering and timing of the proceedings. Timely word was spread that 'It is just one of Justin's little jokes!'[42] The oratory to come and indeed the music was salvaged.

It should be said in view of subsequent events that Prince Andrew was riding high in the public esteem when he came to the E-AG and his speech, which is on the Group website, touched exactly the right note. His whole approach was affable, eloquent and dignified. It may not have been the view of the Azerbaijan delegate whose expensive carpet HRH immediately said he could not accept as a gift.

The Director was gratified to receive the following accolade after the event: '…Elma Dangerfield would have been very proud… I know you like Theatre and Drama. It was a colourful touch to bring in the Pikemen and Musketeers…'[43]

---

[41] *19.11.2009 – Letter to Mr Glass from Alastair Watson, Private Secretary to The Duke of York, Buckingham Palace. The equerries were extremely helpful and, on the night, HRH Prince Andrew was excellent, with his major contribution received with marked appreciation.*
[42] *Identical wording was used at the Savile Club on 18.9.2007 by the Chairman Sir Michael Burton, the former Ambassador, when introducing the Speaker, his namesake Sir Michael Burton, the Judge.*
[43] *Letter to Mr Glass from the Hon Sir Clive Bossom, Bt. 11.11.2009 (See photo n NATO Picture gallery). Sir Clive's father was Sir Alfred Bossom who, in the 1950s,*

NATO Banquet 2009. Left: **HRH Prince Andrew** *with* **Christopher Arkell,** *Trustee,* **Paul Joyal,** *Head of US Homeland Security,* **Hon Mrs Zeenat Rous,** *Ladies Committee,* **E-AG**[44]. *Right:* **Lady Symons,** *E-AG Chairman;* **John Bradley** *at table centre*

Prince Andrew's 'relaxed formality' came across as very human, right up to the moment at almost the end of the proceedings after dinner when he said he had to go as Fergie (the Duchess of York) was waiting for him. He joked pleasantly with the Director "So, you're the one who caused all the trouble!" as a result of Justin having 'booked' so many Speakers as opposed to reserving only one slot for HRH. His office had requested it and often a person at the top takes the rap for following the advice of underlings.

---

offered the Group hospitality at the Anglo-Belgian Club. Churchill famously remarked 'Bossom! Neither one thing nor the other!'
[44] The Ladies Committee had an Annual Ladies Luncheon but by this period the undoubted help, of Mrs Rous, Lady Burton, Katerina Jeffrey & Doreen Willis Bailey et al, was on an individual footing.

Top Left: **John Quick** with **Princess Zohra**; *Top Right:* **Lord Dykes**, *E-AG President*
Bottom: **Dr Julian Critchlow**, *Trustee*

Life would be dull indeed if political decisions were reduced to abstractions without human interest or a degree of entertainment value. The UK debate over Europe was heated well before 'Brexit' divided the country. As Sir Philip Goodhart[45] put it: 'By the end of the evening the hostility temperature was climbing very satisfactorily. If

---

[45] *Sir Philip Goodhart did Trojan work for the Group as a Trustee and was amenable to instructions, writing to Justin on 13.2.2001: 'I always just follow your lead whenever I can understand what you are writing or saying.' Sir Philip was on the all-important 1922 Committee of the Conservative party but joked that his real bid for power would be through his family: his descendants of his and Valerie's seven children, each being fecund, was numerically such that he said his family by the end of the century could be a majority of the population in his borough.*

the Savile Club had produced another couple of courses, our principal speakers might have hit each other....'[46]

Here again is Sir Philip, this time writing after a debate about Climate Change:

'I am all for reducing sea levels (except at Frinton and Bognor Regis) .... Anyhow, after Tuesday night's blizzard, I am in favour of more Global Warming.... We have had considerable success with our Afghanistan projects but we have never discussed the attitudes of Afghanistan's northern neighbours... Ought we to be quietly pressing the Ukraine to give the Crimea back to Russia? This time the Light Brigade should stay at home...'[47]

Sir Phillip Goodheart. CREDIT: Photo: Rex Features

---

[46] *Letter to Justin Glass 5.7.2007. Professor Stephen Haseler and Derek Scott was speaking to the E-AG about the EU at the Savile Club on 19.6.2007.*
[47] *The Light Brigade famously charged into withering fire of Russian canon in the Crimean War. Letter to Justin Glass 30.10.2008. Sir Philip was on the 1922 Committee. He wrote 'A Stab in the Front' the account of how, as a journalist and then politician, he discussed with the protagonists of the Suez War, Nasser, Eden, and Eisenhower, their perspectives, his conclusion being that their moves were miscalculated and on the basis of faulty Intelligence.*

Consideration of practical issues could play second fiddle to underlying attitudes. As the Russian Ambassador[48] put it, quoting Count Sforza:

'There are times at the opera when you should enjoy the music, and not worry about the words.'

The Russian Ambassador went on to explain the Russian reaction to the build-up of armaments by the West by quoting the theatre director, A. Stanislavsky: 'It is an almost inevitable rule that where there is a gun hanging on the wall that is seen in the first act, it will be fired in the third act.'

There were 'guns' enough awaiting a pull on the trigger in times past; it is instructive to see what the Men and Women of the Moment thought about issues such as Brexit and the refugee crisis, as reflected in E-AG transcripts, at times prior to the crossing of a plentiful supply of Rubicons.

Above: **Glora Martin**, *a loyal attendee of the E-AG, with the blind Home Secretary,* **David Blunkett** *and his dog at the E-AG in January 2006*

---

[48] H.E. Mr Yuri Fokine, the Russian Ambassador, spoke to the Group on 26.11.1998.

Chief Ajmal Khan of Paktia, Afghanistan, met through the E-AG top military and diplomatic UK and US personnel including General, later Lord, David Richards, Commander-in-chief at the time. The 'Chatham House Rule' inhibits quotation but he, like many, owned to being swayed by Khan's platform. A paper was produced by the Group on Khan's plans, the target audience being the upmost echelons of the political and diplomatic world involved in the issue. Behind-scenes meetings were set up by, or following from, E-AG discussions, including a TV panel with Ajmal Khan and Sir Paddy Ashdown, a hero on the Hindu Kush.

Paramount Chief **Ajmal Khan Zazai** spoke to the Group in the House of Commons in 2018 (above) with E-AG Trustees **Mili Gottlieb** and **Justin Glass** in the House of Lords unveiling a scroll of signatures of tribal chiefs in Afghanistan subscribing to his League of Afghan Tribes.

Ajmal Khan's predictions in that debate and the E-AG project on Afghanistan [49] were highly prescient. They still hold force in 2020. Will Afghanistan be affected by Khan's experience or his experience of the West at the E-AG? Will implementation of his ideas be the salvation of his country? It is yet too early to say.

---

[49] See the website of the Group with hard copies in the office records for the E-AG paper on Afghanistan and the E-AG debates on this topic.

Behind-scenes meetings instigated by, or spawned by, the E-AG featured in E-AG Newsletters but this was not part of the public *persona* of the Group. T'was ever thus in the E-AG as can be seen from the Annual Record of 1959:

'Round Table Dinner Discussions have given the experts such as Sir Paul Gore-Booth (one of the "The Group of Four") and Mr John Tuthill (of the United States Delegation to O.E.E.C) the opportunity to speak frankly "off the record" to smaller gatherings as they could not do at large open meetings.'

Churchill believed that secret history not in the history books explains the course of history. In this shrouded area the E-AG perhaps can lay greatest claim to influence.

In 1987 Sir Geoffrey Pattie, Minister for Space, spoke in the Grand Committee Room to the E-AG in Parliament. He told of how the cosmos drew closer through scientific invention. The temperature of enthusiasm plummeted as the in-house telescreen broadcast that the Prime Minister, Mrs Thatcher, intended to scrap the whizz of a project, 'Hotol', an 'air-breathing' rocket. Spirits at dinner in the St Ermin's Hotel were revitalised when representatives of the industry stood up, microphone in hand, to pledge private funding.

THE E-AG IN WASHINGTON

The Group has planted its flag on American soil. Chief Ajmal Khan Zazai spoke on 16 April about Afghanistan at the beautiful home of the Count and Countess de Bessenyey. The Chairman was Harold Sands, Hon. Treasurer of the E-AG, Justin Glass, Director, Opened the Discussion, and John Gouriet gave the Vote of Thanks; they were among many E-AG members or friends who travelled far for this fascinating event, which included a first class buffet. There were some 40 people including diplomats present. Chief Khan was on an extended visit by invitation to the USA during which senior E-AG officers arranged consultations with crucial people in Washington and elsewhere. This *démarche* has won friends for the Group and extended its influence in a worthwhile cause.

John Gouriet giving the Vote of Thanks on 16 April

***European-Atlantic Group Newsletter** – from Page 2 – **May 2009 edition**[50]*

Left: **Ajmal Khan** with **Donald Rumsfelt**, US Secretary for Defence, in Washington
Right: **General Joseph Ralston**, Supreme Allied Commander Europe and Commander-in-Chief and US European Command, who spoke to the Group on 16.4.2002, holding E-AG cuff links

---

[50] *John Gouriet was a co-Founder of 'The Freedom Association' and author of 'HEAR HEAR!' which won the Elma Dangerfield Prize for literature.*

The Rt. Hon. Margaret Beckett[51] at the E-AG set store by the principle, 'There is no end to what you can achieve if you don't mind who gets the credit for it!' Where save perhaps as a footnote to history does the name of George Guise appear? Guise, a vice-President of the E-AG, was generous with high level contacts. He was a 'head chef' in Mrs Thatcher's so-called 'Kitchen cabinet' and played a key advisory role for instance in the UK's financial support of CERN as well as in 'Thatcherism' generally.

The Iranian Ambassador appointed shortly after Ayatollah Khomeini came to power was to address the Group but pulled out at the eleventh hour, having decreed that none of the two hundred or so guests should have alcohol, it being contrary to his religious tenets. The Director had acceded to the request, thinking it eloquent of new Iranian attitudes. A panel of experts made good the loss of the billed speaker but it was the Number Two at the Iranian Embassy who gave the real game away. Julia Couchman, a photographer and an E-AG Assistant over many years, some of whose photographs adorn these pages, sat with him over dinner at a table for two in the hall outside the banqueting room as he had refused to sit at the table where wine was being served. When Julia tried to pour him a glass of water he refused; and he later poured one for himself. That said, he accepted her family's Christmas card.

Three hours in total for the presentations in a two-header – an hour and a half in Parliament, and the same again at the ensuing dinner – was too long for any controversial policy let alone sloganising to pass unchallenged, especially with audiences like those at the E-AG. Here is Lord Runcie: 'I am confronted by a very distinguished gathering …who could speak with greater authority than I about so many of the

---

[51] *The Rt. Hon. Margaret Beckett, former Labour Foreign Secretary, spoke to the Group on 6,3.2007.*

issues I will raise.' Once the Speaker did not show up, a German banker who had had a heart attack. A panel rapidly was pressed into service from the 200 present in the Grand Committee Room and also Sir Frederick Bennett who happened by Parliament just at the time. Asked what would happen if the speaker arrived in the middle of the fascinating debate, the Director, tongue-in-cheek, replied, 'We would bar him ingress!'

Rare it was that an easy run was accorded Speakers from the experts or delegates. It was expected, and asked, that E-AG questioning should be feisty. The Archbishop of Canterbury, Lord Runcie, was under no illusions: "I am comforted by the thought that if I tread ignorantly or confusingly you will not simply smoulder; you will be up and at me!"[52] The Head of the Ditchley Foundation[53] with two senior colleagues made out a case of logic that seemed hermetic for moving with caution as regards Western responses to Iran over its nuclear build-up. Some at the E-AG felt that in this context Fortune Favours the Bold. One of this ilk had to be Louisa Hutchinson who, speaking from the floor, did not mince her words:

'Tonight we have heard three Neville Chamberlains![54]'

Sometimes, official policy brooked no scintilla of deviation, especially during the Cold War. Positions then were mired in amber. An intellectual exercise was in savouring the manner in which Cold Warriors such as Sir Frank Roberts could expound doctrines, saying little new but a way that sounded fresh-minted and garnished with a

---

[52] *February 25th 1997. NB E-AG Debating Conventions are at the end of a Sample Guest List below.*
[53] *Sir Michael Quinlan GCB.*
[54] *Sir Neville Chamberlain famously waved a piece of paper signed by Hitler and declared 'Peace in our time!' shortly before WW2. Louisa Hutchinson, an E-AG member, was in the property business.*

bon mot. Those who hated Germans so much that they wanted the Berlin Wall to stay standing were characterised as loving Germany so much that they wanted two Germanys to love! Sir Frank who had been the Private Secretary of Ernest Bevan attacked a policy of Mrs Thatcher in diplomat-speak:

'Great people can make great mistakes!'

Sir Frank, whose lack of inches probably pressed his candidature to deal with Stalin, notoriously height-conscious, would talk of 'We', impressing into considered words a putative weight of the Foreign Office, and endowing the stiletto gleam of a courteous smile and the odd musicality of his hacksaw vocal chords with an unspoken threat.

Foreign visitors usually were heard out with politeness and respect, such as the Chinese Ambassador[55] when stigmatising at length the Dali Lama as 'a war criminal' in her talk about Climate Change. Perhaps she had had 'word' that Tibetan religion was the safer topic? An unusually placid discussion was about the stand-off between Pakistan and India at a time when the Temple at Amritsar was engulfed in sectarian violence.[56] The *De haut en bas* debate lasted till the E-AG President, the Earl of Limerick, in whose person fine breeding sat well alongside his fine intelligence, wound up proceedings with a customary, well-crafted limerick. A Sikh mesmerised by all the intricacies, to go by his ever-widening eyes but zipped-up mouth, could bear it no more. Lord Limerick's light-hearted swan song was barracked in anger! Passions inflaming the topic were brought home with a bang to the would-be map-drawers present, a moment when light was shed on heat.

---

[55] *H.E. Mrs Fu Ying, Ambassador of China, spoke to the Group on 24.4.2008.*
[56] *Sir David Goodall GCMG spoke to the Group on 25.3.2002. His speech is on the website of the Group with hard copies in the office records.*

A jet-lagged South American Ambassador began by saying 'I will be boring!' It was the most pertinent thing he said. So well did he make good his word to the nine increasingly somnolent South American Ambassadors present that it surely was no co-incidence he was recalled that week to the country from which he had just come. It could happen in a Group that was as high profile as the E-AG, as Sir Anthony Buck knew. Sir Anthony, former Minister of the Navy and red-blooded scion of the House of Gentleman Jack, eighteenth century pugilist, was a staunch E-AG Vice-Chairman in the mid-1980s. He had eyes for a comely lady (as seen in the photo below). He laid claim to two causes of personal sadness, the first when he retired as an MP, his Tory successor in his constituency 'had the colossal cheek to increase my majority!' The other was his marriage to gold-digging, kiss-&-tell, fuck-&-publish Bienvenida, a Spanish harlot. The photograph splashed in newsprint of the Spanish Minister sitting beside Bienvenida Buck in the E-AG horrified his compatriots when confronted by this evidence. He was ordered straight back to Madrid. His Diplomatic Controller who knee-jerked in damage-limitation from the scandal is hereby informed that all E-AG seating plans were conjured up by the E-AG Directors. A picture can tell a thousand dubious words. Sir Anthony Buck is caught on camera[57], below left, in the act of simply looking at Princess Michael.

---

[57] *Photo taken at a Gala organised at the Hilton with the E-AG in tandem with David Griffiths.*

Hat trick

FINLAND'S jovial Ambassador was an arresting sight at a dinner on Wednesday night in the St James's Court Hotel in London, where diplomats had congregated in hordes. Leif Blomqvist wore the menu on his head throughout the meal.

Diplomacy was the watchword among fellow diners, including Lord Montgomery of Alamein and the guest speaker, Lord "Ivor" Richard, who raised not an eyebrow at this apparent eccentricity.

Blomqvist tucked merrily into the avocado mousse and chicken, then sat through the speeches and questions and removed his headwear for the royal toast. "There was a cold draught," he explained. "I haven't much on top so I was protecting what's left."

(Left): **Sir Anthony** looks at **Princess Michael;**
(Right) 'The Times Diary' on 21st October 1994

The E-AG's eclectic mix of social grace and expertise sometimes interacted at cross purpose. A stage-whisper of a titled lady 'Is he talking about Monet, the painter?' raised intellectual beetle-brows half way through Pierre Duchene's thought-provoking account[58] of Jean Monnet, founding father of the European Union. E-AG archives are not yet open to the public for her name to be revealed. Humour could surface even before guests arrived, in debate titles like Sir Malcolm Rifkind's *'When Bush Comes to Shove'* or the Middle East Peace Process being billed as 'Multi-faced' as opposed to 'Multifaceted' [59], a Freudian Slip if ever there was one.

---

[58] *See Lord Dahrendorf's book review. Duchene spoke at an E-AG luncheon-discussion Group on 17.7.1995.*
[59] *The Rt. Hon. Sir Malcolm Rifkind QC MP, Secretary of State for Defence, spoke about President Bush's plans to the Group on 13.7.1993. He wrote in July 2020 '... I can claim to be fons et origo of the title "When Bush Comes to Shove". It came to me, like an epiphany, when I was thinking what I might say....'*
H.E. Mr Mohammed Shaker spoke to the Group on 12.12.1994.

The German Ambassador, Herr von Richthofen, did not come to address the Group as planned. He was summoned to Germany by the Chancellor, Herr Genscher, when the Berlin Wall fell. The following committee meeting featured as usual a list of some 20 applicants for E-AG membership. Von Richthofen had applied. The custom was for a Chairman, in this case Lord Rippon, to read out each name and accompanying thumbnail CV slowly, then pause, ostensibly to give those present a chance to voice objection to the candidate's suitability. Lord Rippon, with customary gravitas, read out the names, as (a hypothetical) example: 'James Smith, (pause)...The Director of Smith, Smith & Smith Heavy Industry PLC (pause)'. Lord Rippon's recital of names and justifications of fitness for membership went on: 'His Excellency Baron Hermann von Richtfofen'. He continued giving the qualification for entry with solemnity: '...The German Ambassador who did not come, as promised, to address the Group'. Lord Rippon saw if too late that he was hardly advancing the cause of the applicant. The chance of blackballing the Ambassador was not seized, amid a gust of laughter.

Left to Right: **The Lord Mereworth,** poet and playwright, **The Earl of Limerick KBE FBA,** Chairman and then President of the Group 1998-2002 at an E-AG Reception on 24.11.1997 for the Hon Peter Caruana, Chief Minister of Gibraltar

The Lord Chancellor, Lord Irvine, quoted from an E-AG dinner in *'The Times Diary'* of 14th December 1999 aroused the synthetic ire of Lord Limerick.

LORD IRVINE of Lairg has offended the Earl of Limerick. The peer is furious about an analogy the Lord Chancellor recently made in which he said the concept of heredity in the Lords was as absurd as having hereditary poets. Limerick, an enthusiastic penner of light verse, says: "I think I would make a good hereditary poet and might even get elected, which is more than I achieved as an hereditary peer."

MARK INGLEFIELD

Left: The 'Times Diary' 14th December 1999; Right: **Lord Limerick** and **Lord Irvine** looking in different directions. Averting his gaze in the foreground is **Admiral Sir Julian Oswald**.

Below is the letter of protest from Lord Limerick printed in 'The Times'

Peers, Plumbers and Poets

Sir,

Your Diary column has it (14 December) that I was "furious" over the Lord Chancellor's after-dinner assertion that hereditary peers were as ridiculous as hereditary poets (or, by more notorious comparison in debate, hereditary plumbers). Not at all. But his attempted *reductio ad absurdum* did make me reflect that any hereditary plumber would have shared with an old-style peer the advantage of studying his trade from relatively early age, under the mentorship of an experienced practitioner.

As for poets: The virtues of genes, I insist,
                Should not be too lightly dismissed;
                    If a poll's on the cards
                    For hereditary Bards –
                My name will be found on the list.

Yours faithfully,

LIMERICK

Patrick Limerick ran a risk of acquiring the mantle of being 'the Earl of the Limerick'. It may not be fair; his poetry branched out, as seen in the E-AG Journal, *Politics Tomorrow (see below)*, and the acumen he brought to restructuring the Group in line with new legislation illustrates abilities that took him far in business and diplomacy.

E-AG delegates offered much food for thought with lighter moments and *bonhomie* that made it all go with a zing did not go for the food for eat. Obstinate souls cavilled at the chicken, for years the main course. A former Minister of Iran under the Shah, prepared for the worst, was delighted to behold *'Poussin'* bedecking the menu. As other guests at his table knew, it means 'Baby Chicken'.

'Ah!' cried that dignitary with satisfaction: '...*Poussin!* At long last! ... FISH!'

No one enlightened the gourmand as to the translation of 'Poussin' preferring instead to await with glee his disconsolate reaction on being served, yet again, the E-AG's dish of the day and every other day. His fellow guests were not disappointed as his face fell on seeing the plate put before him. It is a little-known success story of the E-AG that he kept coming back for more.

*The former **Iranian Minister** when off duty could be the life and soul of a party. Photo not taken at the E-AG*

© Copyright April 2020 All Rights Reserved - Justin Glass; <u>justinglass2020@gmail.com</u>

3. BEHIND THE SCENES

THE E-AG OFFICE IN CHELSEA 1987-2006 – the Group at work and at play

The E-AG office under the aegis of Mrs Dangerfield was in a basement[60].

Who worked there? Lord Limerick observed in writing that it was '...the energetic, but solitary Justin'. This was not so at the start of the Justin era. The office was staffed by a blue rinse brigade whose name was not 'Efficiency' – a word, like 'Networking', that was somehow rather common. But one didn't say so, of course. One by one they departed. One advantage of this was that it cut down on the interminable wall-to-wall chatter. They had curtsied before the King in their Debutante days, but in harder times they were in thrall to Mrs Dangerfield and to a paltry stipend. The work was demanding. Fulsome praise in thirty pages of letters attest to this but the exigencies of the long working days did not permit any resting on laurels.

Maxine Vlieland, late of the British Königswinter committee, and Jane Page, whose letters exude an upstanding graciousness, were on the E-AG staff and the Ladies Committee in the 1970s, but they had departed and those left *in situ*, domestic staff aside, when Justin arrived were Daphne Olorenshaw and Clarissa Lada-Grodzicka. Clarissa's grandeur was softened by a touching humility, largely born of the demands of a tough modern world on a lady alone in straitened circumstances. Tall, fine of feature and form, she had once been a

---

[60] *Elma's home at 6 Gertrude Street, Chelsea, SW10 0JN. The office was previously was at 64 Kingsway, WC2.*

beauty. It sounded as if her early adult life had been spent drifting through Edwardian drawing rooms: 'Not a very nice man, Evelyn Waugh!' she recollected, having been snubbed by that writer. Her exchanges with callers on the telephone often began thus: 'Who are you!' It was a proclivity finally remedied when Lady (Shirley) Williams[61] snapped back 'And WHO are YOU?' Clarissa knew 'how to behave', but this did not mitigate her Scandinavian depressive tendencies. An insect flew into the office. Clarissa gasped, 'Oh my God! It's a WASP!' Her lugubrious facial expression and vocal tone descended to mock-horror as if in anticipation of noxious fumes rising from a newly-opened coffin as she concluded darkly: '...SPRING must be coming!'

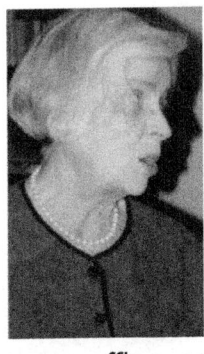

Sneering at Clarissa *(pictured left)* oh-so-politely was no-nonsense Daphne Olorenshaw, slightly less grand, more portly, the very model of a modern English gentlewoman, with a career in embassies behind her. The term 'gentlewoman' could not in her case easily be associated with its two worded consort 'gentle woman'. 'That's a nice dress you have on!' Justin exclaimed after years of working with her in the same office, only to be put back in his box with, 'Don't make personal remarks!' Mrs Glass, being French, was impressed by the tough English specimen in the person of Daphne, having seen her after an event on a midwinter night wearing a light chemise with not so much as a scarf round her neck, an octogenarian shrugging off the freezing cold while people half her age were shivering in furs. Daphne did have a friendly side, but could always be relied upon to 'keep her end up'. She needed to watch the pennies – only known to others after her

---

[61] One of the 'Gang of Four' who broke away from the Labour party to form the Liberal Democrats.

demise – but this disposition became her as a proper deportment for those brought up to take on the mantle of 'The Lady of the Manor'.

The garden at Gertrude Street

Photography by Julia Couchman: <u>juliacouchman@hotmail.co.uk</u>

The physical surrounds and quaint garden seemed to recall the period of the Boer War, when the house was built. Fustian furnishing, the clanking, ancient boiler in the kitchen, and an *olde worlde* feel, lent to modern gadgetry a semblance of incongruity. The voluminous Helen, Elma's domestic assistant, a ball of irrepressible fun like her great-great-uncle, Dan Leno, the Music Hall comedian, played her part in this parallel universe of the Edwardian age, being transfigured by Elma into the obligatory Parlour Maid. One day, the boiler clanking began rising in volume by the second; Helen scared the living daylights out of everyone, rushing into the office in the prescribed manner of a Below Stairs drama queen, the many folds of her body wobbling in so-un-English panic, screaming out in her best cockney: 'ITZ GONTA BLOW!', before diving for cover – outdoors.

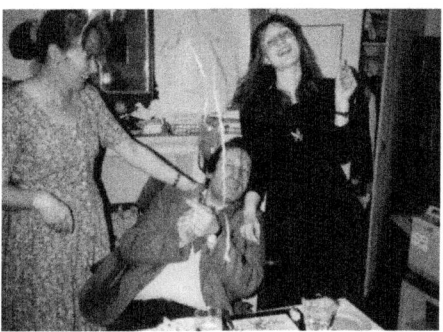

*Office Christmas party 1995: Left: A 'Parlour Maid' (**Helen**) caught in the act by **Elma** (Comment added in jest later by Rosemary); Right: **Rosemary, Justin,** and **Lisa***

Elma was impervious to the advantages of new technology. 'Where is Justin?' Elma was once asked. The tone of her answer – 'Fiddling with his computer!' – was ample testament to her scorn. It was an anxiety-laden part of preparing painstakingly the detailed guest lists, a job Justin made inviolably his, that the grand result might be snookered by mechanical failure in any or all of the three printers crammed into a tiny space. And sure enough, they all went wrong the day before an event, necessitating a 7 a.m. rendezvous in a publisher's office.[62] Some 200 names, post-nominals and exact credentials (no errors allowed) with 'tribal notices' of extra-mural Group activities were feverishly listed for delegates with deadlines ever looming, and non-stop telephone calls and the usual business correspondence.

---

[62] *Nothing of mechanical failure in that period was as nail-biting as when years later the computer imploded with all the information on it pertaining to the NATO banquet in St James's Palace – it would have been lost but for the 16-hour repair session of Mr Seris Leonidas, not so much as eating until he had it all restored. He also helped to sub-edit this book.*

The office furniture was rudimentary and functional, with old wooden tables and stiff chairs, and the only thing that changed over the years was the content of the clutter. On one wall a painting of an imaginary South American scene encouraged thoughts of flight from dreary old England[63].

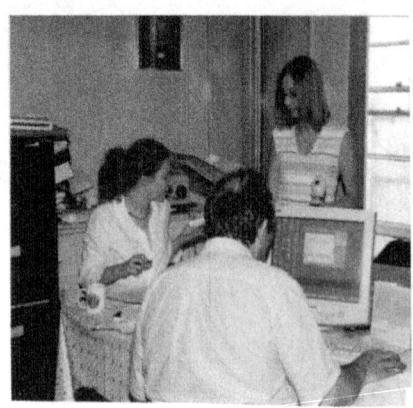 

Downstairs and Upstairs

Left: **Justin** *'fiddling with his computer'[64]; Right: Elma's living room and office*
Photographer: Julia Couchman. juliacouchman@hotmail.co.uk

Elma, no foodie, pointed approvingly to the example of the Circassian dancers who drank by sucking a finger dipped in water. Helen's culinary aspirations, however, were decidedly not Circassian. Elma ordered broccoli and fish fingers for every single lunch. Helen, aided and abetted by Lisa, whose cheerfulness was a breath of fresh air in the office, cooked up a revolution which was evidence of the truth that all triumphs in life are worth a struggle. Solid food was borne on trays into the office. American interns could not believe the contrast

---

[63] *The painting is beneath Elma's Obituary below.*
[64] *Kimberlee is the US intern standing; the other young lady was passing by, briefly helping out.*
Carmen Bouverat, a very helpful and efficient professional, was working at the E-AG at a later date.

between the spartan workaday surroundings and what they had been told, and saw, of the elevated status of those with whom the Group dealt. Justin told them that they were to live primarily in a cerebral world. There was no Skype back then. Callers on the phone could not see that the Empress had no Empire. When speaking to Elma it was hard to believe that the Empire was no more or even that Mrs Dangerfield did not own it. Elma, receiving her OBE[65] at her investiture, broke with protocol to say to Prince Philip how odd it felt to be made a member of an Order of a non-existent Empire. The royal response was after Elma's own heart:

'We don't talk about that sort of thing!'

'Where is the E-AG?' asked a recently retired Colonel when meeting Justin by appointment in that basement office. He had earmarked the E-AG as an upward career move on being demobbed, having never forgotten the grandeur of the E-AG 50th anniversary celebration of the founding of NATO at Guildhall, and his dinner placement near Robert Maxwell – famous then for his zillions not his frauds – or the Royalty, the glitter, and what appeared to be an organisation that ran like clockwork.

'It is right here; you are here!' Justin answered.

'Yes, of course, but where is the E-AG?' the Colonel persisted.

'Right here!'

'No but, I mean, where is the E-AG?'

---

[65] *The Report of 1959-60 lauds Elma for her honour in the New Year's Honours List of the O.B.E. ('Order of the British Empire'). It is rare to be advanced, as was Elma later, in 2002, to the CBE (Order of Commander of the British Empire).*

The man simply could not believe he had penetrated the *Sanctum Sanctorum* of the institution that had featured prominently in his fond ambitions for a decade. He must have been thinking that it was surely not feasible that 'So Much Had Been Achieved By So Few For So Long in this … this … NISSEN HUT!' Until he fathomed the man's problem Justin thought he was dealing with some fruitcake in mufti.

The genesis of many E-AG policies that held sway for decades can be traced back to its early thinking. A tradition that survived for many a long year was put in round terms in the E-AG Minutes of 1964: *'In view of the unsettled world political situation it was felt that Meetings should not be planned too far ahead'*. Thus the programme of events was never 'six months ahead', as some wanted, unless planning for Royalty. Urgency, therefore, was endemic in the system. The 'Unforgiving minute' was revengeful if frittered away nattering over fry-ups. This was understood by the charming, efficient Rosemary, a secretary who withstood all the pressure for two years; the blame for her retreat to Ireland cannot be laid at the door of the E-AG. Whatever the burning topic of the day, let alone year, it was all grist to the E-AG mill. It was life on the cliff-edge. There was the constant danger that in four weeks from any given time a yawning gap in the monthly programme might appear. The seedbed that germinated E-AG events needed constant watering lest it became a desert. Elma's greeting almost every morning in her active years right up to her early nineties was, 'What are the horrors today?'

Once a speaker succumbed to an invitation, the few hands available scrambled to the tiller until an all too brief anchorage – a good hour or so was generally given to the castigation of some misconduct at the event of the previous evening – and then course was set for the choppy waters of the next international crisis. This involved homing in on a new set of experts, sweet-talking them into coming. Can the millennial generation envisage the sheer amount of time consumed researching and identifying new specialists in a new topic before the internet took hold? The divide that separated those, high or low, who could present a forensic or impressive case from the doers who got things done, was thrown into sharp relief. Results, not intentions, were everything. The unforgiving minute seemed to metamorphose into the unforgiving second, and the spirit of Elma's father lived on in the E-AG in the regimen of his daughter. He had run the famous Jardines in Hong Kong, and permitted no chair in his office apart from his own, as a hint to would-be chatterers. Justin had to summon up all his reserves of self-restraint in order not to snap, 'GET TO THE POINT!' at a telephone caller starting to blather on with a, 'How are you?' An Oxford writer, on being told that E-AG work of the utmost importance was pressing, earned his place in office legend due to his perspicacity in matters relating to deadlines. 'Of course ... yes ... I very well know what it is to be busy ... yes indeed ... Oh I say, that's funny. There seem to be a lot of planes flying overhead today....'

Who today would think to follow the example of Elma's father, doyen of the Hong Kong Stock Exchange who, after a crash that harmed investors, gave them most of his own money rather than have the imputation levelled at him that 'He's done alright out of it!' The E-AG was run in the old way, with the old sense of upright morality and trust in someone's word even if at times and in a less ethical world this could verge on naivety.

There was no better way of recording minutes of a meeting than in Elma's prescribed way. Elma would look aghast at Justin's efforts when he first joined the office, her pursed lips the prelude to her slashing through words and sentences in red ink, replacing them with the infinitely better ones of her choice. Several weeks after a committee meeting, Elma forgot that the minutes being prepared for circulation had been edited already by her. Justin presented them to her and omitted to mention this fact. Imprecations spurted from the pursed lips until, after the inevitable dressing-down was well under way, Justin enlightened Elma as to the true authorship of said minutes. Not for a second did Elma falter. On and on, unchecked, went the slashing and the imprecations with no hint, but for a realignment of gender, that she knew that she had been hoisted by her own authorial petard.

'...The silly bitch! Honestly, HOW could she write such TRASH!'

Their abiding cause, the E-AG, was shared, but it may well be wondered how Justin managed to withstand such a human tempest as Elma if disagreement arose over policy, even if Elma had a soft spot for him and a very sociable side to her nature. His expedience worked like a charm; perhaps 'charm' is not quite *le mot juste*. Justin in his first years would agree with Elma. And, until he took over, he would continue to agree with Elma through thick and thin ... unless ... he was sure, 100% sure, that he was RIGHT! Then Tempest met Typhoon:

'If you were a gentleman, you wouldn't SHOUT like that!'

'If you were a lady, I wouldn't have to!'

Elma was not one to brood or sulk. The curtain would be rung down on protestations from any injured party by her ending the conversation with: 'FINISH! FINISH! FINISH!'

Elma came to know that when Justin stood his ground he had reason on his side. She once backed him against heavyweights on the

Committee. He was proved right.[66] One of their number left under a cloud. Elma then informed the Committee of Justin's appointment as her Joint Director[67]. Lord Rippon told Justin that he had never seen anyone look so surprised.

Royalty, said not to sully itself by carrying money on its person, had a spiritual disciple in Elma, no doubt fortified by a family trust and a concept of money pegged at pre-inflation value. It sat oddly with a parsimony manifested by her never buying a Christmas card, preferring instead to cut off the picture on the front of cards that had been sent to her. She pressed them back into service as stand-alone cards. It happened only rarely, but it did happen, that Elma sent such a card to the person who had just sent it to her. Her personality characterised the Group *persona*. Corporate members paying a small subscription, relatively speaking, of between £100 and £200 per annum were to Elma the life-blood of the Group, even when sponsorship truly worthy of the name came under Justin's aegis. He entered the State Bedroom one day flourishing a donor's cheque for £25,000. Elma looked straight through it, seemingly uncomprehending, a reaction akin to that of nineteenth century Tongan islanders as a European warship docked in their harbour – it was a thing so utterly alien, so immense, that they did not even see it. Tens of thousands of pounds came from Meg Allen's trust and from sponsors of dinners at some £2000 a throw. These included Steven Philippsohn[68], Jan Boulting[69], Graham Cole[70], and Sandi Baxter[71], to

---

[66] *Invaluable help came from accountant, Colin Baker, over how to stop VAT bankrupting the Group.*
[67] In 1992.
[68] *An extremely competent solicitor, a Partner of PCB Litigation.*
[69] *Director P & JP & Company; See photograph at end of previous section.*
[70] *Government Liaison officer, Augusta Westland, and on the E-AG Committee.*
[71] *Sandi Baxter is the Guiding Light of Baxterbear, the mascot of the British Military Tournament. 300 bears were handed out at the dinner for The ABF The*

name but a few, but, nothing daunted, the life-blood of the Group to Elma remained ever 'The Corporates' with their annual £150 for the coffers.

Dinners made a handsome profit, part of the secret of which can now be revealed. People came at the last moment without a dinner place, but bearing cheques. Some ten people out of 150 who had booked almost always failed to turn up. A few minutes after the start of a dinner, Justin, *qua* Pied Piper, would enter the dining room, ten anxious people trailing behind him, nosing out the 'ghosts' in unoccupied seats.

All changed for the better following the bequest in Mrs Dangerfield's will and – *Voila!* Now guests like President Kaunda could have their travel expenses reimbursed. Kaunda's son, however, demanded three first class return tickets; the subsequent refusal nearly became a diplomatic incident. The Group could issue *gratis* invitations to the FCO and the Diplomatic Corps for the 2009 NATO Banquet. In the early days, donations from Lord Chalfont and his Dulverton Trust, which paid the costs of the European-Atlantic Journal, and the handouts from Henry Tiarks and other well-wishers, rarely topped the £200 mark. Their generosity was acknowledged in the minutes in prose that came closest to purple in the Record.

Elma with damp cigarette dangling from lower lip was clad daily in a many-holed, old dressing gown. Jove, the Thunderer of the Phone, was described as 'Fag-ash Lil' by Helen. Such a sacrilege was hardly for the ears of Elma's personal assistant, Mary Melville[72], of dormouse manner, the daughter of the Solicitor-General and a Spanish mother

---

Soldiers Charity EU Dinner. Baxterbear sponsorship is acknowledged in the NATO brochure, featured herein.
[72] *See references to Mary Melville above and photograph below.*

who had said to her, 'Mary, you must never take a paid job and steal the bread from someone who needs the money!' A certain toughness ruled Elma's head and heart. Lady Killearn, Jackie, a close friend of Elma, unburdened herself to Justin on the phone. 'What did I do! Elma slammed the phone down on me!' Soothing balm was to hand. 'But Elma does that all the time!' Mary didn't show up for work or phone in. She could have had a stroke. 'Can't be helped!' said the Blue Rinces. Thought of Mary vanished in a haze of the latest society gossip. The lovely Carole, Elma's assistant, prompted Justin to ring the police. They broke down Mary's door and she had indeed had a heart attack. Helen never quite 'got' the upper crust and their genuine emotion and was surprised how, at the drop of a hat, charm taps were turned off and on. Helen's people mucked in together. *Autre temps autre moeurs*! Lady Killearn who died aged 105, always asked after Justin's wife of 25 years, 'How is the blushing bride?' Elma invariably suppressed heartfelt emotion, yet at her Dennis's death in 1973 (see below for stories about Elma's paramour and colleague) she sobbed her heart out and was so loath for him to leave her that she forbade removal of his body from her bedroom until it became imperative.

Tough as old rope Elma might appear but Simon David, a young poet recently arrived in the UK and who met Elma at the Royal Society of Literature then stayed with her, tells a different story: 'She introduced herself poetically as 'Tryphosa' (Elma's middle name). Her passion for poetry and politics was instantly infectious. She rolled out what turned out to be a decade-long welcome mat. Elma's belief in my writing never dimmed just as my gratitude for her kindness and unwavering passion never will.'

It was clear that by 1988 the E-AG was on the slide, navel-gazing within its old, familiar circle whilst membership numbers shrank[73]. Elma invited Justin into the E-AG as a *cri de coeur* when, with only days to go, hardly anyone had booked to come and hear Sir Geoffrey Pattie's talk on the space race. In the event it was a sell-out due to the fact that Justin went to the library and sifted through a variety of manuals and compendiums concerning those involved in this sphere, and then contacted them all. Surprised at the burgeoning number of guests unknown to him, Lord Bessborough famously remarked: 'Who ARE all these people?'[74]

Achievers, not necessarily with a 'handle' to their name, had to be coaxed into the office mix. Gaby gave computer training; Jeffrey Long sourced E-AG ties. Destiny would not deny the E-AG its haul of grandees. Not long thereafter Gaby became Countess de Bessenyey and Jeffrey was appointed MBE. In Anthony Westnedge OBE, Justin's successor, the criteria combined, again with a satisfactory outcome.[75] Bluebloods like Anne Hodson-Pressinger *(left)*[76] could 'meet and greet' E-AG guests as did her mother, Lady Torphichen. *Le crème de la crème* was part of the Group's success

---

[73] *Evidence of this is in the choice of Book Reviewers, almost all being Group affiliates.*
[74] *Speeches and Book Reviews of Lord Bessborough are on the website of the Group with hard copies in the office records.*
[75] *Some did not make the Honours List. Cliff 'Brains' Ireland, for instance, was an internet expert whose help was invaluable. Jeffrey Long became an E-AG Vice-President. Anthony Westnedge had enjoyed a successful career in Johnnie Walker whisky.*
[76] *On one occasion Anne Hodson-Pressinger, a successful PR lady, suggested the Speaker and bought 30 guests, a record. Anne was always helpful and ready with advice on protocol. Anne became an E-AG Vice-President.*

story. It was not a recipe to be jettisoned without adverse consequences. The prevailing fashion rules the day. It was the way things were. Justin once got chatting with a public lavatory attendant. 'I love my job!' she said happily. 'Every morning when I come in, I never know what I will find new to clean up!' Hers too 'not to reason why....!'

E-AG exclusivity was gradually ameliorated. Boris Andonov, a Russian-Bulgarian joined the office straight from school, stayed as Financial Director and became a Director of European-Atlantic Publications Ltd[77]. His patriotism, too, could be tolerated within the new Broad Church: Taxed about the millions of his own compatriots murdered by Stalin, Boris muttered in a voice pregnant with innuendo, "He may have had his reasons!" The 'Double Arch' theory of international relations (see cutting below) expounded by the Shadow Foreign Secretary – 'No two countries with MacDonald's ever go to war with each other!' – could have gained in impact by Boris's growl, 'That was why we bombed Chechnya. They don't have MacDonald's!'

---

[77] *He much helped with the sister Publishing House of European-Atlantic Publications in publishing a biography of Michael Jackson, the pop singer. General Sir Mike Jackson was most displeased when his publisher did not deliver his autobiographies in time for his E-AG speaking event but he almost exploded when Justin, never one to knowingly short-change E-AG guests, offered to distribute this book as an alternative.*

Globe toting

SHADOW FOREIGN Secretary Francis Maude was in robust form last night at the Ermin's Hotel where he was speaking in favour of globalisation to a gathering of the European Atlantic Group. "Until very recently no two countries which both had a McDonald's have gone to war with each other," he declared. "Globalisation is the most potent force for progress but it makes the nation state more not less important than before."

Maude also took a swipe at New Labour's supposed ethical foreign policy. "It was a bad day for Britain when the Metropolitan Police felt themselves obliged to arrest lawful protesters against the Chinese President during his visit to London," Maude said.

Dinner

European-Atlantic Group
The Hon Francis Maude, MP, Shadow Secretary of State for Foreign and Commonwealth Affairs, spoke on current Foreign Policy issues at a dinner discussion held by the European-Atlantic Group last night at the Hilton St Ermin's Hotel. Lord Judd presided and other speakers were Sir Michael Burton, Admiral of the Fleet Sir Julian Oswald and Mr Geoffrey Yeowart. Among others present were:

The Ambassadors of Luxembourg, Estonia, Mongolia, Romania, Macedonia, Kyrgyzstan, Bosnia and Herzegovina, Indonesia, Poland and Morocco, the High Commissioner for Cyprus, Baroness Hooper, the Hon Dominick Browne, the Hon Sir Clive and Lady Barbara Bossom, the Hon Barnaba Leith, Sir Ronald and Lady Arculus, Lady Bellinger, Lady Carnwath, Sir John Fretwell, Sir John and Lady Osborn, Lady Newsam, Sir Robert Peliza, Sir Andrew and Lady Stark, Dr Denis MacShane, MP, Mr Robert Worcester, other Diplomats and representatives of the Foreign and Commonwealth Office.

Left: **Londoners Diary, Evening Standard**; *Right:* **The Telegraph** of 31st October 2000

Not all the committee judged mainly by results. Sir Reginald Hibbert felt that the HQ was too much of a personal fiefdom and, for all its *politesse*, this was simply not the way to do things. He weighed in to bolster the power of the Committee. Sir Julian Oswald, with good reason, knew where and how the real work was being done. He and the Chairman, Lord Dahrendorf[78], saw off Sir Reggy. Such insurrection was rare, but not unknown. Lord Montgomery as Chairman, the example of his father of El Alamein fame before him, had a short way of dealing with any hint of jibbing at duly appointed Authority so long as they didn't question that of the Directors, and woe betide them if they questioned his.

A cast of extras, interns or friends in the main, would stuff envelopes and turn a hand to whatever was needed – bemused moths at the

---

[78] *Baron Ralf Gustav Dahrendorf KBE, FBA.*

flame of this powerhouse run in the gentleman amateur tradition long after the world had moved on to worship at the shrine of professionalism. Some were most helpful as well as unpaid – starting with Justin's wife, Catherine – such as Graham Jarvis who wrote reports on meetings, designed the website and, as a journalist, planted articles in the press. None of it satisfied an incoming Chairman, a General and a Peer, who preferred the show run in a manner more akin to the army.

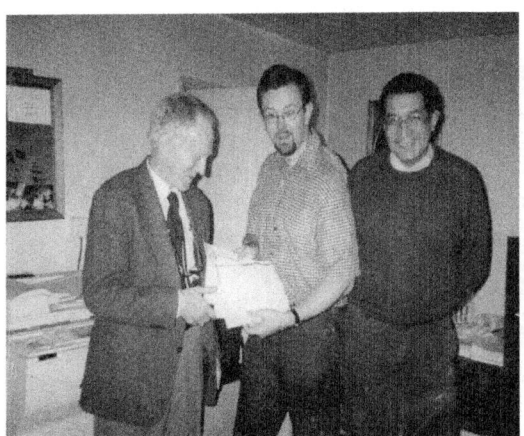

*Office adherents: the **Hon Dominick Browne, Graham Jarvis, Patrick Emek, Raymond George***

This was not going to wash. The supernumeraries sharpened their spurs. A man of deeds, not words, was Patrick Emek[79]. Trusty webcam in action, he sent a recording to the office of his portrayal of 'Luigi', the Mafiosi with a wardrobe of cement underpants that were tailor-made for recalcitrant E-AG Chairmen. Raymond George, an actor not to be out-performed, followed this with his video portrayal of

---

[79] *Patrick ran a private school, a career spiced up in vacations by trips to Indonesia, the Philippines and Sri Lanka, There he interviewed terrorists and thereafter wrote up findings for those charged with dealing with such threats.*

a Hun Stasi agent. Alas, his prey, the target of his grim, deadpan warnings, never heard them. Melissa, an American intern, complete with fern in her hair, which was cracked up to have been used as camouflage during an FBI agent field trip, got in on the act with an on-screen blast at the Chairman worthy of a female 007. A free-for all ensued, unleashing hitherto dormant acting ambitions. It was three tense weeks before E-AG top brass, notably the Earl of Limerick, ended the run of home movies by piloting through the Chairman's resignation, completely unaided by E-AG staff.

Elma had a flock of Big Beasts whose horns she could bring to bear on other Big Beasts, few admittedly, who tried to give her grief. It would put Justin Glass in an invidious position if he singled out those 'of his party', but apart from Sir Julian Oswald, who had so keen a mind and so warm a side, and with the profusest apologies to others not listed here, Sir Geoffrey Clifton Brown MP, Lord Judd, Sir John Osborn and Sir Neville Trotter have his undying gratitude.

The letters from, among others, Lady Hooper, Sir Michael Burton, Lady Symons and Lord Montgomery, and the other Chairmen, bespeak a commitment and a dedication beyond the call of duty, and much good sense. They were wonderful people. The same could be said of Trustee Christopher Arkell and Dr Julian Critchlow of the Elma Dangerfield Trust. Thanking them here properly is beyond the reach of Justin's pen.

The organisation was one for flying the Union Jack. Sir Michael Burton told the Group: 'What is clear is that Britain will always be at the centre'.[80] Sir Michael, a brilliant analyst among many other

---

[80] *Quoted in 'The Diplomat', February 2001. Sir Michael Burton, a former Ambassador and Chairman and President of the Group, was giving the Vote of Thanks at the E-AG meeting with the Shadow Foreign Secretary, the Rt. Hon. Sir Francis Maude. Sir Michael's attempt to call up a gunboat was when he was a*

qualities, picked the right stage, the E-AG, to tell of how he once attempted to call up a gunboat to make a diplomatic point. He was the last of a line of diplomats, vaunted in the nineteenth century, as exponents of the practice of 'Gunboat Diplomacy'.

Left: **Sir Michael Burton GCMG GCVO;** *On his left are* **Lord Limerick** *and* **Lord Judd**.
Right: **Sir Neville Trotter** *with* **Lord and Lady Hamilton** *at NATO banquet in 2009*

The speeches at the heart of the St James's Palace NATO 60th anniversary banquet in 2009 can be found on the Group website but this part of our tale is about what it was like to be backstage in the organisation. The letter of Julia Couchman to her friend Everett Hoffman describes what it felt like to be involved in the event. One can imagine her tension from her matter-of-fact account:

---

junior Diplomat in the Trujal States, now the UAE, because he felt that it was a sensible way to intercede in a dispute between ruling sheikhs. NB Lord Brammall told the E-AG in 1991: "...It is my experience from eight years in Whitehall that 'Send a gunboat' is still a seductive option in any political leader's armoury."

'The Palace was cold and drafty when I arrived at 5pm. What do you expect in an ancient building of stone and brick! Thirty of us were drilled on our duty and then Justin delegated posts. Mine was to be part of the Security Check at the entrance. The E-AG had 1000 members and I didn't know the NATO outsiders and I said that within those constraints I'd do my best.

'Lord Carrington came early and was stopped from entering the Palace before the official start of proceedings. He is 91. The police were very pleased that they'd managed to admit him with his chauffeur and car in the courtyard but now there he was, left out in the cold! You look after the car and forget the VIP! Nothing for it, I just took command treating policeman and staff like I used to drill horned, Welsh black cattle into submission. There is nothing like an element of surprise and I surprised myself as I was mad as hell. I seized him by the arm and said in an authoritative voice, "Lord Carrington, what an honour, can I take your arm." He looked so pleased to be rescued. He later complained since that there was no table named after him. Nothing like forgetting our home-grown NATO former Secretary-General! (Justin afterwards told me that every table was named after a former NATO Secretary-General and he hadn't wanted people to joke that they 'had sat on Carrington').

(Everyone had to have photographic ID but It transpired that the security team had a guest list that was a week out of date) 'If the police could turn you away, they certainly did! The Chilean Ambassador came up and thanked me for my help, they'd never have made it inside but for my help. Shenda Amery-Khazal's credentials were fine but those of her husband, Sheikh Nezam, were on an Iranian passport, or something of that nature. I knew him and was able to reassure the Palace security staff. The police, luckily after the couple had made their way inside, rushed up: "The Sheikh! The

Shiekh, you haven't let me him in!" I eased the path for General Sir Peter de la Billiere, and his wife said to him sweetly: "That should teach you dear not to leave things behind." Quite fun to see the likes of several other military including General Sir Mike Jackson being grilled. To their credit they took in in good part. Lord Hamilton then came up to me. "Take me through to Justin!", he commanded. So I abandoned my post....'

The nonpareil of those who discharged their self-imposed duty to the full was the stalwart person of The Rt. Hon. Lord Hamilton of Epsom. 'Archie' was inveigled into the E-AG Chairmanship on what transpired to be a false prospectus – 'Don't worry, Justin does everything.' For the first time in two decades, serious troublemakers – two who knew each other – arose and whose attitude called to mind Elma's oft-quoted biblical reference: 'All is vanity.' Up against Archie, all demonstrably erroneous contentions were swept into the dustbin of E-AG history, the smell lingering a short while as a last vestige of the bellyache. Cometh the hour, cometh the man! A veil is drawn over the time consumption and effort involved in seeing off one insurrectionist on the principle quoted by Dr Julian Critchlow with his typical erudition from the Rubaiyat of Omar Khayyam: 'to no such aureate earth are turn'd' / as, buried once, men want dug up again'. A recollection of Hugh Stewart, a corporate member, is saltier: 'When I sat opposite her she held out her hand for me to kiss. Much to her disappointment I took it in my hand and gave it a good shake'.

Lord Judd, the former Labour Minister, as Chairman was kind, indefatigable, and meticulous. His attitude can be seen in his lines to Mr Glass after Elma died: 'With admiration for all you are so excitingly doing for the E-AG.', as can that of the Admiral of the Fleet Sir Julian Oswald GCB in 2011: 'Looking back and thinking about all my happy years of membership, I think the most outstanding feature is my friendship with you personally.' Frank once said that politics was a profession more important than any other. On being reminded of this at a later date, he denied having made the assertion – perhaps it was just a view he happened to hold on the day of being asked.

Left: **Sir Julian Oswald** and **Roni, Lady Oswald**, with **Mrs Catherine Glass** (on the left); Right: **Lord Judd**, reading an E-AG Guest list

The Group was part of a social whirl. Work and amusement went hand in hand.

Elma and Dennis Walwin Jones, apart from their stays in Malta, spent weekends on the Thames usually in country houses along its banks. On Dennis's memorial tablet Elma had the lines of Lord Byron from Childe Harold inscribed: 'I live not in myself but I became portion of that around me'. It is a prime example of selective quotation. Elma chose not to add the sentiment in the next line of that poem: 'and to me…the hum of human cities (is) torture'. A dedicated urbanite, Elma's claim to fame may hinge on her being the first nonagenarian who was out on the tiles every single night. Elma was wont to remark of her socialising – 'Didn't we have FUN!' Not that a sense of humour was a noticeable trait in her. The only joke that Elma made that Justin can remember was after he told her that he had met a friend in the West End. She gasped, 'I hardly thought you would have friends in the …EAST End!'

Friends in high places had friends in high places, as well as clients. The E-AG was recommended with confidence by friends as well as successive E-AG Chairmen and Committee stalwarts like Sir Neville Trotter. Where better than the Betty Boothroyd Room in Portcullis House for the Speaker of the House of Commons, Betty Boothroyd, to speak, eyed by her likeness as rendered by Shenda Amery-Khazal's art?[81] Lady Killearn spoke of 'My lovely guests'. Her parties were the toast of the town, and when she died at the age of 105, mourners at her funeral seemed to feel short-changed by being deprived of their usual carousing laid on by this Queen Bee. After a morning service the reception in the church courtyard went on and on almost till dusk. The Hampstead mansion of Princess Gagarin-Moutafian was another port of call for Elma. There, she could hobnob with the likes of Boris Pankin[82], the Russian Ambassador. He had also been a 'lovely guest' of Lady K.

---

[81] *The Rt. Hon. Betty Boothroyd, MP spoke to the Group on 'Women in Parliament' on June 21st 1993.*
[82] *The speech to the Group of H.E. Mr Boris Pankin on June 12th 1995 is on the website of the Group with hard copies in the office records.*

> AT HER open day at Haremere Hall in East Sussex on Saturday, the 70-year-old Jacqueline, Lady Killearn was delighted to receive from Russian ambassador Boris Pankin the gift of a teapot, but was less lucky with some chocolates presented to her, which were consumed by the hard-of-hearing pianist entrusted with their safe keeping. When asked for their return, his reply was: "Thank you so much; they were quite delicious."

Left: **Lady Killearn** at an open day at her fourteenth century country seat, Heremere Hall; (centre); **Lord Kitchener**; (right) **Mr and Mrs Boris Pankin**, the Russian Ambassador and his wife

The elegance and wit on the party circuit usually drove talk of the hard realities away, much the same, it is said, as revels at the Palace – 'We don't do misery here!' Inevitably, there were some characters who enlivened the social scene of the E-AG. Dennis Bardens, to take one example, had been in the Secret Service in WW2, and his many books include a biography of Elizabeth Fry published by *European-Atlantic Publications*. His authorial and espionage credentials were enough to endear him to a Russian Ambassador wanting advice on publishing his memoirs. Dennis (pictured below at his home)[83] was trusted by Mr Pankin, not least because he rated him a member of the inner E-AG circle. His wit was laced with a trace of the laconic. No phrase of his evokes this trait better than the note (see below)

---

[83] *A poem by Dennis Bardens is at the end of the Section on the E-AG Journals.*

appended to the front door of his mews house in Kensington, for any passer-by to see.

A sense of this E-AG mix of social and political worlds reached into '*Hullo*' in its article on the event of the E-AG for Otto von Habsburg.

HELLO!

HABSBURG BANQUET

EDITED BY JOHN RENDALL

The Banqueting House, Whitehall, was the venue for a European Atlantic group dinner held in honour of Dr Otto von Habsburg, MEP and son of the last Emperor of Austria and King of Hungary, Archduke Charles von Habsburg. Principal guests included HE the Austrian Ambassador Dr Walter Magrutsch and the Hungarian Ambassador Mr Tibor Antalpeter.

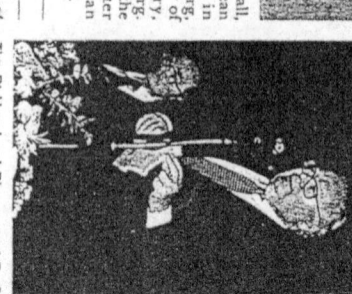

The Rt Hon Lord Rippon and Dr Otto von Habsburg, seated (above). Countess Casimir Grocholski and Count Nikolai Tolstoy (above right). Michele, Countess Griaznoff and Mr Michael Webb-Bowen (below right)

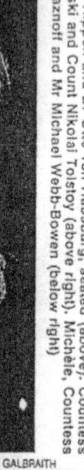
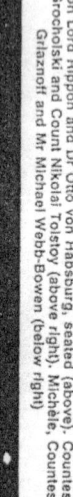

Mrs Daniel Prenn and the Duke of Valderano (below). Count and Countess Bertil Bernadotte (below right)

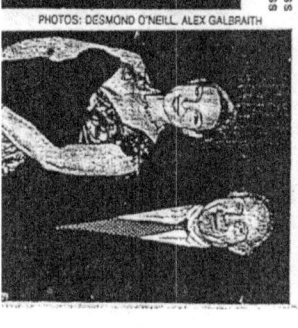

PHOTOS: DESMOND O'NEILL, ALEX GALBRAITH

HULLO - December 15th 1990

Jorge Luis Jure, the ambassador of Uruguay in Paris in 2024, and who was a Counsellor and Consul in London 1990-95, reminiscences in 2024:

Following a warm invitation by Mrs Elma Dangerfield and Mr. Justin Glass was my first time at those exciting and well attended EAG diners, with which I was invariably accompanied by Lilly Sigall[84] *(see below)*.

From the elegant entrances of London hotels to the perfectly prepared protocolar setting of tables, we could appreciate a wisely mixed crowd, composed of top politicians, foreign and local, senior and relatively junior diplomats (I was in that group at the early 90's…), who mingled with journalists and influential business people. It didn't matter who was the speaker (my goodness, we had big names), the

---

[84] *On page 218 is a photo of Sir Clive Bossom, and records can be found on page 61 and in the President's Report on page 176.*

understanding was that we were clearly 'North Atlantic', meaning believers of the good old alliance for democracy and decent human compassion: the order that encompassed the 50 years post 1945. Diplomats were trained to believe in a global system created to make international law respected and respectful.... We would help make a small world a gentler place, as we should expect the real world to behave.

Coming from Uruguay, I couldn't imagine myself further away on earth than Afghanistan, Egypt, Lithuania or Mongolia! But here there were leaders of those countries, talking to us! They surely were charmed by Elma and Justin to come and enlighten us about their World.

Listening to those top officials from 'exotic countries', we felt that the World was doing its best to ensure that 'the evil ones' would become better people and that the virtuous (namely us, those listening) were to be consecrated in the process. Humour, good food and wine together with Justin's efficiency would help relax the 'confessor' (the foreign lecturer) and cheer up 'the jury' that we felt ourselves to be.'

Jorge referred to Lilly Sigall. It prompts a keyhole peep into the cultural worlds interlocking with the E-AG. Lilly Sigall was the doyenne of social hostesses in her exquisite home. She was a gracious Hungarian lady, Jewish, of zestfulness, charm, gentleness and a melodic voice. Her *milieu* was the world of arts, as her *Times* obituary spelled out. Opera singers of the ilk of Placido Domingo, TV producers like Christopher Raeburn, critics like Ned Sherrin thronged to see her. She always looked on the bright side, once commenting to the celebrated actress whose husky voice dripped with suggestive sexual allure, Fenella Fielding: *'Darling, such a terrible accident that brought you to hospital – but at least you were run over by a Mercedes and not by a bike!'* A caring, upright lady was Lilly: *'I never committed adultery! After all, the men I only slept with when I was married were famous!'*

Tales from Behind Scenes had a certain charm, if not always. Countess Elizabeth Ledochowska, of high sensitivity and refinement, a composer and pianist in direct line of descent from the Earl of Carnarvon, came to Lilly's *soirees* as well as the E-AG. Elizabeth was seeing her cousin at Highclere Castle when Her late Majesty was visiting. Elizabeth asked Lord Carnarvon to introduce her and was rewarded, if that is the word, by hearing the Queen say in the next room on being asked to come and shake her hand: *"Oh No! Not Another!"*

This was what the Group circles were like and there were many of them. Mention is in these pages of Sir Clive Bossom Bt, whose contributions to the E-AG marked his public *persona,* and that of his father. In their jovial and learned presence, even smut became gracious. Aged 98, he spoke about Max Mosley who was being pilloried in the press about his no-longer-private peccadillos: *"And I said to Max, 'Max, we have been friends for 50 years so why is it that you have never once invited me to one of your spanking parties!'"*

The Director received an invitation to the Iranian Embassy for a private luncheon after a dinner-debate previously mentioned. Conviviality was the order of the day. This included talk of private proclivities of the four Ayatollahs whose large framed, stern photographs in black and white glowering from the dining room wall belied stories of what they got up to at night. The Minister, possibly sniffing a latent louche streak in his guest, went on to hint that he undergo religious conversion; indicating the belles in summery skimpy clothing in Kensington Park outside the window, he opined that it was holy writ that men following the Teaching should enjoy themselves to the hilt. The waitress, having served lunch, glided from the room, backwards. If her eyes goggled her subservient demeanour did not betray her.

The thousand or so E-AG members, impeccably respectable to a man and woman, in general were happy to sniff the rarefied air in which most E-AG high-ups lived and all members had the Cavendish Club near Marble Arch in the centre of London as a perquisite of E-AG membership. Talk among E-AG aficionados often had much to do with the political world. Evidence of this is in letters written at length and often with acuity which attest to wishes of members[85] to bring concerns to the melting pot of debate with those in the centre of political affairs.

Elma Dangerfield at Newstead Abbey, home of Lord Byron

---

[85] *Sonia Ayres of the Harpenden United Nations Association was a good example of an avid and very sensible correspondent. Her summary of the speech by Sir Kieran Prendergast in 2000 is in the Speeches section. Other Members such as Darius Furmanovicious and Lilly Sigall, in many ways, gave of their time and valuable advice.*

The Byron Society, since its re-founding by Elma in 1972, had its part to play in the way things were. Michael Foot, leader of Her Majesty's Opposition, was a Byron Society Vice President, poetry being a love of his, but he surfaces as a book reviewer in the E-AG Journal. In choosing Viscount Montgomery of Alamein as his subject, this Left Winger picked out a safe choice for the E-AG.[86] Lord Bessborough reigned almost supreme in the European-Atlantic Group hierarchy when Justin Glass plunged into this world. It was by way of a Byron Society invitation to a play about Lord Byron in the private theatre of Eric Bessbough's country seat, Stansted. He arrived, knowing no-one save, barely, Elma just as an altercation between His Lordship and Elma was heating up to its sorry climax. Eric Bessborough refused point-blank to go on stage and play Byron, opposite Elma as Byron's lover, Lady Caroline Lamb. Mr Glass first set eyes on a tall man in a smoking jacket who angrily divested himself of that garment and, placing it around Justin's shoulders where it took on the look of a dressing gown, demanded, imperious forefinger pointing at him:

'YOU! You will play Lord Byron!'

They are not the words that Mr Glass will remember till his dying day. These came shortly afterwards. Mr Glass, bemused, script in hand, was onstage beside Elma, in character, sobbingly protesting her thwarted love for him in front of a Byron Society audience mainly of respectable ladies of a certain age. Mr Glass was desperately looking down the page to see what he was about to reply and then saw, looming up – in an age much more prudish than now – the awful words that explained the belted Earl's sudden cold feet:

---

[86] *See Speeches on the website of the Group with hard copies in the office records and Review section.*

'YOU NEED NOT JUST KISS AND TELL! YOU CAN **FUCK** AND PUBLISH!'

As far as Justin was concerned, Lady Caroline had to be blinded by love to describe Byron merely as 'mad, bad, and dangerous to know!' In interpreting the way Byron slammed into his whimpering mistress, Justin's whisper was elevated almost to an art form. Years later Lord Bessborough addressed him as 'my Lord in waiting!' Justin's induction into this *métier* and embrace by the E-AG hierarchy owes much to the Byron Society.

Above: Evidence of the indelibility of early memories, the one person of whom Elma was seen to be in awe, **Maria Gussago**, known as 'Nanny' and whose every word to Elma was as a command. On her right is **Lady Killearn**

The apotheosis of the Upstairs Downstairs *geist* permeating the office came when Penny, 'the maid', had had her fill of an attitude so out of step with the times. After an altercation, Elma's words 'Finish! Finish! Finish!' or their equivalent, for once did not weave their customary spell. Penny lodged a complaint against Elma and it went to an Employment Tribunal. It was water off a duck's back to Elma. Justin suggested her plea be on the grounds of the greater respect surely due to one of her advanced years and background. Addressing the Judge, he was pointing out that Mrs Dangerfield was 90 years old. Elma would not stoop to anything short of the truth even if to gloss over it was in her interest. Penny's case, which was faltering by then, took wings when much merriment was caused in court by Elma's angry rebuke, clear as a bell and louder than most, enfeebling the punch behind his presentation:

'I AM NOT 90! I AM ONLY 89!'

Elma's competitive spirit extended even to the sphere of longevity. She remarked on turning 98 and so outliving the rest of her family: "I've beaten the lot of them!"

It was not a case of 'All play and no Work'; there was no obvious boundary between the categories. Work and play were intertwined and never stopped.

Michael Wade tells the story of his going with Elma to the country house, Knebworth, as the guest of Lord Cobbold. His mother, a most gracious lady, Hermione Cobbold, *née* Hermione Bulwer-Lytton, came to tea. At the time of our visit in the early 2000s, she was the last living Vicereine of India. She lived in a house in the grounds, which was the old stables converted into a very comfortable bungalow. She remarked to Elma words to the effect that they were getting on a bit. 'I'm 96. *(give or take a year)* How old are you?' Elma was horrified and retorted in her inimitable way, 'I NEVER disclose or talk about my age!' Light was shed on Elma's anti-ageist thinking when Justin threw a surprise party for her 90th birthday and she burst out: 'I don't WANT to be 90!'

Elma reigned in her living room and, wary of invading its sacrosanct space, interns slaved below stairs and later in the Finchley office *(see comments below)*. Most of them were American; another one, Keay, was a credit to South Korea; they were birds of passage who provided invaluable assistance. To these interns, the pick of the Centre which sent them, who helped make the E-AG flourish during that period, the Director must say a very big THANK YOU!

Comments from the E-AG interns

> ***Sent to the E-AG by CAPA, the Centre for Academic Programmes Abroad*[87]**

The E-AG seems to really be humming along. The newsletters looked *fantastic*. Kaunda seems fascinating and I'm sure he did not disappoint. As you noted in your newsletter, the E-AG appears to be on a new trajectory of providing up-and-coming leaders a platform with which to promote their ideals. Has this become the E-AG's new mandate or was this more of a coincidence? You've also managed to procure promising people from nations that need liberal leaders who can inspire their citizens – *(Griffin)*… I want to say again thank you so much for letting me work with you – *(Tania)*… I hope you've found a bit more peace and quiet coupled with a little less stress with all the inherent responsibilities that come with the E-AG and the dinner-discussions. They were definitely an intriguing part of my experience abroad and I'm very thankful I got the opportunity to sit in on them and take it all in – *(Bryan)*…I just wanted to write to you to thank you for everything over the course of this internship. You are a wonderful boss who works and runs a great organisation – *(Kristin)*…Thank you so much for everything – *(Kasia)*… I wanted to write a note and

---

[87] *The department concerned in CAPA was run expertly by Terry Sheen, who understood exactly the E-AG requirements and singled out candidates every one of which fulfilled amply the expectation of them.*

thank you for everything. Working with the Group was wonderful and proved to be much more than I ever expected. I appreciate the time and patience you allowed me. I feel I learned a lot and gained valuable experience due to your efforts. Thank you for the responsibility and trust. I hope to have kept the standard high. Also thank you for the 'push' in asking the question at the second dinner. As I spoke I heard your voice saying 'Speak slowly, loudly and confidently. This allowed me to keep my composure' – **(Kim)**… I was saddened to read that Lord Limerick had passed away. He was a great man and we were privileged to have known him. I think about my time in London often. If ever you are planning to visit the Chicago area and need a place to stay, just let me know. – **(Robert)**… Thanks for a great new experience – **(Gabe)**… I have really started to miss being at the office. I trust that the summer conferences have gone well and I hope the E-AG website will be at full service to give the transcripts a look in the future – **(Ryan)**… I just wanted to say thank you so much for a terrific internship experience. I still can't believe the amount of work that you and Boris put into the events and I think that you should demand more credit. I really appreciate how you trusted us to handle very important tasks, and in all honesty will remember the experience forever – **(Sarah)**… I would like to take this time for having me part of the company for the internship. Having this internship has been an invaluable experience and one that I will treasure for a lifetime – **(Kyle)**… I am feeling so grateful to you as the placement at The E-AG has been real asset on my C.V. Now about the next meeting, of course I could come and help you out – **(Assitan)**… I just wanted to say 'Thank you' again. Thank you very much indeed for the great opportunity! It was a fantastic time and a very awesome work climate! – **(Christiane)**… Thank you so much for everything. It was such a pleasure to work for you – **(Amber)**… Thank you for all of the opportunities that you have given us – **(Nicole and Jenn)**

From Vivenne Todd, European College of Business and Management):

Thank you very much for providing a work placement for Juan. The feedback from the group was extremely positive, and we are most grateful to you for making Juan so welcome and for the time you have given to make the experience worthwhile.

©Copyright May 2020 All Rights Reserved – Justin Glass justinglass2020@gmail.com

4. THE EUROPEAN-ATLANTIC GROUP JOURNALS

European-Atlantic Review, New European, European-Atlantic Journal, Politics Tomorrow

In the early days of the Group its Journal, *European-Atlantic Review*, covered the gamut of taxing international issues, including accounts of a few debates at E-AG meetings. Later, the *European-Atlantic Journal* was devoted mainly to transcripts of speeches at E-AG events – much may have been lost to posterity due to the ensuing debates being off-the-record. It also carried reviews of books by illustrious E-AG members on the hot topics of the day. Both trends finally flowered in the journal of the E-AG, *Politics Tomorrow*, which was almost exclusively on subjects debated at the Group inclusive of transcripts, together with articles of more general political and international interest written by informed members and specialists.

The Group entered into a partnership in 2005 with the publishers of *New European*, which was subtitled anew as 'The Journal of the European-Atlantic Group'. Mr Glass became a co-Director with John Coleman, an Oxford-educated publisher of the 'old school'. His meetings, despite his commercial bent, were flavoured with intellectual curiosity. Augustus Caesar's thinking often seemed to cast light on issues scrutinised by the E-AG. A reverence for the traditional segued into the Review section policy: authors garnered a spurious authority through their own summaries being printed as 'reviews'. After all, E-AG journals had always boasted a Review Section...

John Coleman

The following pages give samples of covers and editorials of the E-AG Journals.

Please note that:

(a) The poems by Dennis Bardens and Lord Limerick mentioned previously as being in 'Politics Tomorrow' are reproduced below. (b) the 'E-AG Journal' had no bespoke editorial aside from the Group Aims, and (c) the 'European Atlantic Review' is discussed in the 'E-AG Foundation' section.

EUROPEAN-ATLANTIC REVIEW

First journal of the Atlantic Community and of European economic co-operation

Headquarters of the South-East Asia Treaty Organization in Bangkok. See ASIAN...

Contributors to this issue include

LUNS · AIICHIRO FUJIYAMA · LAURIS NORSTAD
PIERO MALVESTITI · PAUL-HENRI SPAAK
...UDE GIBB · POTE SARASIN · SIR GERALD D'ERLANGER

EUROPEAN-ATLANTIC REVIEW
Vol. 8, No. 4. Winter, 1958-59

EDITORIAL BOARD

The Earl of Bessborough
President, European-Atlantic Group

Sir Edward Beddington-Behrens, C.M.G., M.C.
Chairman, United Kingdom Council of the European Movement

Sir David Kelly, G.C.M.G., M.C.
President, British Atlantic Committee

The Rt. Hon. Lord Pakenham, P.C.
the Hon. Michael Layton; Nigel Nicolson, M.P.
R.T. Paget, Q.C., M.P.; the Hon. Sir Steven Runciman

EXECUTIVE EDITORS

Elma Dangerfield; Howard Russell

Editorial Office
61, Gloucester Place, London, W.1.
Tel.: Welbeck 9753

Publishing Office
64-78, Kingsway, London, W.C.2.
Tel.: Chancery 9227

Editorial Commentary

GENERAL DE GAULLE's courageous decision to put the French economy on to a realistic footing has important results in the international sphere. It means that France is fulfilling her obligations as a member of the Organization for European Economic Co-operation, by lifting restrictions on ninety per cent of her imports from all seventeen O.E.E.C. nations. It had been known for some time that de Gaulle did not see eye to eye with those influential French industrialists who were intent on preserving the greatest possible measure of protection for French industry. He has been credited with the privately expressed aim of ending the situation in which France was "always in the dock" at international economic conferences. That aim has been achieved. When the nations meet now, France can hold her head high.

Welcome as this transformation is, it does not, in itself, do anything to end the deadlock over future economic arrangements in Europe which had developed when the Council of O.E.E.C. adjourned its meeting in December. That deadlock had developed over short-term arrangements to nullify the discrimination in European trade resulting from the inception of the Common Market on January 1. On that date, the six Common Market countries began mutual tariff and quota concessions which would not all apply to the other eleven countries in O.E.E.C. With goodwill on both sides — and goodwill has been engendered by the French actions — this short-term problem may be resolved, for the world of tariffs and quotas is a complicated one which lends itself to intricate compromise. But the task of putting Europe's economic arrangements on to a satisfactory basis will only have begun. The long-term solution has still to be sought.

THE need for this long-term solution cannot be evaded. It will come inexorably closer. As Signor Malvestiti, Vice-President of the Commission of the Common Market, points out in an article in this issue, further tariff and quota concessions are due under the Common Market treaty next year. Discrimination will progressively increase. Unless ways are found to avoid it, the other eleven O.E.E.C. countries will inevitably seek ways of cancelling out its effects upon their own economies. A trade war in Europe could all too easily be the result.

It may be possible now to take a new look at the principles on which that solution should be sought. Some complicating factors which had helped to confuse the issue have been cleared out of the way. The fact that France was taking on new commitments under the Common Market treaty while, at the same time, protesting that she was unable to fulfil her long-standing commitments to O.E.E.C. to liberalise her trade, had done a great deal to sour the atmosphere of negotiation. This has now been recti-

Editorial Commentary CONTINUED

fied. More important still, the question of the future of the European Payments Union is no longer an issue.

The Union was probably the most effective instrument which had been devised in the postwar years for furthering economic expansion in Europe. Switzerland had already given notice of her intention to withdraw from it, if the Common Market came into operation without some form of multi-lateral agreement embracing all the O.E.E.C. countries. It is doubtful whether many other nations would have followed the Swiss example, and certainly Britain would not. But it was widely recognised that if the Common Market continued to develop, divorced from the rest of Europe, the Payments Union system would almost certainly have proved unworkable. The consequences for all the European countries, in the Common Market or outside, would have been severe.

All this is changed by the decision to make the major European currencies convertible in a limited sense. As was planned as long ago as 1955, the Payments Union is ended and the European Monetary Agreement takes its place. One of the important effects is that the Payments Union arrangements for automatic credit are gone. Another of its effects, however, is that a system which would have been unworkable if the Common Market countries had proceeded with their plans in isolation, has been replaced by a system which would not be unworkable in those circumstances. In this sense, the hand of the Common Market countries has been strengthened for any future negotiations.

But the new arrangements will, in any case, demand even closer co-operation between all the European countries in monetary policies. Such co-operation, particularly between Britain and France, has been apparent in recent weeks, and the task now is to extend it to the solution of trading disputes. It is here that a new look at the true nature of the problem is needed.

ONE of the first needs, perhaps, is to get rid of what might be called the rival theologies of the six Common Market countries and the remaining eleven O.E.E.C. countries. Attitudes have become too frozen. The sense of impending doom needs to be dissipated. The importance of co-ordinating economic and financial policies in Europe far transcends matters of trade arrangements, vital though sound decisions in this sphere may be. Above all, the unity of Europe in political and defence matters remains the over-riding consideration. No rival theologies in trading arrangements should be allowed to undermine it.

What are these rival theologies? Only a few aspects of them can be mentioned here, but one important differences is over the nature of a Customs Union (which the Common Market is) and of a Free Trade Area (which the other eleven nations want). Both of these forms of association are recognized by the General Agreement on Tariffs and Trade and by O.E.E.C., although a Free Trade Area in which there was discrimination between the members would be contrary to G.A.T.T. In essence, the Common Market partners take the view that the members of a Customs Union mus treat the countries inside the Union differently from the countries outside; otherwise the Customs Union becomes meaningless and ceases to exist. This is true. But hov important is it?

It has often been pointed out that the objectives of the Common Market go fa beyond mere matters of trade. It aims also at great economic advances in terms of the rationalisation of industry and the stimulating of an era of expansion in the hea of Europe. In addition, it has tremendous political objectives. It should be the fin act of Franco-German reconciliation, creating a supranational political entity in Euro which will end once and for all the national rivalries of the past. It looks forward

Editorial Commentary CONTINUED

the day when a great European Parliament, elected by direct suffrage, will set the seal on a European unity such as has never ben known before. This is a great ideal. Is it really dependent upon niggling over a quota of three per cent of national production in this or that sphere? Is it wise, or right, or even expedient, to bring about a new split in Europe in the name of European unity? These are questions which the Common Market countries need to ask themselves anew.

THEY are not the only ones who need to do some self-questioning. Another clash between these rival theologies is over the relations of nations in a free trade area with the rest of the world. The French view, simplified, has been that a free trade area is a preferential system in which each of the members has guaranteed preferences in the markets of the other members. It follows from this that none of the member countries can have freedom over its external commercial policy. The British view has been that, whatever else a Free Trade Area does, it should not inhibit the trade of members with the rest of the world. This is a natural view for a country which does only one-quarter of its trade with Europe and three-quarters of it elsewhere. But, again, how important is it?

Clearly, Britain, and other nations of the potential Free Trade Area could not agree to submit their trading policies to a supranational body with powers of the kind the Common Market countries envisage. But the bridging of the gap between these rival theologies should not be difficult. The French concern is that the Free Trade Area may, in turn, become almost meaningless through the external trading policies of some member countries. Britain, or any other country, should be willing to agree to a procedure by which complaints of this nature could be thrashed out in some appropriate body — and O.E.E.C. would seem to be the most appropriate.

Fortunately, there is time for reflection of this kind, regardless of what happens at the imminent discussions on the short-term objective of eliminating the discrimination which at present exists. It is the long-term solution which matters most. Professor Hallstein, President of the Commission of the Common Market, has been charged with the task of producing proposals on behalf of the Common Market countries, and he has to submit his report by March. This method of working has some disadvantages, at any rate for the non-Common Market countries. It gives something of an air of unreality to other negotiations and, while Ministers are talking, they cannot but be conscious that other talks are proceeding at different levels. But its great advantage is that the Hallstein report will, at last, produce a common attitude among the six Common Market countries. This should be a big step forward.

It remains to be seen whether or not the Hallstein proposals will be acceptable to the remaining eleven countries. It is, perhaps, too much to hope that this will be so. But they should form the basis on which, given goodwill on all sides, a long-term multilateral agreement can be negotiated. That must be the hope of all who care for the future of European unity.

CONTENTS

A revolution begins	Piero Malvestiti	7
Three elements of Western strategy	General Lauris Norstad	10
Is Nato equipped to face the future?	J. M. A. H. Luns	12
Future of Atlantic air travel	Sir Gerard d'Erlanger	17
Survey of European nuclear developments		23
Risks for Nato in political co-operation	Paul-Henri Spaak	32
Viewpoints from the Asian nations		36
European-Atlantic Information Service		45

THE EUROPEAN-ATLANTIC JOURNAL

The Section on Speeches and Articles contains speeches printed in the European-Atlantic Journal as well as the following book reviews

BOOK REVIEWS

The Earl of Bessborough DL *On:* **EUROPE: A HISTORY OF ITS PEOPLES** *By:* Jean-Baptise Duroselle

The Earl of Bessborough DL *On:* **MACMILLAN: 1957–1986** *(Volume Two) By:* Alistair Horne

The Rt. Hon. Lord Chalfont, OBE, MC, PC *On:* **OUT OF STEP** *By:* Michael Carver

The Rt. Hon. Lord Chalfont, OBE, MC, PC *On:* **IN SEARCH OF CHURCHILL** *By:* Martin Gilbert

The Rt. Hon. Lord Chalfont, OBE, MC, PC *On:* **ALBANIA'S NATIONAL LIBERATION STRUGGLE: THE BITTER VICTORY** *By:* Reginald Hibbert

The Lord Dahrendorf KBE FBA *On:* **JEAN MONNET: FIRST STATESMAN OF INTERDEPENDENCE** *By:* François Duchêne

Michael R. D. Foot *On:* **THE LONELY LEADER** *By:* Alistair Horne *and* David Montgomery

Sir Curtis Keeble GCMG *On:* **DEALING WITH DICTATORS** *By:* Sir Frank Roberts GCMG GCVO

Judith, Countess of Listowel *On:* **THE EVIL EMPIRE** *By:* Count de Marenches

Sir Frank Roberts GCMG GCVO *On:* **HITLER AND STALIN: Parallel Lives** *By:* Alan Bullock

Sir Frank Roberts GCMG GCVO *On:* **THE WESTERN EUROPEAN UNION AND NATO** *By:* Alfred Cahen

Sir Frank Roberts GCMG GCVO *On:* **VOICE IN THE WILDERNESS: Imre Nagy and the Hungarian Revolution** *By:* Peter Unwin

Christopher Robson *On:* **CHURCHILL A LIFE** *By:* Martin Gilbert

Christopher Robson *On:* **THE CHALLENGE OF EUROPE – CAN BRITAIN WIN?** *By:* Michael Heseltine

***Christopher Robson**, Review Editor, European-Atlantic Journal*

European-Atlantic Journal
1994-1995 ISSUE

CONTRIBUTORS:
Dr. Kevin Klose
H.E. Ambassador Mohammed Shaker
Deputy Secretary-General Sergio Silvio Balanzino
Rt. Hon. Hon. Lord Richard QC
H.E. Mr. David Tatham
Former Ambassador- H.E. Boris Pankin
H.E. Mr. Kent Durr
The Hon. Roy Maclaren
Sir Patrick Mayhew QC, MP
H.E. Ambassador Perez de Cueller

BOOK REVIEWS
Rt. Hon. Lord Dahrendorf KBE, FBA
Rt. Hon. Lord Chalfont, OBE, MC, PC
M. R. D. Foot
Christopher Robson

EDITORS-IN-CHIEF
Rt. Hon. Lord Dahrendorf KBE, FBA
Rt. Hon. Lord Chalfont, OBE, MC, PC
Rt. Hon. Lord Rippon of Hexham, QC, PC

EXECUTIVE EDITOR
Elma Dangerfield, OBE

REVIEW EDITOR
Christopher Robson

Published by The European-Atlantic Group, 6 Gertrude Street, London SW 10
Registered Charity No. 274898   Price £5.00
In Association with European-Atlantic Journal Ltd.

NEW EUROPEAN

THE EUROPEAN-ATLANTIC GROUP
ON AFGHANISTAN
   General Sir Mike Jackson
   Chief Ajmal Khan
   General Sir David Richards

David Howell
   TOWARDS ENERGY AND
   CLIMATE REALISM

Rob Hopkins interviewed
   THE TRANSITION MOVEMENT

QUARTERLY REVIEW
Journal of
THE EUROPEAN-ATLANTIC GROUP

Price £4.95   **Winter/Spring 2008/9**

EDITORIAL

The most important section in this issue hinges on Afghanistan. Clearly the Middle East as well as the whole of Asia have a significant bearing on what happens there. As the former Ambassador to Afghanistan, Sir Jeffrey James said, in referring to the roots of terrorism, when we went into Iraq 'we took our eye off the ball' as far as the true cause of terrorism is concerned. Al Queda saw its tactical advantage as lying in Afghanistan and northern Pakistan. General Richards and Chief Ajmal Khan have a very promising answer to that troubled area. It is greatly to the credit of Justin Glass that, when he came across Ajmal Khan struggling to tell Western authorities what he believed to be the true nature of the Afghan situation, he quickly drew him into the E-AG circle and introduced him to the appropriate generals who also knew the realities from the point of view of soldiers on the ground. Perhaps one of the greatest failings of our Western societies is not to see the realities at that level. Maybe this is a lesson that should also be learnt from our experience in former Yugoslavia.

On the environmental front we begin with David Howell's new book, *Out of the Energy Labyrinth; Towards Energy and Climate Realism*. As the author a few years ago of *On the Edge of Now*, his views on the coming energy crisis are particularly significant and as Deputy Leader of the Conservatives in the House of Lords his influence on his Party's policy on energy must be considerable. Brian Lewis gives a fascinating account of how sail power can be harnessed more effectively today with the use of modern technology. Finally Rob Hopkins suggusts how a change in lifestyle can actually lead to more satisfying life. He started the Transition Movement in Totnes and it has now spread to many towns and cities all over Britain. A combination of this and the appropriate modern technology may well be the way to prepare for the difficult challenges of the future.

The Rev. Anthony Freeman, author of *God in Us – a Case for Christian Humanism*, gives us an insight into the thinking of Daniel Dennett, the fiercely critical opponent of creationism in America. Christopher Ormell, the editor of the educational journal *Prospero*, questions the way in which education today tries to be 'value-neutral' and concentrates on teaching skills alone. He believes the moral effect of this to be disastrous. It reminds us perhaps of Florence Nightingale's comment: 'If you teach the three R's without morality, you can add a fourth R, Rascaldom.'

In New European we aim to include articles by authors about their own books. Lord Howell's book is obviously in this category. Margaret Pawley, whose article hardly does justice to her excellent book, *The Watch on the Rhine*, provides us with another example. As the daughter of the last High Commissioner she grew up in post First World War Germany and was directly acquainted with the situation on the ground. She chronicles the warnings of her father and the military commanders out there about the growing Nazi network, and how they were disregarded by those at home in their political ivory towers.

A straightforward book review by Jim Bourlet of the Economic Research Council follows. The interesting thing about *A Farewell to Alms* by Gregory Clark is that it gives Thomas Malthus, not Adam Smith, centre stage in economic history, The short reviews which follow mainly refer to themes in the present issue of *New European*.

John Coleman

Politics
TOMORROW

THE JOURNAL OF THE EUROPEAN ATLANTIC GROUP

In Focus:

The Euro-Atlantic and the Middle East
Prince Hassan of Jordan, page 20

America's Relationship with Europe
Larry LaRocco, page 6

Faith and Conflict in the New Europe
The Lord Bishop of London, page 37

The Challenges Facing UK Armed Forces
Admiral the Lord Boyce, page 46

ISSUE 1 · JULY 2005

Contents

Insight

Editorial, *Sir Richard Body & Justin Glass* 4

Articles

America's Relationship with Europe, *Larry LaRocco* 6
In Favour of a Strong Transatlantic Partnership, *Dr. Karl H. Pagac* 8
Deepening after Enlargement of the European Union, *Dr Glen M. Segell FRGS* 12
An Assessment of the Current Political Climate in the USA, *Prof. Alan Lee Williams* 13
Astrophysics: The Way Forward, *Lucy Irimy* 16
Britain and the European Common Market, *Elma Dangerfield & Howard Russell* 18

Debates and Speeches

The Euro-Atlantic and the Middle East, *Prince El Hassan bin Talal of Jordan* 20
The Council of Europe: The Way Forward, *Dr. Walter Schwimmer* 32
Faith and Conflict in the New Europe, *The Lord Bishop of London* 37
New Conceptual Thinking Required for the Armed Forces, *General Sir Deverell* 40
The Challenges Facing UK Armed Forces, *Admiral the Lord Boyce* 46

Book Reviews

Asymmetries of Conflict, *John Leech* 50
Fighting Through to Kohima, *Lieutenant-Colonel Michael Lowry* 52
On Being a Conspiracy Theorist, *Tim Slessor* 55
Rising Tides, *Rory Spowers* 58
The Politics of the Forked Tongue, *Aidan Rankin* 62
Nurturing the Natural Laws of Peace, *Ted Dunn* 65
Give and Take, *David Sogge* 69
The Last Hours of Ancient Sunlight, *Thom Hartmann* 73

European-Atlantic Aims 76

Politics Tomorrow
Journal of The
European-Atlantic Group

Published by Chanadon Publication Ltd.

PO Box 37431
London N3 2PP
Telephone: 0207 3528300
Fax: 0207 9006660
Email: info@chanadon.co.uk
www.chanadon.co.uk

In association with New European Publications

14-16 Carroun Road
SW8 1JT
Telephone/Fax: 0207 58239996
Editorial Board

Editorial Board

John Coleman, Chairman
Sir Richard Boy, Editor
Josephine Pearse, Deputy Editor
Lord Norton of Louth
Dr Ann Robinson
Professor Philip Schlesinger
Diana Schumacher
Professor Christopher Thompson
Lorraine Williams
Tracey Worcester
Luise Hemmer Pihl

Journal of The European-Atlantic Group

Elma Dangerfield CBE
Justin Glass
Boris Andonov
Christopher Robson
Irene Banfield
Christopher Ling
Melissa Zanmiller
Scott D. Withycombe
Catherine Moorhouse

Production by Innovative Labs

3 · *Politics Tomorrow*

Editorial...

Conscious that our readers have felt the doom and gloom of so many of the books we have chosen in the past, we now strive as best we can to avoid dismal genre. The trouble is that optimists are not motivated to sit down for months on end to write about the good things; given their perspective, they find more pleasurable ways to spend their time. However, we have selected a few books tending towards pessimism but with the hopes of a solution.

Modern technology also comes into Asymmetries of Conflict: War Without Death. This is a timely book on a subject that exercises the minds of most of us. Wars are never likely to be fought again by two great armies facing each other more or less evenly balanced. Modern technology and rapid means of transportation have enabled a handful of suicidal terrorists to fight a battle on a scale that only several army divisions could have fought in the past. There are also quite a few nuclear bombs once in Russia that seem to have disappeared into unknown hands. Although some kind of warfare will never cease, other less murderous means must be found to defend a nation. In the nineteenth century Disraeli and after him Lord Salisbury knew how to bluff and cajole powers much greater than their own; and long before them Queen Elizabeth skilfully took on and defeated all Europe one, by one, without a death. The twenty-first century needs to refashion those skills.

Neo-classical economics having become respectable even in Beijing, a reaction has to be inevitable. Seven Steps to Justice is a critique of the system, and in advocating monetary reform it is surely opposed to only a by-product of the system that is now reaching levels that could not have been imagined by a previous generation. In short, only about twenty per cent of spending power in the UK was in the form of bakers' money (overdrafts, credit cards, and the like), whereas for us it is now 97 per cent. Reflecting upon that for less than a minute we realise it is something that simply cannot go on without the whole edifice crashing down. As the authors say, it is also unjust.

The proportion of the working population now employed in one or another form by the state is one in five, higher than it has ever been except in time of war. Anyone involved in this huge sector knows of the ways of self-protection; criticism from outside can be redirected down a cul-de-sac. Tim Slessor has served us well in On Being a Conspiracy Theorist, a title he has taken ironically, having been so described by a government minister, 'discomforted' by Slessor's penetration of the truth about his department's incompetence. His is a book that deserves to be read very widely.

What a surprise? Rising Tides – a History of Environmental Revolution – Visions for an Ecological Campaign is not more doom and gloom, for it ends with a healthy (in the original sense) degree of optimism, albeit with a caveat. Rory Spowers blends history and philosophy to give us much to think about.

Some of us laugh at political correctness; others simply believe it to be politeness taken a bit too far. Aidan Rankin, however, shows it to be something quite different – a new ideology purporting to be liberal but dangerously authoritarian. He takes three examples – race, homosexuality and feminism – and argues that each is compartmentalised, so that minorities within those three groups are denied those two precious freedoms, of Speech and of association. Orwell saw this coming. Politics of the Forked Tongue needs to be taken seriously.

Sadly Ted Dunn died just days before his Nurturing the Natural Laws of Peace was published. It is a legacy for which we can be grateful. Natural law is not easy to define, but readers may grasp the essence from his contribution in these pages and then see how it can reconcile those old adversaries, individual freedom and government power. Both can be transferred to the world stage, to freedom of nations to behave towards others as they chose and inter-governmental

4 • *Politics Tomorrow*

or supra-governmental authorities. The power of the law though, can so often be abused in a welter of fine language. The new International Criminal Court seems to be on the verge of doing just that.

David Sooge is well qualified to write about foreign aid. In Give and Take he points to much of what is going wrong in the way that tens of billions of dollars a year are spent on foreign aid. Professor Lord Bauer died not long ago: he spent virtually the whole of his distinguished academic career in showing that foreign aid was based upon a series of fallacies. Fair trade, he said, was much better for the Third World. But that means the rich countries and especially the EU and US, dismantling their tariff and non-tariff barriers against poor countries. And there is no sign of either of them wishing to do that in the way it should be done, for there are too many powerful interests with other ideas.

The clash between the Old and New Cultures is the theme of the Last Hours of Ancient Sunlight. There is poignancy in every page, and anyone reading this book will surely realise that our present-day zest for materialism is suffocating the spiritual values of ancient tribes. In those little pockets of the world where they have survived until now they are being exterminated, without exception, and by cultural warfare. Are we really homo sapiens? ■

Sir Richard Body
Editor, World Review

European-Atlantic

European-Atlantic Group debates are a quest for solutions to difficulties in international relations. Many of the monthly addresses to the Group over the last few months have been electric. It is perhaps invidious to select from these the worthiest for inclusion in these pages but the problem of selection has been eased by the fact that much of E-AG proceedings cannot be published because off-the-record. We have included in this edition an edited transcript of a debate with Prince Hassan of Jordan as well as the text of his on-the-record speech, and those of the Secretary-General of the Council of Europe, the Bishop of London, and two texts on the Challenges facing the UK armed forces giving the perspectives respectively of Admiral the Lord Boyce and General Sir Jack Deverell.

Further texts or transcripts of addresses to the Group over the last few months – and for over the last 20 years -- can be found by visiting www.eag.org.uk in the section on 'Speeches.' The development of ideas on many areas of concern to international policy makers in recent times can be gauged in large degree by reference to these texts.

There is need at the present time for Europeans and Americans to understand and appreciate their respective positions on a range of issues. Two articles have been commissioned for this Journal on the way forward for European-Atlantic relations. They are to be seen as individual rather than exhaustive accounts. We are grateful to The Honorable Larry LaRocco, President of the U.S. Association for Former Members of Congress - many of his eminent organisation having spoken at the Group - who, together with their Executive Director Peter Weichlein, has presented a key view of what can be done to further co-operation of the transatlantic partners from an American perspective. Dr Karl Pagac, a European-Atlantic Group member for many years, tackles the same question but from a European standpoint.

International relations being ever more inter-connected, the European-Atlantic Group does not only consider specifically European-Atlantic issues. The Group represents a wide range of expertise. In these pages, Dr Glen Segal outlines views on the deepening of the European Union after enlargement. Professor Alan Lee Williams OBE draws on his recent findings during a tour of the USA to assess differing views within the USA, the subject of much relevant controversy. The E-AG is nothing if not forward-looking and perhaps the last frontier left for Mankind to explore is Space: Lucy Ivimy charts in brief where we are in this odyssey and what's next.

The authorial summaries of Politics Tomorrow have set the pattern for E-AG members to follow suit. Colonel Mike Lowry MBE MC, who saw action on the Burma front in World War Two, has given us a piece about his recently published book that gives the action-packed flavour of his experiences and some of his thinking about their ramifications. With many in the Group writing books, this promises to be a regular section of forthcoming editions.

In this, the 50th anniversary of the European-Atlantic Group, we include an article by Elma Dangerfield CBE from the European-Atlantic Review of which Mrs Dangerfield was Executive Editor in the 1950s, on an issue, Europe, still so relevant today.

There are over a thousand members of the Group. It nevertheless contrives in an important sense to be a family. We do not include an In memoriam section for those who passed away over the last year but affectionate remembrance may be evoked of the late Dennis Bardens whose poem about seeing life afresh after his soldiering appears in print for the first time towards the end of the journal. It is followed by a poem by the late Earl of Limerick KBE. It was a grievous loss to very many when Lord Limerick, a most able and beloved President of the Group, passed away. His 'trade mark' of a limerick rounded off many an event on a note of bonhomie. This is consonant with the way in which those of differing viewpoints can meet under the aegis of the E-AG to discuss contentious matters without rancour. ■

Justin Glass
Editor, European-Atlantic Journal

5 • *Politics Tomorrow*

A poem by the late Dennis Bardens written in Kensington Gardens in the spring of 1941. He wrote it down on Nov 11th 2003 from memory. Dennis was a member of the Group for many years. He was the founding editor of TV's Panorama. Dennis Bardens worked in Intelligence during and after the War; was an influential journalist; he wrote fifteen books amongst which were Churchill in Parliament and The Ladykiller. His biography, Elizabeth Fry: Britain's Second Lady on the Five Pound Note, will be published in August 2004.

A bright and sunny day had found its close
And I who through long winters and grey days
Had felt the chill of Earth's quiescence chose
To wander in the park, where I might gaze
Upon the sun whose rays in parting, kissed
The drifting clouds with red and amethyst

Yes, there is war and yet these beauties stay
Endemic in all life. So haste the day
When all who walk the world will know the joy
Of these - God's works which somehow we had missed.

77 · Politics Tomorrow

A day in the Country

A poem by the late Lord Limerick written to divert his friend and assistant, Jasmine Boxall, on a rather unfortunate exercise in path-finding on one of her return journeys from his country seat of Chiddinglye.

When Jasmine B. and Sally H. set out, their faith was high
To find the southward route from Barnes that leads to Chiddinglye.
And so they did. [But - jump ahead - it somehow was, alack,
A somewhat different question when it came to getting back.]
They maple syrup brought with them, and lovingly did bake
From lemon and from coconut, a quite delicious cake.

Ms. Boxall had an envelope, with paper overflowing,
Whose contents would not wait, she said, and she's the best at knowing.
While Boxall works, Miss Heap set forth to garner generous yield
Of blackberries from the hedgerow and of mushrooms from the field.
Next, lunch upon the terrace, after which were ladies brimming
With energy for tennis, and then still enough for swimming.

At last it's sadly time to go - wave goodbye to the car
With spectacles upon the roof to help to spy a star.
The running time is just the hour, for those who know the way.
But if you take the B - H route, it does extend the day.
At almost any venture those who shine, but yet, perhaps,
There's just a hint of weakness when it comes to reading maps.

If someone traced the route they took, you'd swear it was a hoax,
That night they went to Balfour Place by way of Sevenoaks;
If someone sought to rationalize, you'd say it was a con.,
To take the road through Dulwich on the way to Wimbledon;
It has to be original - quite probably a first -
To plot a course to get to Barnes by way of Chislehurst;
'Cos if you are in a hurry to get back to your abode
Then Catford's not the quickest route to Upper Richmond Road;
And if time were of the essence, it might well be deemed a pity
To cross the Thames from Brixton, just to re-cross from the City.

It matter not, so long as you can laugh, and truly say
It ended nigh tomorrow, but 'twas still a lovely day.

5. THE EARLY DAYS OF THE EUROPEAN-ATLANTIC GROUP

The Foundations of the Group

The Group began with a Bang and if it is due to 'end with a whimper' that would be a pity from the standpoint of a putative historian quarrying into its archive centuries hence. Letter after letter throughout the period of 1954 till 2010 attests to both the interest and affection with which the Group was held by the Great and the Good. Many say little else but fulsome thanks for its interest-value. That people penned such sentiments in such profusion is an indicator of how times seem to have changed from a more gracious age. The President's Fifth Report from 1958 to 1959 is to be found in the Addendum of this History. The breath of topics that bespeak what looks like turbo-charged activity and all the measured conclusions give a snapshot of the political perspective of the times. Elma had admiration for those who called the shots. The Group was exalted, not designed for Everyman who Elma, defying a tenet of democracy on an off-day, dismissed as 'the dribs and drabs'. It was part of the glue that held together the highest political circles. In this it was perhaps comparable to the gatherings of Sir Philip Sassoon that were of such relevance in the 1930s in an age of greater deference and when travelling and communication were not what they are today.

Thoughts on the Founding of the E-AG by James (Lord) Abinger[88]

'Although the EAG was the inspiration of Lord Layton, in reality it would never have come to fruition without the dynamism and energy

---

[88] *The family name was 'Scarlette' and his forebear was among those in command at the famous Charge of the Light Brigade.*

of Elma Dangerfield. She contacted myself and Eric (Lord) Bessborough and we met with Lord Layton in my Chelsea House. It was to be a non-party political pressure group to bring British interest together with European and the USA and Canada. (At that time the debate was very much either or).

In no time the Group was inaugurated by Elma's amazing drive and initiative. Meetings were arranged at the Anglo Belgian Club in Belgrave Square, an influential Council and Committee were recruited of well-known politicians, academics, economists and journalists. Elma did most of the work in a tiny office in Bloomsbury with much help from her journalist partner Dennis Walwin Jones. The main worry was finding enough money to fund this enterprise; (for me at least as I had drawn the short straw of becoming Treasurer!) We struggled to keep up with Elma's expansive plans. Luckily Henry Tiarks joined me as joint Treasurer and things looked up at once.

I now look back with enormous admiration for Elma and great satisfaction at being connected with such a successful and fun enterprise. I wish it further triumphs in its next 50 years.'

Hon. Director & Co-founder
1954-1991
Mrs. Elma Dangerfield, O.B.E.

Elma Dangerfield wrote the first history of the Group in 1955, in words that she put in her handwriting into the mouth and the pen of the Earl of Bessbough. It is below:

CHAIRMAN'S REPORT

The EUROPEAN-ATLANTIC GROUP was founded in London last June year (1954) by Members of the present Committee, headed by Lord Layton, Lord Abinger, Lord Birdwood, Commander Sir Stephen King-Hall and Mrs Dangerfield. This Group drafted the Aims and Objects and issued invitations to the first Meeting of the Group in July, 1954, at 6. Belgrave Square. There, with Sir Stephen King-Hall in the Chair, the Group was joined by a number of the present Members, and was addressed by Lord Layton on the necessity of European-Atlantic co-operation. At that Meeting I was invited by the Committee to be President and Chairman, a position which I accepted with some trepidation, owing to various other commitments, but I may say I felt very honoured to be invited, and I have greatly enjoyed the Meetings at which I have presided. We are holding our ninth Meeting this evening.

Our Meetings, as you know, have been held monthly, with only occasional interruptions for last Summer's holidays and the General Election last May. Otherwise we have held Meetings each month, dealing primarily with European and Atlantic subjects connected with NATO and the Council of Europe. We have been fortunate enough to have been addressed by Lord Ismay, Secretary-General of NATO, last November, and by General Alfred Gruenther, Supreme Commander of S.H.A.P.E. in the House of Commons last March. This Meeting was attended by most of the NATO Ambassadors in London and by many Members of both Houses of Parliament, including the present Foreign Secretary, Mr. Harold Macmillan, who moved the vote of thanks to General Gruenther, seconded by Sir David Kelly, President of the British Atlantic Committee.

Our subsequent Meetings have covered quite a wide field, including the influence of Television on European and Atlantic unity. For this we were fortunate enough to have the former Postmaster General, Earl De La Warr, in the Chair, and a Panel of T.V. experts from Canada and the United States, as well as from the B.B.C. and Commercial Television, on the platform. Other Meetings have dealt with Sessions of the Council of Europe, Western European Union and the Atlantic Treaty Association, at which some of us were present. Our Speakers have been chiefly Members of Parliament who have been delegates to these European and Atlantic Conferences.

Our Membership, which commenced with twelve Founder Members last June year

Portrait of Elma Dangerfield CBE and bust of Dennis Walwin Jones MC

This history that you are reading is the second history written of the Group. Beverley Nichols, tongue-in-cheek, once wrote that the oldest anyone should be when writing their autobiography was 25. A biography as above of Elma's brain-child, the E-AG, was written only a year after it was born. From then till now, with an exception of the one passage from Elma quoted below, and though the archives are still extant, the history of the Group as a narrative was a *tabula rasa*.

The first decades of the Group are largely a story about Elma Dangerfield. Lord Bessborough's comments below, often repeated in much the same terms in the Minutes, call to mind Macauley's 'Great Man' theory of history: for all the talk of underlying trends and decisions of key institutions, and the rest, it is ultimately the individuals who really make the difference:

'I must, as usual, pay a very special tribute to the untiring efforts of Mrs. Elma Dangerfield, our Honorary Organiser and her able Assistants, without whose energies and enthusiasm the Group would certainly not be as active as it was.'

Elma Dangerfield wrote the following piece about the founding of the Group when it was suggested to her by her co-Director in the 1990s that this should be done.

'The European-Atlantic Group was the inspiration of the late Lord Walter Layton, then the first British Vice-President of the Council of Europe in Strasbourg. He then suggested the idea to Elma Dangerfield, at the time Foreign Correspondent of The Manchester Guardian at the Council. Lord Layton had been instrumental in inviting American and Canadian Senators and Congressmen to debate with European Members of Parliament in Strasbourg, and suggested to Elma Dangerfield that she should start a group in London with leading Representatives of all the Anglo-European and Anglo-American and Canadian Societies in London. Elma Dangerfield had been assisting him over Human Rights issues in Strasbourg, and on returning to London, she approached Lord Abinger, other Peers, MPs, Academics, Economists and Journalists. The Group was founded in London at Abinger's London House, with the first Meetings held at the Anglo-Belgian Club in Belgrave Square. A Committee and Council were formed of well-known British, American and Canadian personalities.

Lord Layton's original idea was to have such an International Group in each Capital of Europe as well as in Washington and Ottawa but the Founders discovered it was enough to have one active Group in London and have left it to the other countries of the West to form their own Groups....'

It was pretty scant as histories go, but the past was passed over save for the odd occasion, as when Elma spoke at the funeral of Mary Melville about the inception of the Group:

'I first met Mary during the war, with her mother, Lady Melville, the Russian wife of Sir James Melville, M.P. (who had been Solicitor-General in Ramsay Macdonald's Labour Government). It was at the Duchess of Atholl's (the 'Red Duchess') flat in Inverna Court where she had founded with me and Rowmund Pilsudski 'The British League for European Freedom' to help East European Refugees in this country – especially Polish ones. Mary also helped us with 'The Deportees committee' – together with Rose Macauley, George Orwell, Rebecca West and a few MPs of all parties such as Ellen Wilkinson, Eleanor Rathbone, Ivor Thomas and Sir Victor Raikes, who first brought up the question of Deportations from Eastern Europe to Siberia in the House of Commons, followed by all of us at meetings in Caxton Hall and in the press. Mary also helped us found the 'London International Group' with the Duchess and Sir Ronald Story which later became The European-Atlantic Group.'

Here is Elma introducing herself to the Hon. Angus Ogilvy In a letter[89] by way of a curtain-raiser to the invitation that was her purpose in writing it:

'...My husband, Captain Edward Dangerfield, R.N. was a great friend of Alexandra's father George, when they were together in H.M.S. Hawkins, together on the China Station in the 1920s. Later, in London, he and I used to lunch at Belgrave Square with George and Marina when Alexandra was a child... The Group is celebrating its 30th Anniversary with a Reception. Barbecue, short concert with Jehudi

---

[89] October 1983.

Menuhin and Dance at Hurlingham Club, on Wednesday June 27th....'

The earliest reference to Elma in the Group archives dates from 1929 and it is from HRH Prince George, Duke of Kent, KG, KT, GCMG, GCVO who was godfather to Elma's daughter, Gay. Prince George nearly a decade later writes to a mutual friend about the loss of Elma's husband, Ted, a Lieutenant-Commander who served with him: 'I know what this must mean for Elma. It seems so sad and unnecessary just now when so many are being killed by enemy action that he should be taken by illness when he was doing so well in the Navy. How long ago those days at Hong Kong seem and all our jokes and dinners – quite like another life… I wonder what Elma will do but she has many interests which will occupy and help her.' Elma destroyed her letters from the Prince but kept an envelope, embossed with the Balmoral crest, he addressed to her.

The earliest days in the main were happy, also to go by a letter of 1942[90]:

'… How we disliked Dr Grove… I shall never forget our Buttock jokes. I am glad Elma is getting on well with her job and is happier. Being busy must be a great help. A son has cheered us up amidst all the depressing news…'

Who now can entertain us with the buttock jokes, though to go by what else is in the files, they probably were not all that *risqué*. The record deals with weightier matters.

---

[90] *July 11; a letter from 3 Belgrave Square.*
Prince George, according to Chips Channon's diaries, had the most elegant dining room in London.

One year on from the foundation of the Group, it was up and running, sprinting more like. Here is further rubric from the Chairman's Report of 1955:

'The EUROPEAN-ATLANTIC GROUP was founded in London last June year by Members of the present Committee, headed by Lord Layton, Lord Abinger, Lord Birdwood, Commander Sir Stephen King-Hall, and Mrs Dangerfield. This Group drafted the Aims and Objects and issued invitations. (This is added in the handwriting of ED) to readers of the European-Atlantic Review to the first Meeting of the Group in July 1954 at the Anglo-Belgian Club, 6 Belgrave Square. There, with Sir Stephen King-Hall in the Chair the Group was joined by a number of the present Members, and was addressed by Lord Layton on the necessity of European-Atlantic co-operation…'

Tasters of this type of account can be read of those early days. They are putatively from Lord Bessborough, in A Record of Events in 1958 – though, if later E-AG usage can be trusted, the words were put into his mouth, or at least his pen, by Elma.

'The Nordic Common Market': This was the first time that this subject had been discussed at such a meeting in London. In view of its importance in relation to the proposed European Free Trade Area, this meeting was, I think, of considerable value and usefully informative to members and guests.'

'I would like at the outset to refer to the great honour which the Prime Minister and Lady Dorothy Macmillan have done us in accepting to come to the Group's reception in their honour on July 15th.'

Passages like the above abound in the E-AG Minutes and the Reports. A picture of the first flush of achievements by the Founding Fathers and Mother can be glimpsed, congealed beneath flat if patrician prose. In a period style that *inter alia* subliminally conveys unimpeachable respectability even a triumphalism, the entries can seem turgid to a modern sensibility.

HRH Prince George of Kent writing about his god-daughter, Gay, the daughter of Lt Cdr and Mrs Dangerfield

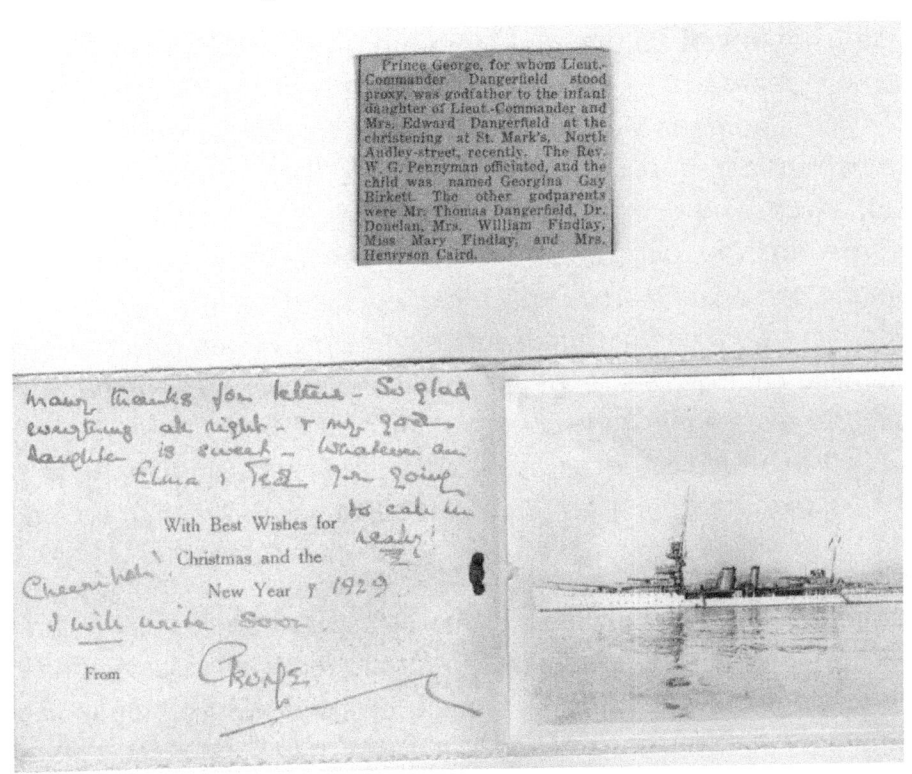

'Many thanks for your letters (to a mutual friend). So glad everything all right – & my god daughter is sweet – whatever are Elma & Ted going to call her really!

Cheerihoh!

George'

The above was found in 2020 in a cache of surviving letters addressed to Mrs O'Conor Donelan (Joseph O'Conor Donelan was buried in the same grave as Elma's father). The correspondence was from the 1920s to shortly before the end of World War Two. The correspondents had partied in Hong Kong together and Prince George served in the Royal Navy with Elma's late husband. This circle was broken up shortly before the end of World War II by the untimely demise of Lt-Commander Dangerfield from illness and that of Prince George in a fatal plane crash. A typed and signed letter in this packet is from his brother, the Duke of Windsor and the former King, expressing deep sorrow at his death. The letters from Prince George are the unguarded correspondence of a good friend, a humane person, and are mainly about personal matters. In the course of penning sentiments without waste of words, Prince George voices relief when the UK is strengthened with powerful allies against Hitler. This gravitates against the controversial depiction of the Prince on TV in 2020 and elsewhere as being a sympathiser of Germany at the time, let alone allegedly en route at the time of his crash to do a deal with Hitler.

Unlike the statute depicted in Shelley's *Ozymandias* only part of which, aeons after it was sculpted, protrudes from desert sands, it seems as if the granite-like verbiage in the E-AG archive is like a monument that was constructed in a desert in the first place. After the unveiling of 'The Word' the sense grows that it was destined to lie there un-interred, its fate all but lost in the sands. It was destined for burial beneath the next and the next event, in the unforgiving Present. Sage pronouncement on, and grappling with, the politics of State seem chiselled on an unending but disused tablet of stone, as if left to a Time Traveller to marvel at a procession though labyrinths lit by E-AG torch-bearers with names worthy of recording because of their illustriousness. Today, how many household names of the time will be recognised?

If this writer may breach convention by interjecting a personal note, he admits that the results of his quarrying into the compost of the Group record surprised him. There had been no time, given the exigencies in the heat of the office needs, to be spent in going over old ground or mountain peak. I worked cheek by jowl with Mrs Dangerfield for over a decade and was with her at gatherings such as the one at Guildhall where our association began. Elma took to me as a species of kindred kith and kin when I told her my surname, Glass, the same name as the Scottish town graced by her family seat, Beldorny castle, as if I was related to the bricks and mortar surrounding her from the cradle. I had no full idea till writing this history of how much the Group and Elma accomplished from Day One. Mrs Dangerfield's dynamism even well into her mid-eighties makes one wonder how mighty her dynamo must have been in her youth and middle age!

Elma Dangerfield when young

Lord Russell Johnson, the President of the Parliamentary Assembly, told the Group on 19th July 2001: 'I would like to pay particular tribute to Elma Dangerfield sitting in front of me, whom I remember as a flibbertigibbet in the 60s when I first became a Member of Parliament. She does not seem to have changed all that much.'

The 'Archives' that had lain untouched for years before Justin joined the E-AG were captured for posterity by the art of Julia Couchman. What prescient genie, it may be wondered, whispered in her ear of their rightful niche in Group history?

Outer office Clutter

Photographer: Julia Couchman. juliacouchman@hotmail.co.uk

Much of the 'archive' survived for some six decades the depredations of mildew, burglary and unintentional camouflage in the anonymity of unmarked cardboard boxes in Gertrude Street, and was transported lock, stock and barrel to the Finchley office. As an example of the way there was no looking back or sentiment: a mere two years before Justin joined the staff in 1987, the Group hosted the Prime Minister, Margaret Thatcher. He had no idea of that, or of so much else accomplished in the Group's antiquity – if harnessed to that term may be the idea that a week is a long time in politics. It was of even less contemporary relevance, then, that the Group mounted an event in the Albert Hall, as far back as in 1956. It never came up even in chat about possible future venues, but then nor did County Hall or Central hall, Westminster, where the E-AG had also held debates.

The E-AG overriding achievement in 1956 was in making the mercury shoot up the barometer of public consciousness of the Hungarian Uprising. The Group's keynote speaker was the Archbishop of Canterbury. A politician might have seemed the obvious choice to present the Western cause, but the subject was Human Rights, long before President Jimmy Carter made of it a staple of international political discourse. If later custom is anything to go by, Elma bagged 'the Archbish' as a speaker then worked backwards, suiting a title of debate to her prize collared. Grand as were the second-tier speakers – the Archbishop of Liverpool, the Rt. Hon. Viscount de L'Isle, PC, VC, Sir Robert Boothby, KBE, MP, The Rt. Hon. Kenneth Younger, PC, MP, Miss Jennie Lee, MP – it may be suspected that the 'Tail-end Charlie' at the bottom of the roster, 'Hungarian speakers', was indicative of Elma's Rule Britannia mind-set. Foreigners were fine in their place beneath the salt of British loam. It admittedly could also be that the Hungarians during their uprising against their Russian overlords were too busy in their own counsels or manning barricades to rally a British chorus of support.[91]

Elma was not against foreigners particularly if they were aristocratic or Polish. Elma had so soft a spot for Poles the story went that she forfeited part of her inheritance because of family disapproval of this wayward penchant. Her slant on society was that it was, metaphorically speaking, cone-shaped, Royalty at its apex, and a base comprised of 'the dribs and drabs'. Elma on occasion went in for personal reminiscence but was not one for boasting. Allusions to her 'Great Connections' were effective enough, and a certain mannerism let slip that they were of the air that she breathed. Had Elma wished to impress deliberately, a passing phrase or two might have passed her lips about, say, the holiday she took when younger with Dame Rebecca West, who was on the E-AG Ladies Committee and who wrote a preface to Elma's book, *Beyond The Urals*. Elma did say of Prince George, Duke of Kent, in a rare revelation, that he would never read a word of what was written in the press about the Royal family: 'All of it is untrue', he told her.

One of Elma's cousins only ever related a single anecdote about her to Justin. He chanced upon her in Parliament, a rare meeting, and this was her fleeting greeting:

'Can't stop now! Must rush! Seeing the PM!'

---

[91] *Sir Frank Roberts in his review of 'A voice in the Wilderness' (See Book Review section) offers a personal perspective on Imre Nagy who was at the centre of the Hungarian revolution of 1956.*

*The Prime Minister, the **Rt. Hon. Edward Heath**, with **Mrs Dangerfield***

Below is an entry that gives a sense of divers matters exercising the corporate mind of the E-AG:

'We have held Meetings each month, dealing primarily with European and Atlantic subjects connected with NATO and the Council of Europe. We have been fortunate enough to have been addressed by Lord Ismay, Secretary-General of NATO, last November, and by General Alfred Gruenther, Supreme Commander of S.H.A.P.E., in the House of Commons last March. This Meeting was attended by most of the NATO Ambassadors in London and by many Members of both Houses of Parliament, including the present Foreign Secretary, Mr. Harold Macmillan, who moved the vote of thanks to General Gruenther, seconded by Sir David Kelly. President of the British-Atlantic Committee.'

The Group was an arm of NATO spokesmanship in London. The Atlantic Council, co-founded by Mrs Dangerfield, arguably took on the mantle around the mid-80s, but the Group was always affiliated to NATO, in particular in the task of organising the Anniversary Celebrations every five or ten years up till 2019 when the Atlantic Council put on an event in London to mark the 70th anniversary of NATO.

The anniversary celebration of the founding of NATO became a fixture in the E-AG programme. Lord Bessborough[92] had his work cut out to describe the 1959 event in suitably restrained terms but the excitement of it can be deduced from his prose:

'This has been a momentous year for the Group. The North Atlantic Treaty Organization and the Council of Europe – the two chief international bodies which the Group was founded to support – have been celebrating their tenth anniversaries, and the Group is honoured by being invited to organise the NATO Banquet in Guildhall on 11th May, which was attended by H.R.H. the Prince Philip Duke of Edinburgh, H.R.H. The Prince of the Netherlands and the Lord Mayor and Lady Mayoress of London, cabinet Ministers of this and other countries, the Supreme Allied Commander Atlantic and the Supreme Allied Commander Europe together with a number of other NATO Commanders... The speeches which lasted an hour were relayed 'live' on both B.B.C. Television and Radio, as well as later on Independent Television, and the proceedings were shown on Movietone Newsreel. A full-length film of these has been made

---

[92] *Transcripts of speeches by HRH the Duke of Edinburgh to another E-AG NATO Anniversary celebration banquet are on the website of the Group with hard copies in the office records, as is a speech on the same occasion, and a Book Review, by the Earl of Bessborough.*

available to the Group by the B.B.C. and will be shown after the Annual General Meeting on 30th July.'

David Griffiths, Director of Atlantic 2000, remembered that as a young man he attended the E-AG NATO banquet in 1959. It determined his choice of career, so enthralled was he by it. Behind the glitter and glamour, there was serious stuff:

ARTICLE FROM 'THE TIMES' OF MAY 1959 ABOUT THE E-AG GULDHALL NATO EVENT

GERMAN DEMANDS

Last month I exposed the London Guildhall dinner, at which the Duke of Edinburgh spoke, and at which Hans Speidel was one of the guests. The William Hickey gossip column in the *Daily Express* for Tuesday, April 12, 1959, had two enlightening items concerning this dinner:

With a crash and a blare and a ta-ra ra-boom-de-ay the band of the Scots Guards crashed into life at London's Guildhall last night with a fine roar of sound. . .

Prince Philip was there, so was Prince Bernhard of the Netherlands, so were a medal-chested procession of ambassadors, diplomats, politicians and military nabobs.

The big guns came from 15 separate NATO countries. That controversial German General Hans Speidel was there, for instance.

Pointing out that Herr Strauss also attended the ceremony, as representing West Germany, the *Express* columnist added:

Last night's aperitif march was based on that worrisome NATO hymn. There has been some undiplomatic trouble over the NATO hymn, you may recall. When 5,000 schools were asked to sing it 10 days ago at prayers there were strong protests.

So Lord Bessborough, who as president of the European Atlantic Group was organising the dinner,

had that hymn tactfully bowdlerised. He asked the man who wrote it, Thomas Preston, to write a wordless march on the same theme.

NOW GERMANY WANTS BASES IN BELGIUM, HOLLAND AND FRANCE

Britain, Belgium, and (of course) Germany are deep in a behind-the-scene squabble about the siting of forward arms dumps.

West German Defence Minister, beefy butcher's son Franz Strauss, is waltzing from capital to capital to "sell" his army build-up.

He insists that his new Wehrmacht must have 90 days' march supplies available instantly — and that to reduce the number of potential targets in Germany, two tons in three must be stored in safety West of the Rhine — that is, outside the Fatherland.

So, besides Belgium, he wants to lease bases in Holland and in France.

Top left: **Sir John Rogers Bt**, Joint Hon Treasurer, 1975-1985; The **Rt. Hon. the Earl of Listowel**, Chairman 1961-1963; The **Rt. Hon. Lord Abinger**, Hon. Treasurer 1954-1960 & Founder member. Bottom left: **Sir Frank Roberts GCMG, GCVO**, Chairman 1970-1973, President 1973-1983; The **Lord Layton CH, CBE**, Founder and President 1964-1965; The **Rt. Hon. Lord Rippon** of Hexham QC Chairman, President and Vice-President in the 1980s and 1990s. Below: **David Griffiths** (see comments above) with **Lord Layton**, the grandson of Lord Layton.

Below are further entries that indicate the lie of the land described by those in the cockpit of the E-AG, a land they made their own, thus that of the Group, and so it would continue: 'The new British Secretary-General of the Council of Europe, Mr. Peter Smithers, (a former Member of Parliament) honoured us with a special visit from Strasbourg and spoke on developments over the past years in the Consultative Assembly and in the Council of Ministers. Lord Layton, our President, and a former Vice-President of the Assembly (from 1949 to 1957) presided, and a most interesting discussion ensued on the role which the Council of Europe is playing, being the only forum in which Parliamentary representatives of all the E.E.C. and E.F.T.A. countries are able to debate publicly… problems affecting the whole of Western Europe, economically and politically.'

'Following a proposal of Lady Violet Bonham Carter, one of our Vice-Presidents, the Lord Privy Seal, The Rt. Hon. Edward Heath, M.P., kindly agreed to receive a Deputation from the Council last March to discuss the European-Atlantic situation since the Brussels breakdown. After giving the Deputation, led by our President and Chairman and including some of other Officers, more than an hour's resumé of recent events, Mr. Heath emphasised the need for the United Kingdom to work with all existing European and Atlantic Organisations rather than setting up any new Institutions. He was good enough to show his appreciation of the activities of the Group in supporting and publicising the work of these international organisations such as the G.A.T.T., the O.E.C.D., the W.E.U., the N.A.T.O., the Council of Europe and the E.F.T.A. Mr Heath fully endorsed the Hon. Director's proposals for Meetings on these subjects during the rest of the year, and kindly agreed to address the Group himself at a future date. He also appointed a permanent liaison officer in the Foreign Office to assist in obtaining Speakers from abroad. Furthermore, he approved the suggestion of a large N.A.T.O. Dinner in the near future as a demonstration of support for the Atlantic Alliance, as well as other Meetings on Atlantic Partnership.'

Another entry from the Record shows *inter alia* how the thinking of the Group was to be at the forefront of the events that mattered:

'The "Control of Western Strategy" was discussed by Monsieur Maurice Schumann, President of the French Foreign Affairs Committee, under the Chairmanship of General Sir Richard Gale, former deputy Supreme Allied Commander, Europe. This was the first occasion since President de Gaulle's veto on Britain joining the E.E.C. that a French politician had addressed us and was a promising sign of an improvement in Anglo-French understanding.'

If ever conventions can be a framework within which an institution moves forward, the E-AG is an exemplar. Policies and Group guidelines were consistent in the main over a period of some sixty years. As seen above, the Group was set on a course of inviting speakers at the last moment, when it was clear what the questions of the greatest topicality would be. Another idea of the Group was objective discussion run not along party political lines but according to the dictates of common sense. Might Democracy itself not gain if parliamentary thinking followed suit? The Group was inclusive and independent, not adversarial, and was free-thinking, all shades of opinion being represented. It was a boast that it was a Non Governmental Organisation. When in 1973 Sir Frank Roberts proposed Lord Chalfont as incoming Chairman, the reasoning was to redress the imbalance when, on Sir Geoffrey de Freitas' retirement as President, Lord Layton and Sir Douglas Dodds-Parker MP did not represent all three major political parties.

The Group was among the first of the registered All-Party Parliamentary Groups. It had a long list of vice-Presidents comprised *inter alia* of all the Chairmen at the helm of the Societies representing a link between the UK and other European countries. Thus in 1957:

'Our object... is to form a common meeting ground for these various organisations, which I think I may say we have happily succeeded in doing.'

The tradition continued on to 2015. The remit of European and Atlantic focus was cast ever wider. By 1957...:

'...The Group had a vital and important role to play. The recent ratification by Germany and France of the Common Market and Euratom Treaties have crowned the efforts of many Europeans in this field. These steps towards European integration show more than ever the tremendous need in this country for a forum for the discussion of all such questions, while maintaining and strengthening our links across the Atlantic...'

The idea of fostering amicable and useful relations was ever in the background. In the following year Lord Bessborough, with Elma no doubt his copy-writer, says:

'... Since its inception four years ago the Group has held... thirty-six meetings and the number of members as of 30 June 1958 stood at 445. Increased interest in the past year has been demonstrated – not only by the size of membership but also in the Group's influence in the international field both at home and abroad. It is already well-known in most capitals of Western Europe as well as across the Atlantic.'

There is something to be said for a principle hallowed in Ancient China where legal disputes were settled while breaking bread with an adversary. The Group at its best was a form of glue helping bind together leaders and opinion-formers. Whatever the advantages of cosy chats and dinners in a society of members who had got to know one another well over the years, the ideal outcome was not always forthcoming. Frank discussion did not always produce the desired results or chemistry. The meeting of the two Italian renaissance princes to resolve their differences through talking rather than warring illustrates the problem – after their discussion they understood one another perfectly... they both wanted Italy! The Group, for all its convocations conducted in unfailing courtesy to try to get to the bottom of what caused differences of opinion, was just as vulnerable to this as anyone else, as can been seen in the following account:

'Professor Hugh Seton Watson led off the discussion on Relations with Soviet Russia giving us a fair and objective picture of what was happening in that country and in some of the satellite countries. It was clear during the course of the ensuing discussion that some members and guests were so strongly anti-Communist that the meetings only served to widen the gulf between those who consider that we should trade and have cultural relations with Communist countries and those who consider that such relations are only used by the Soviet Union for propaganda purposes.'

It was not just guests who might disagree with one another. There were rumblings behind the scenes in the upper echelons of the E-AG, not about office politics, but international politics, as is evident in the following passage concerning two eminent men who until then had been supportive of Group Aims:

'We greatly regretted the resignations from the Committee of Lord Birdwood, one of our Vice-Chairmen, and Mr Gilbert Longdon M.P. on matters of principle in connection with East-West Trade.'

It was logical in view of the goal of furthering of good relations with opposite numbers abroad that delegations, eleven between 1955 and 1970, to other countries played a part in the life of the Group.

Thus Lord Bessborough – or his E-AG muse, Mrs Dangerfield – again:

'These yearly visits to Europe are, in my opinion, amongst some of the most valuable of our activities. It is only by such exchanges that we can obtain first-hand knowledge of the countries with which we are endeavouring to have ever closer relations… This summer I, myself, had the honour of leading a Delegation of our corporate and individual Members to the headquarters of the European Economic Community in Brussels, where we were most cordially received by Professor Walter Hallstein, President of the Commission, and by other officials of the Commission. At this time, when the problems of the "Sixes" and the "Sevens" (EU and non-EU leagues of countries) are uppermost in our minds, it was invaluable to have the benefit of this personal contact with the leaders of the European Economic Community…. For these are surely some of the most pressing problems before us today and which the Group has to consider and discuss. For these reasons… some of our Members… visited the United States this summer for the British Trade Exhibition in New York.

'In 1956, the Group sent a delegation of representatives of those industries, such as Oil and Nuclear Energy, that were most interested in the proposed European Free Trade Area to the Council of Europe in Strasbourg. It was the first industrial delegation from the United Kingdom to attend a session of the Consultative Assembly.'

DELEGATIONS ABROAD:

The Group has sent its yearly Delegation abroad this year to NATO, SHAPE and OEEC in Paris, which we had not visited for four years. This time the Delegation was received and briefed by the Supreme Allied Commander Europe, General Lauris Norstad, and others of his Staff at Versailles, including Sir Richard Gale, the Deputy Supreme Commander, who addressed our Group last year. Sir Frank Roberts, the U.K. Permanent Representative to NATO, was kind enough to give a cocktail party for the Delegation, as did Sir Hugh Ellis the U.K. Representative to OEEC. Lord Coleraine and Sir Evelyn Shuckburgh entertained and briefed the Delegation at NATO, and Monsieur René Sergent, Secretary-General of OEEC, did likewise at the Château de la Muette. Such visits abroad are one of the highlights of the Group and I only wish it were possible for all the Members to take part in them.

From the European-Atlantic Group Annual Report of 1959

The verdict of Lord Bessborough was: 'I think I am speaking for all members of the delegation in saying that the visit was a most useful as well as an interesting experience.'

Russia, the focus of much ongoing concern, featured in the round of E-AG visits abroad. Findings were awaited with interest by the Group at large:

'Rt. Hon. Aubrey Jones MP (former Minister of Power) Mr Maurice Edelman MP. Sir John Rothenstein, Geoffrey Kitchen (Chairman Pearl Insurance) JB Scott (Director of Crompton Parkinson) each gave their impressions… of their visits… the President of the Board of Trade Rt. Hon. Reginald Maudling M.P. and Sir James Hutchinson Bt addressed us on East-West Trade with specific reference to the British Trade Fair in Moscow to which a dozen of our members went at their own personal expense to see for themselves what possibilities exist for better trade and cultural relations between our two countries. …Mr Henry Tiarks, our Joint Hon. Treasurer, kindly showed us the excellent colour film which he had taken during the visits to Leningrad and Moscow. (It) was the first time we had had the benefit of T.V. screens in three rooms…'[93]

Delegations abroad had dwindled to a dribble by 1970 until, led by the Mid-Atlantic Group in the early 2000s, an E-AG contingent of members went on a fact-finding mission. Numbers the E-AG could certainly provide, given its peak membership of a thousand. That said, it was a first for the Group that a meeting of the E-AG in Washington in 2009 was held *(see previous section)*.

Here are some details of a 1963 event:

---

[93] *The next time that there were three TV screens in three different rooms for an E-AG event was in 2009 at the E-AG NATO banquet in St James's Palace.*

'This 'Old Dominions' Dinner and Discussion was followed by a small Reception at Overseas House for some of the Commonwealth Prime Ministers and their staffs who were attending the London Conference. Lord Layton and Lord Colyton (one of our Vice-Presidents and a Former Minister of State, Colonial Office) received our distinguished guests who included the Prime Ministers of Jamaica and Malta as well as a number of leading African Commonwealth representatives. Again, each emphasised the importance of increasing their trade with Europe, but some of them reiterated their objections to 'Association' with the European Economic Community from the political and 'neutralist' viewpoint. Lord Listowel (former Secretary of State for India) took the chair of the African Commonwealth (2nd meeting), but some of them reiterated their objections to 'Association' with the European Economic Community from the political and 'neutralist' point of view.'

The marriage between 'Captains of Industry' and the Group was more of a platonic affair than one consummated, let alone with a Golden Egg emerging from this union. A flaw of the Group from the start was its limited purse. Justin was parachuted into the Group in 1987 initially as Financial Director, partly to head off a take-over bid by Robert Sigmon, who went on to run the Pilgrims, but mainly to sort out the woeful finances of the Group. It was a 'cosmetic' appointment as Justin's real contribution was to help reverse a slide in attendance at E-AG events due to Elma's declining years. He also eventually reversed the trend pointed out in the statement of Alan Smith, the E-AG treasurer, for 1957, a recurring refrain down the years:

'Although we are solvent, our finances are still dependent on the subscriptions of our members and generous donations from members of the Council and Committee. These however are insufficient to extend our activities in any way.'

E-AG activity was much extended without need of largesse from a visitor from El Dorado or elsewhere. At AGMs, Alan Smith put in different words and for different reasons an oft repeated story of straitened finance. Geoffrey Smith, treasurer some 40 years later, was able to strike a more upbeat note, but had an advantage over his namesake because of income through a level of sponsorship that both dwarfed the previously vaunted corporate and individual membership subscriptions and replaced them as the key to sound finance.

Left: **Harold Winthrop Sands**, Joint Hon Treasurer 1977-2001; The **Lord Grantchester** Joint Hon Treasurer 1985-1993; **Terence Browne**, Joint Hon Treasurer 1985-1992

The Achilles Heel in the early period of the Group, was its insufficient income. The paltry sums involved holed some extra-mural activities below the water-line – specialist work-study groups, and in particular the early publications. These had flourished for a while then petered out, and it is not difficult to see the explanation in Alan Smith's words in 1963:

'The European review shares offices and the services of a short-hand typist with the Group. Recently the review has been unable to meet its share of the joint cost and now owes the Group about £115.'

The living room and office in the Chelsea home of Elma Dangerfield
Photography by Julia Couchman: juliacouchman@hotmail.co.uk

It comes as little surprise that the partnership of Group and Review dissolved:

'The working arrangements of the European Review would now be separated from the Group and that it would no longer share the

Group's Office (in Kingsway) or Secretary. It was agreed that the Group should have a full-time Secretary and Assistant.' [94]

The Review did valuable work but their respective ways parted. The Review sank, not the Group. The fact that 'the Group should have a full-time Secretary and Assistant' shows what was afoot. 'The Group' was run by the same person as the editor of the Review. No prizes for guessing the identity of this person. She was ...

'...Mrs Dangerfield is also Joint Editor of the European-Atlantic Review on whose editorial board are some of our members. The Review continues to be published in association with the Group and is reaching a wide public both here in Europe and across the Atlantic'

It is doubtful if a barren treasure chest explains why the Group in the person of Elma detached from the publication arm. The great day, after all, finally had dawned when sanction was given for payment of Elma's office staff. More likely an explanation is that there was divergence in philosophy about the work, as done respectively by Group and Review. The Review for at least ten years was immensely informative, as excerpts below show, but it did not discuss issues so much as explain them. It was didactic, in the manner of such publications. It was about international relations and it expounded the views of top commentators, whereas the main idea behind the Group was to interact with the wire-pullers and influence them. Personality no doubt also entered into it. No Queen Bee should have to put up with a King Bee, still less stomach another Queen Bee, certainly not if the foremost Bee was Mrs Dangerfield.

The latter contentions are reinforced by two factors. Had the Review primarily been an organ for views expounded at the E-AG's High

---

[94] *The Editorial and advertising base was at 61 Gloucester Place, London.*

Table then the presentations of its Speakers surely would have been flaunted in its pages. This was not the case, as it was with the European-Atlantic Journal of later date, which showcased speeches given at the E-AG. To the contrary, in the Review very few E-AG Speakers got a look in. This bespeaks independent editorial hands at the helm of the Review who were beyond the authority or at least the focus of Elma and her partner, Dennis Walwin Jones MC. Pedants may find a further example or two but almost the only Speakers at the Group – among whom were top-notch personalities – accorded space in the Review were Leo D'Erlanger, Chairman of the Channel Tunnel Company, Sir Claud Gibb, Chairman of the Nuclear Power Plant Company, and Monsieur Paul-Henri Spaak, Secretary-General of N.A.T.O. That is not to say that Elma's editorial say-so was overlooked. Had Elma's voice not been one to heed it may be wondered how, among the reams of close analysis in the European-Atlantic Review, a whimsical article like that penned by Elma and quoted at the foot of this section could have appeared.

… The review Members of the Editorial Board were very happy that Lord Pakenham accepted to join them in succession to Lord Listowel and that Sir Edward Beddington-Behrens and Sir David Kelly likewise agreed to be among their number. Mrs Dangerfield and Mr Dennis Walwin Jones[95] have continued to act as executive editors of this highly successful publication. Issues this year have included special supplements on Scandinavia, Benelux and Switzerland, and it is now initiating a series of industrial supplements.'

---

[95] *Dennis Walwin Jones MC (b1913-d1975): Chairman, the Byron Society 1971-1975; Executive Editor, Byron Journal 1973-1975; Founder Member, European-Atlantic Group 1965-1975; Director-General, British-European Movement 1960-1970; British Secretary, European League for Economic Co-operation 1960-1970. Dennis and Elma lived together and were partners also in the early fusion of the worlds of the Byron Society and the European-Atlantic Group.*

Dennis Walwin Jones. His memorial tablet in Putney Vale in front of the tombstone of Henry Birkett, Elma's father, is described on the internet as 'more like a CV than an epitaph' (see footnote)

It is a tendency in language to conflate an end-of-day conclusion with a final verdict. The accountant often has the last word. Mealy-mouthed talk of 'the bottom line' may be only a part of a whole story, and sometimes a misleading one. It describes the engine but does not run it. The European-Atlantic Review did good work in its day and was associated with the European-Atlantic Group up to 1964.

Movements in the *zeitgeist* found a champion in Elma. The Ladies Committee and its annual House of Lords Ladies Luncheons was weaponised into an espousal of the cause of women, with platforms gender-oriented to those scaling to the apex. Baroness Elliott, Janet Fookes MP, Lady Chalker, Christina Foyle, the list is as long as the decades the Ladies Committee thrived before it descended, more or less, into an inspection of seating plans on Guest Lists. Ideas and suggestions came. 'Lola', Lady Lidderdale, for instance wrote to Elma with a newspaper cutting on Katherine Graham; invitations all but identical to the output of the E-AG 'menfolk' ensued. Lola wrote 'Horrified that you should be up at 4am working. We are not grateful enough to you.' In her prime, Elma's researches had gone further. Elma's book *Beyond The Urals* (published in 1946) was a survey of the persecution and deportation of over a million Polish citizens from Eastern Poland by the Soviet authorities during their occupation there from September 1939 to June 1941. These deportations affected about 10% of the population in that country. It was a solid work of research, as indeed were Elma's *Mad Shelley* and *Byron and the Romantics in Switzerland* about these poets.[96] All the more surprising

---

[96] *Elma's treatise for Oxford University on 'The Romantic Movement' (1789-1830) was followed by her first book entitled 'A Diary of the Forty-Five' (the Jacobite Rising). She was Assistant Editor of the 'Nineteenth Century' during the war (as well as being a liaison officer between different war departments), then became editor of 'Whitehall News' (as well as founding The British League for European Freedom' with the Duchess of Atholl). She edited 'European Affairs', 'The European Digest' and 'European Review' after the war, and the Byron Journal (as well as standing for Parliament as a Liberal candidate for Aberdeen*

then, that in the European-Atlantic Review, there was only a light piece from her pen, in an article entitled *The Heart of Little Europe.*

'... The modern Geneva of supra-national organisations... this strongest fortress in Europe was successively incorporated in each succeeding European empire from the Middle Ages down the last war... Christianity first came to Luxembourg from England, being brought to the town of Echternacht in 968 by St Wilibrord of Northumbria... there is, in truth, a nineteenth century air about the whole atmosphere of the Grand Duchy... No one is in a hurry and everyone is courteous. Even the taxi-drivers doff their hats when they open the taxi door with a bow, wishing you Bonjour... Not luxury but good solid comfort. ... The Grand Ducal family spend most of their time in their stately Chateaux, as do most of the wealthy families, and foreign ambassadors often rent pleasant homes in the countryside. On the whole, however the well-to-do Luxemburger lives either in a solid, Victoria-style mansion in the city itself, or in one of the ultra-modern villas which are springing up on the outskirts, Luxemburgers are a thrifty people, spending more on their homes than their backs.'

Thrift might be all very fine but it was hardly a characteristic prominent in Elma's social set, intertwined as it was with the Group. Get-togethers in mansions of friends such as Princess Helena Gagarin-Moutafian were of the air Elma breathed. Elma to the end thought afresh about deeper questions: in conversion to the Bahá'í faith she saw a light shed of religion's key riddles. And who can deny that the *imprimatur* of Society, a knighthood, has been conferred only on one religious leader: Abdu'l-Bahá.

South (1959) and Hitchen, Herts (1964). Elma also founded The International Byron Society.

*A Bahá'í gathering visited by **HRH the Duke of York**. **Elma Dangerfield** and **Lord Mereworth** (right); the **Hon. Barnaby Leith** (left) a high-up in the Faith and an E-AG Corporate member*

Elma retired from hyperactive service at 92, not that a Rastafarian who tried to steal her handbag would have judged her to be so elderly after she gave chase to him in her car. Her participation in the running of affairs had been handed over by then, but as late as 2002 Elma would put on her finery and come to events to lap up all the adulation for her at the Group.

THE DIPLOMAT - January/February 2001

dispatches

Francis Maude
Out of the shadows

LONDON

If you were the ambassador who fell asleep during the Shadow Foreign Secretary's speech at the European Atlantic Group (EAG), fear not. James Robertson was there taking notes.

Britain's shadow foreign secretary, The Rt Hon Francis Maude MP, opened his speech at the EAG in a manner befitting the new, more humble Conservative Party. "There's always a knot in the stomach before you make a speech to a new audience," he confided. "The fear is, will there be anyone there at all?"

He needn't have worried. The ballroom of the Hilton St Ermin's Hotel was packed, the guest list swelled with nearly thirty foreign diplomats, including eleven heads of mission, doing their homework as the General Election approaches.

Mr Maude began with a declaration that the era of superpower politics had ended and that in a globalised world, the nation state is now more, not less, important. "We shouldn't think of Britain as being on the periphery of anything – not of Europe, nor as the 51st state of America. Britain has a new life at the heart of the global system."

Whereas citizens were willing, ultimately, to lay down their lives for their country, it was too much to expect such vigorous allegiance to the European Union. The Danish rejection of the single currency was a signal that must be taken seriously. "The EU working assumption of 'one size fits all' is going to have to change. We need a flexible, multi-system European Union. How can uniformity imposed from the centre work for up to 30 member countries?"

Britain had to keep the pound "because control and agility is everything...The EU is eroding the ability of nations to govern themselves." Nevertheless, Maude had no regrets about being one of the ministers who signed the Maastricht Treaty.

There was remarkably little about the world outside of Europe in the speech, that if you are poor, it is your own fault: "Nations and groups of nations can choose whether they succeed or fail. Those that choose the rule of law and an open economy will succeed. Nations that trade together tend to stay together. The flashpoints around the world are all closed economies."

Maude's audience was intrigued by his authority, "the Golden Arches Theory, which states that no two countries which both have a MacDonald's have ever gone to war together."

While trade created human relationships which are "almost by definition mutually beneficial" Labour's ethical foreign policy was a "grand, gesture-ridden and simplistic strategy," inconsistently applied, the speaker argued. "We [the Conservatives] would restore the annual motion at the UN which draws attention to China's very poor record on human rights. We'd back that up with constant pressure. It was a bad day for Britain's influence for good in the world when the Metropolitan Police felt themselves encouraged to arrest legal protesters [during President Jiang Zemin's state visit]. The test of an ethical foreign policy is not how you treat small states but large and strong ones."

But that didn't mean frequent overseas interventions: "The doctrine of humanitarian law is a novel and ambiguous one...Solutions in most cases come from within, not outside."

While it made sense for Britain to act jointly in particular cases, the Conservatives were against subsuming the country into a single European foreign policy. Nato already provided the ideal flexible structure for multilateral defence and there was "absolutely no military case for a European army or giving the EU a role in Europe's defence capabilities. The idea that we gain influence by giving up power is inherently absurd."

A "chilling and growing anti-Americanism" could be observed in the EU, which had no chance of being a rival

Shadow foreign secretary Francis Maude and EAG founder Mrs Erma Dangerfield.

provoking America into seeking a replacement ally, "turning its eyes to the powerful allure of Asia." Instead, "Britain should lead Europe in making the case for America's NMD (National Missile Defence)."

While generally against the deepening of the European Union, the Conservatives were strongly in favour of enlargement. "Countries like Poland etc. fought far harder than we did in the War for a peaceful Europe." They deserved to be swiftly hauled aboard the EU mothership, and feeble excuses were being made for not doing so. The "single huge roadblock" on the path to enlargement of the European Union was the Common Agricultural Policy.

Questions rained down on Mr Maude. Did he feel that the word 'British' had inherent racist connotations? "There are episodes in our history that would be better glossed over – but so what? We should not feel weighed down," the shadow foreign secretary declared cheerfully. Most of his friends came from immigrant families and Britain's racial diversity was a cause for celebration.

The former Chief Minister of Gibraltar Robert Peliza complained: "The Spanish have built a wall stopping Gibraltarians from being Europeans" and wondered what a Conservative British government would do about it. Maude's answer was that Britain had no legal right to give full independence. "It is just a bit silly really for Spain to take a rather old-fashioned view."

Another impassioned questioner argued: "We destroyed international law by our attack on Yugoslavia. Even the

We are unlikely to see her like again[97]. Elma would quote the bible: 'And the Lord walked abroad in the cool of the evening'. It is an apt metaphor for her twilight days.

And that is the story of the end of Elma's life, but not the end of the story of Elma. The office clutter had more secrets to yield up and if anything it eclipsed what was found in 'the scullery' as it was known – a large cubbyhole that had lain untouched for decades, save for when an electrician had tried, and all but failed, to clamber over grubby suitcases into a pile of junk inside. At the end of that 'scullery' lay a mouldy trunk, much like all the others. It contained the family silver, the horse racing trophies won or to be distributed by Henry Birkett, Elma's father, in Hong Kong, a crested tray bearing the genealogical tree of the family's ancestors, and so much silverware that it covered a dining table when laid out in Justin Glass's house, he having brought the trunk home to see what was inside. Elma never referred to it. Any such heirlooms were thought to be long gone in 'the burglary'. The family, retrieving the silverware, were amused by its tale that they had thought accounted for its loss.

A friend of Elma who was connected to Nureyev, the ballet dancer, had been staying in Elma's house and he was said to have some dubious acquaintances, one or more of who were probably responsible for what happened. It looked as though a madman had broken in, beginning with the front door, which was shattered open by an axe. The house, though not quite upside down, was certainly inside out. Elma had gone home to dress for dinner in a Polish café called *Daquise* with a Polish friend, Richard Kazuba, when she came

---

[97] *This phrase modifying Shakespeare (gender apart) was coined by Barry Downing for the Autumn 2018 Repton School magazine obituary about 'Johnnie' F. M. Walker, a popular, dynamic housemaster who, like Elma Dangerfield, was an intellectual and who exemplified the virtues and attitudes of the Old Guard.*

upon the utter chaos. Her ansaphone message to Justin has to be heard to be believed.

'Justin, Justin, come immediately! A mad axeman has broken in! He has stove in the door! EVERYTHING has gone. The place is in UPROAR! You've never seen anything like it!'

There followed a short pause in the breathless recital, a minute pause, before Elma continued on a different tack, and on a pleading note:

'...We're just off to *Daquise*. You know how you like it. Richard is coming. You know you like Richard. Oh, do come! It will be such fun! Please come!'

A lady of Elma's generation not born to rule an empire or two could have had a swooning fit or called for smelling salts. A more modern lady would contact her shrink for counselling. Elma was of different clay. 'Onward Britannia!' was a phrase still *au courant*. Her attitude may account in part for the surprise find of the 'Letters to Mrs O'Connor Donolan' (see above) which throw light on her early days in high circles.

justinglass2020@gmail.com © Copyright April 2020 All Rights Reserved - Justin Glass

Obituary of Elma Dangerfield in *THE INDEPENDENT* on 24th January 2006

ELMA DANGERFIELD

Writer and campaigner

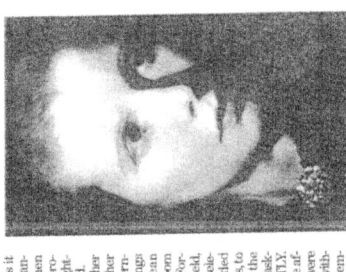

Dangerfield: determined to get her way

Elma Dangerfield was an energetic participant in London political, literary, and business life for more than 60 years. Until housebound by declining health, she attended a social occasion almost every weekday evening. Many of these events she had devised and organised herself, in one of her several guises, as co-founder of the European-Atlantic Group, perhaps, or re-founder of the Byron Society, lectures in hotels in central London, dinners in the Houses of Parliament, lunches in the City.

She knew everyone who mattered – and had often known their fathers and mothers too – but few who encountered her in recent decades appreciated quite how remarkable her earlier life had been. She disliked talking about the past, partly to conceal her great age, and it was for the same reason, I suspect, that her name did not appear in reference books although she was appointed OBE 46 years ago. Until the end, she was full of new ideas and ambitious projects for the future.

Born in Wavertree, Liverpool, in 1907, Elma Ricked spent her earliest years in the Philippines and Hong Kong, where her father was a banker. In a fragment of unpublished autobiography, she recalled the luxury and loneliness of colonial life, the endless exchanges of social visits, polo, golf, and cards, the omnipresent servants, the lavish presents – she was given a pony by an admirer of her mother who later became her stepfather. She wrote too of finding her own private refuge in the dream worlds of the English Romantic poets. When the inside the country, these articles are still relevant to the historical question of how much the Allied governments knew, and why they did not divert air power from the bombing of cities.

As the Second World War ended, Dangerfield recounted another series of atrocities, the deportation of innumerable Poles by the Russians, a subject that the Western allies were then reluctant to see discussed. Her excellent book on the gulags, *Beyond the Urals*, with a preface by Rebecca West, was published in 1946 by the British League for European Freedom.

The history of that organisation, in which Dangerfield was closely associated with Kitty, Duchess of Atholl and members of Parliament of both houses, has been told by Douglas MacLeod in his book *Morningside Mata Haris* (2005). Although Dangerfield stood for Parliament unsuccessfully as a Liberal candidate more than once, she had discovered her unique talent, the organising of cross-party, extra-parliamentary campaigns, aimed at shaping opinion.

Anyone who thinks that British politics is Westminster, Whitehall and the media can never have met Elma Dangerfield. The European-Atlantic Group, of which she was a co-founder in 1954 and which remains active, helped to shift opinion from the narrowly nationalistic ethos of the post-war years and campaigned for closer British involvement with Europe.

The Byron Society, which Dangerfield re-founded in 1970s with her partner, the late Dennis Walwyn Jones MC (it had had a previous life from 1876, but had died in the 1930s), has never been just literary, boasting such chairmen as Lord Gilmour of Craigmillar and deputy chairmen as Michael Foot. The society publishes *The Byron Journal*, and Dangerfield herself made her own contribution to Byron studies in *Byron and the Romantics in Switzerland, 1816/1976*.

Tiny, thin, dainty in her manners, Elma Dangerfield in her exotic tropical birds resembled some exotic tropical bird darting around the crowded room. Always in command, she kept to the side-should never be seen eating unless it were lobster and champagne: for Dangerfield a few sips of Dubonnet when the evening had proved a success provided her with more energy in the eighties than most people have ever had.

Dangerfield's determination to get her way was extraordinary, and so was her persistence. When the Wilson government was making the first soundings about Britain joining the European Common Market, I once sharing a room with the colleague who drafted the Foreign Secretary's speeches. Dangerfield, whom I did not meet till years later, telephoned him so often that he dreaded picking up the receiver – sometimes, to let him get some work done, I took the calls and heaped his desk with notes seeking him on the back MOSTURGENTLY.

Everyone had their stories, some affectionate, some exasperated, but all were evidence of her extraordinary power with inner empires. A labour peer remembers rushing down from the ski slopes when the hotel sent up word that he was wanted urgently on the telephone – would he be able, Dangerfield asked, to take the chair at a meeting in May? Sheikh Yamani, the Saudi oil minister, who in the mid-1970s was one of the most powerful men in the world, was persuaded to postpone the funeral of a close relative, something almost unheard of in Muslim society, in order to give a talk in London.

I remember when the Byron Society, on a tour of Italy, arrived at the convent where Byron had sent his daughter. The Mother Superior was reluctant to let us in. "This is the Lady of the Queen of England," Dangerfield announced in schoolgirl Italian, dragging forward the widow of an Astronomer Royal who lived in a grace-and-favour flat in Buckingham Palace Mews. The convent gate duly opened, although most members of the society had shrunk away in embarrassment.

This apparent shamelessness was made possible by an absence of any sense of the reverend. When Dangerfield declared she was the reincarnation of Claire Clairmont, who had seduced a reluctant Byron, she was not joking. Ironic too was the aspect of her hero to which she was largely deaf. What did she did share with Byron of creation. Women, even those with titles, ranked well below in the order of things. Those who thought that their PhDs allowed them to participate were shooed away like pigeons. The numerous RESERVED placards that Dangerfield laid on the seats in the front rows impeded fraternisation across her imposed hierarchies, even on a bus.

A few years ago Elma Dangerfield gave a lecture on a delighted international audience on the life, works, and loves of Madame de Staël. She drew a picture of aristocratic drawing rooms, of intelligent men and stylish women, a world of unchallenged social differences, where politics, literature and art mixed, and influential behind-the-scenes women were gallantly courted by ambitious male admirers.

Dangerfield's enthusiasm for the occasions that she tirelessly devised for over half a century derived from some such fantasy of how great nations should be governed.

William St Clair

Elma Tryphosa Birket, journalist, writer

Obituary of Elma Dangerfield in *THE TIMES*

Elma Dangerfield, CBE, writer and campaigner, was born on October 11, 1907. She died on January 22, 2006, aged 98

Intellectual powerhouse embroiled in the literary, political and social life of Britain for more than 60 years

ELMA DANGERFIELD, to those who knew her or merely met her, could seem like a force of nature. Pertinacious, single-minded, formidable, she would take "no" for an answer only when it issued from her own lips. She was a daughter of Empire, both as to her background and her social attitudes. Grafted on to these attributes were a fine intellectuality, a keen political interest and a flair for organisation.

As an author, her works were admired by aficionados and experts; as founder and honorary director for 50 years of the European-Atlantic Group and for 32 years of the Byron Society, she cut perhaps a greater dash in the influential political and academic circles she so admired.

Born Elma Birkett in Wavertree, Liverpool, in 1907, she spent much of her childhood in the Far East. She cherished memories of her *amah*, or nanny, in Manila. Her father was connected with Jardine, the trading company, and a doyen of the Hong Kong stock exchange. It was said that when a financial crisis threatened the savings of investors, he all but bankrupted himself in honouring obligations that were not, strictly speaking, his.

In later childhood and her teens Dangerfield stayed with her uncle, Sir Thomas Birkett. One of his family seats was a vast mansion in

Scotland. A cousin was the Lord Birkett of legal lore[98]; Dangerfield described an episode in which she saw him bring a coffin into court and lie down in it, his forensic point backed up by a showmanship that was much to Dangerfield's taste.

Her husband, Captain Edward Dangerfield, used to joke that he needed to get back to his desk at the Admiralty for a rest after the social whirl of a weekend with Elma. A personal friend of the Duke of Kent, he died of phlebitis in 1941, a tragedy for Elma and their daughter, Gay, aged 12 years, and damaging for the war effort: he had been in the process of commissioning the cruiser *HMS Dido*.

Dangerfield continued to move in the smartest of sets. Though she rarely stooped to gossip about celebrities, she abhorred vanity and once characterised the Duchess of Argyll by her way of never passing a mirror without stopping. Dangerfield herself, tiny and — to judge by her numerous male admirers — captivating, appeared not to give a thought to her appearance after having daubed on her make-up.

During the war she had liaison jobs at the Admiralty, and with MI9 and the Ministry of Information. She was involved behind the scenes with delegations from Eastern Europe.

Her researches and contacts led her to write *Beyond the Urals*, with a preface by Rebecca West, a chilling insight into what befell deportees and dissidents in the hands of the communists. Her articles in *The Nineteenth Century and After* were among the first to alert a wider public to the extermination by the Nazis of Gypsies and Jews.

---

[98] *Justin Glass submitted this Obituary to 'the Times' who printed it as sent with two minor alterations. Several years later he met a granddaughter of Lord Birkett who discounted knowledge of Elma being family.*

Her friendship with Sir Edward Hulton resulted in contributions to *Picture Post*; her editorship later in the *European-Atlantic Review* with the Earl of Bessborough, Sir Edward Beddington-Behrens and Lord Layton among others drew her to subjects so diverse that she even explored in print the unconscionable way that the flower of British maidenhood was inclined to fall headlong into the matrimonial embrace of foreigners. Behind these apparent preoccupations was a concern for the future of Europe and in particular the need to endorse the power of the Council of Europe.

Aside from more direct forays into politics — she once stood for Parliament as a Liberal, something of a lost cause at the time — she formed, with colleagues in 1954, the European-Atlantic Group. Her view was that Europe and America needed more institutions in place as amicable meeting grounds for parliamentarians and opinion-shapers from both sides of the Atlantic.

Lord Layton had been instrumental in inviting US and Canadian politicians to debate with European parliamentarians in Strasbourg, and suggested to Dangerfield that she should start a group in London with leading representatives of all the Anglo- European and Anglo-US and Canadian societies in London. She had been assisting him over human rights issues in Strasbourg and, on returning to London, she approached Lord Abinger and other peers, MPs, academics, economists and journalists. The group was founded in London at Abinger's London house, with the first meetings held at the Anglo-Belgian Club. She remained a director of this group until the end of her life, but was also a co-founding member of other groups with comparable objectives, whose influence is still felt today, namely the British-Atlantic Group (forerunner to the Atlantic Council of the UK) and the Mid-Atlantic Group.

Dangerfield's literary pursuits were as dear to her as those of her political career. Her *Byron and the Romantics in Switzerland* (1978) is a model of concise writing, as is her play *Mad Shelley*. Her penchant for organisation led her to re-found the moribund Byron Society in 1972, together with Dennis Walwin Jones, and they remained partners until his death *(in 1975)*[99].

The society under her helm was an eclectic mix of blue bloods and notable academics. Its programme, devoted to every aspect of Byron's poetry and life, was and is a tribute both to Dangerfield's interests and her organisational genius. She was for many years editor of *The Byron Journal,* and its reputation as a serious publication assisted in the rehabilitation of the poet's reputation.

The powerhouse that was the HQ of both societies, and the human dynamo that was Dangerfield, has been recorded by Muriel Spark. In *Curruiculum Vitae*, Muriel Spark writes: I would have involved myself far more in this exotic enterprise had I not vowed to give my main attention to my literary work. I was with European Affairs full time for a while, and then I had to explain that I could only do three days a week. Monty Radulovitch accepted this offer although Elma Dangerfield, his partner was against it. She was a creature of the 'thirties, petite, with a short, tight, head-hugging coiffeur and short, tight, body-hugging dresses. I kept an ear out for her voice and her terms of expression, as I always do with people. Monty's way of speech was a treasure-house to me. I was not yet writing stories and novels, but I was working towards the narrative art and saved up 'voices' in my memory-file. The phrase of Monty's that I remember

---

[99] *Dennis Walwin Jones's memorial stone is in Putney Vale cemetery, in front of the tomb of Henry Birkett (d. 1932). Its inscription is more a CV than an epitaph, including his roles as Founder of the E-AG and Byron Society and as the Director-General of the European League of Economic Cooperation; and the European Movement.*

most was the warning: 'Elma, you regret thees, you regret thees, Elma. All yout life.' So it was when Elma wanted to refuse my offer of three days' work a week. 'Elma, you regret thees.' Elma gave in and I stayed.

It was not just the lowly who stood in awe of her. The list of presidents and ministers and notables who have addressed the European-Atlantic Group over the years does scant justice to the unrelenting determination with which Dangerfield so often secured their attendance.

In the early 1970s, when OPEC held the West to ransom over oil prices, Sheikh Ahmed Zaki Yamani, the Saudi Oil Minister, wished to bow out of his engagement as a speaker. "If you do not come, it will be an insult to this country," he was informed, before finally capitulating to the Dangerfield *coup de grâce*: "And the Palace will have to be told!" Dangerfield was appointed OBE after the group mounted the tenth anniversary celebration of the founding of NATO at Guildhall; the Duke of Edinburgh, who attended as a guest of honour again at the 30th anniversary, replied to the question: "What do you need to do to have a place in the roped-off enclosure?" by saying: "You have to know Mrs Dangerfield."

For services to international relations, she was advanced to CBE when in her nineties. In 2000 she was given a European Woman of the Year award[100].

---

[100] *This award was given by the European Union of Women.*

She died on Lord Byron's birthday. Members of the Nottinghamshire Byron Society[101], in their annual celebration on this day, drank a toast in tribute to an extraordinary woman.

She is survived by her daughter.

*****

Painting by Gay Fraser, Elma's daughter[102]

---

[101] *Elma re-founded the London Byron Society in 1972 with Dennis Walwin Jones as treasurer and grandees in her circle if not of her political persuasion such as, later, Michael Foot, the former Labour leader with who Elma went on holiday. The imposing list on the Byron Society letterhead was almost such as to rival that of the Group.*
[102] *Gay emigrated to America to the chagrin of her mother who intended her 'to marry well' in the old sense of the phrase, the celebrated Nigel Nicholson being one swain ear-marked. Gay has three children.*

Obituary of Elma Dangerfield in *THE DESPATCH*

A poetic end for leading Byronist

ASHES AT PARISH CHURCH

EXCLUSIVE
BY DENIS ROBINSON

HUCKNALL Parish Church is world-famous as the last resting-place of Lord Byron.

And it now also houses the ashes of Elma Dangerfield, who was one of the poet's leading champions.

The charismatic Elma died at the age of 98 on Sunday January 22, which was the anniversary date of Byron's birth in 1788.

Newstead Abbey Byron Society (NABS) chairman Ken Purslow said Elma confided that after her death she wanted her ashes to be brought to the church.

The casket will now be placed as close to Byron's tomb as possible, together with a commemorative plaque.

The plaque was unveiled by the 13th Lord Byron, who is president of London Byron Society, during a high-profile thanksgiving service in the church last Saturday afternoon.

The event was attended by many distinguished visitors, some representing different nations and faiths. Several civic leaders were among those who took part.

"The plaque will be a lasting tribute to a great lady," said NABS secretary Maureen Crisp.

Devoted to Byron's ideals of freedom, Elma founded the European-Atlantic Group after the end of World War Two and re-founded the national Byron Society in the 1970s.

Honoured with an OBE and then a CBE, she was described on the plaque as a 'citizen of the world.'

In a tribute to Elma, Mr Purslow said she was the very essence of style and charm: who showed total dedication to any task, she set herself and never took no for an answer.

"She embraced the lives of so many people and all are much richer for having known her," he added. She showed an overwhelming desire to form a Byron society locally and NABS is the result.

"Elma's helping hand has been pre-eminent throughout and seldom a day went by without her being on the phone to myself or Maureen.

"I will always remember her keen sense of

sail and Geoffrey Bond on behalf of the London Byron Society, Lord Mereworth, Justin Glass and Prince Mochin Ali Khan for the European-Atlantic Group, Jack Wasserman, of the American Byron Society, and Brigitte Lohmar, of the German Byron Society. Each lit a candle in Elma's memory.

A special address was given by Brother Tello, a Cistertian monk from Wales, who was formerly Michael Rees, secretary of the International Byron Society (IBS).

Ex-Labour Party leader Michael Foot, who is renowned as a stalwart Byronist, could not attend because of ill health but sent his best wishes.

The service also marked the anniversary of Byron's death in Messolonghi, Greece, in 1824. Wreaths were laid by Lord Byron on behalf of the family, David Herbert for the Lytton family (descendants of the poet), Ashfield District Council chairman Coun Charlie Stott (Lab), of Hucknall, Notts County Council vice-chairman Coun Peter Barnes (Lab), Nottingham Deputy Lord Mayor Coun Des Wilson (Lab), Gedling Borough Council mayor Coun Dr Raj Chandran (Con), Newark and Sherwood District Council chairman Coun Richard Alexander (Con), Christine Symeonides for the Greek nation, Justin Glass for the European-Atlantic Group, Maureen Crisp for the IBS, Tina Brace for the Lord Byron School in Armenia, Jack Wasserman for the American Byron Society, Brigitte Lohmar for the German Byron Society, Ken Purslow for the Messolonghi Byron Society, Iraklii Marabishvili for the Georgian Byron Society, Alan Rawes for the London Byron Society, Iris Rees Williams for NABS and Hucknall rector the Rev Linda Church for the Dangerfield family.

Mr Rees was organist for the service and entertainment was given by the Knights of Harmony singing group, conducted by Malcolm Wailes. During the final hymn, offerings were received towards the cost of setting up an international garden of remembrance around the Byron memorial stone outside the church.

A guard of honour was formed by cadets of the 1803 (Hucknall) Air Training Corps squadron and a

174

6. ADDENDUM

President's Report of 1958
Pages 175-180

Names mentioned in the report:

H.R.H The Prince Phillip Duke of Edinburgh

H.R.H The Prince of the Netherlands

Lord and Lady Mayoress of London

The Supreme Allied Commander

Mr John Edwards MP

Sir John Slessor

The Turkish Ambassador

The Iranian Charge d'Affaires

Mr Eric Johnston

Lord Birdwood

Lady Violet Bonham Carter

Ambassador of the Philippines and Thailand

High Commissionaire of Pakistan

The Indian Commissioner-General for Economic Affairs

The Japanese First Secretary

Mr Pote Sarasin

Mr Peter Hope

Mr Richard Goold-Adams

The American Ambassador to NATO

The President of the Carnegie Endowment for International Peace

Mr Geoffrey de Freitas

Commonwealth High Commissioners

Commissioners of the United Kingdom

Sir Ian Horrabin MP

Sir William Cook

Sir Claud Gibb

Sir David Kelly

Lady Kelly

The Supreme Allied Commander Europe, General Lauris Norstad

Sir Richard Gale The Deputy Supreme Commander

Sir Frank Roberts

Sir Hugh Ellis

Lord Colcraine

Sir Evelyn Shuckbergh

Monsieur Rene Sergant Secretary General OEEC

Sir Alfred Bossom

Joint Honorary Treasurer Lord Abinger

Major Anthony Carr

European-Atlantic Group

PRESIDENT'S FIFTH ANNUAL REPORT
By THE EARL OF BESSBOROUGH

JULY, 1958 — JULY, 1959

NATO BANQUET:

This has been a momentous year for the Group. The North Atlantic Treaty Organization and the Council of Europe — the two chief international bodies which the Group was founded to support — have been celebrating their tenth anniversaries, and the Group was honoured by being invited to organize the NATO Banquet in Guildhall on 11th May, which was attended by H.R.H. The Prince Philip Duke of Edinburgh, H.R.H. The Prince of the Netherlands and many other distinguished personalities, including the Lord Mayor and Lady Mayoress of London, Cabinet Ministers of this and other countries, the Supreme Allied Commander Atlantic and the Supreme Allied Commander Europe, together with a number of other NATO Commanders.

The speeches, which lasted an hour, were relayed 'live' on both B.B.C. Television and Radio, as well as later on Independent Television, and the proceedings were also shown on Movietone Newsreel. A full-length film of these has been made available to the Group by the B.B.C. and will be shown after the Annual General Meeting on 30th July.

The NATO Banquet also received front-page coverage in most of the British press, as well as in many other countries throughout the world — cuttings of which are still coming in to the Group's offices.

COUNCIL OF EUROPE:

The week previous to the NATO Banquet was devoted to celebrating the Tenth Anniversary of the Council of Europe. Some of the founder Members of the Group were honoured by being invited by the Prime Minister to the St. James's Palace celebrations and afterwards to a Government Luncheon in Lancaster House. That evening a Commemorative Dinner was arranged by the Group in the House of Commons. The Dinner was attended by Members of Parliament, who have been Delegates to the Council of Europe, as well as other members of the Group who have been associated with the Council since its inception. Our guests included the newly-elected President of the Consultative Assembly, Mr. John Edwards, M.P., a number of Vice-Presidents representing other countries, the Secretary-General and Members of the Standing Committee and Bureau of the Council of Europe.

NATO'S LINKS WITH THE BAGHDAD PACT:

While concentrating primarily on the development of the European and Atlantic Communities, the Group has also explored the links between NATO and the Baghdad Pact. An important Meeting was held last July, immediately after the revolution in Iraq. Sir John Slessor was in the Chair, and the Speakers included the Turkish Ambassador, the Iranian Chargé d'Affaires, Mr. Eric Johnston (Personal Representative of President Eisenhower for the Jordan River Project) and Lord Birdwood, one of our Vice-Chairmen. Many Diplomatic Representatives of the Middle East countries were present, as well as leading Members of the Societies concerned with this area.

ASIAN CO-OPERATION WITH THE WEST (LINKS WITH SEATO):

The Group's horizon has been widened even further this year, as was shown by its extremely interesting Meeting on the above subject in January, when Lady Violet Bonham Carter took the Chair (following her tour of the Asian countries with our Honorary Director). The Speakers included the Ambassadors of the Philippines and Thailand, the High Commissioner for Pakistan, the Indian Commissioner-General for Economic Affairs, and the Japanese First Secretary. We were also honoured by having the Secretary-General of SEATO, who had come from Bangkok for talks with the Government. The Meeting followed a Government Reception at Lancaster House in Mr. Pote Sarasin's honour, to which many Members of the Group were invited. So successful was the experiment that a number of Asians have now joined the Group, and it is for consideration whether a Special Asian Section should now be formed within the Group.

EASTERN AND WESTERN POLICIES FOR EUROPE:

Immediately following the Prime Minister's visit to Moscow last March, the Group was fortunate enough to be able to organize, with the kind assistance of Mr. Peter Hope, then Head of the Foreign Office News Department, a most informative meeting. The Speakers included London Correspondents of the Soviet, Polish, Czechoslovak, German and American Press, with Mr. Richard Goold-Adams in the Chair. The discussion was extremely frank and some hard-hitting questions were put and answered.

NORTH AMERICAN VIEWS ON THE ATLANTIC COMMUNITY:

Two meetings — one held in the House of Commons when the spokesmen were American Congressmen and Canadian M.P.s from the NATO Conference of Parliamentarians in Paris — and the other including the American Ambassador to NATO, the President of the Carnegie Endowment for International Peace and a Member of the Council on Foreign Relations in New York — underlined the continuing interest and importance which leading citizens of both the United States and Canada attach to the preservation and strengthening of NATO. The Group is indebted to Mr. Geoffrey de Freitas, M.P., one of our Vice-Chairmen, for so kindly arranging the House of Commons Meeting.

COMMONWEALTH VIEWS ON EUROPEAN FREE TRADE:

This Meeting held last October, when the spokesmen were a number of Commonwealth High Commissioners and Commissioners in the United Kingdom, was again breaking new ground for the Group. It was the first time in which we had the opportunity of hearing the views of the High Commissioners and Commissioners themselves, as regards the effects of a European Free Trade Area on their own particular countries. It was, I think, particularly illuminating, not only for our British Members, but also for the Diplomatic Representatives of the Western European countries who were present. The discussion was so interesting that many of the participants agreed that a week-end conference on this subject should be held as soon as possible, and this is a suggestion which I would like to put before the Annual General Meeting. A series of week-end Study Conferences on subjects of particular topical interest might well be valuable.

DEVELOPMENT OF NUCLEAR POWER IN WESTERN EUROPE:

Industry has not been overlooked in our work this year, and indeed I am glad to say that a large proportion of our new members come from industrial and business circles — not to mention, of course, our growing number of Corporate Members, which now include many of the companies in this country interested in overseas trade with the European and Atlantic countries. This particular Meeting on Nuclear Power had one of our most distinguished panels of the year, including Sir Ian Horrabin, M.P., as the Chairman, with the Deputy Secretary-General of O.E.E.C., a Member of the Euratom Commission, Sir William Cook (of the

Atomic Energy Authority), and the late Sir Claud Gibb (Chairman of the Nuclear Power Plant Company Ltd.).

I must pause here to say how terribly shocked and grieved we all were to learn of the sudden death of Sir Claud very shortly after he had so brilliantly addressed us. I am proud and thankful that we had the opportunity of hearing his wise words.

EUROPEAN-ATLANTIC REVIEW:

Sir Claud's address was printed in the following issue of the European-Atlantic Review, which is published in association with the Group, and regularly contains the authoritative opinions of leading statesmen, economists and experts, in this and other countries. The Editorial Board includes the Presidents and Chairmen of a number of our Associated Societies, and I would here like to say that the loss of Sir David Kelly from so many of our Committees has been a tragedy. His place will be hard to fill.

LADIES COMMITTEE:

I am delighted, however, to announce that Lady Kelly has agreed to become Chairman of the Ladies' Committee. I know how admirably she will fill this Chair and what invaluable help she will give to our Honorary Director and the other ladies on the Committee in organizing the social side of our functions, which is so extremely important. I hope they will also elect their own Vice-Chairmen.

MEMBERSHIP SUB-COMMITTEE:

This Committee has largely fulfilled its worthy purpose in that I am happy to say our membership has now reached our original target of five hundred members. We also have in addition 20 Corporate Members.

DELEGATIONS ABROAD:

The Group has sent its yearly Delegation abroad this year to NATO, SHAPE and OEEC in Paris, which we had not visited for four years. This time the Delegation was received and briefed by the Supreme Allied Commander Europe, General Lauris Norstad, and others of his Staff at Versailles, including Sir Richard Gale, the Deputy Supreme Commander, who addressed our Group last year. Sir Frank Roberts, the U.K. Permanent Representative to NATO, was kind enough to give a cocktail party for the Delegation, as did Sir Hugh Ellis the U.K. Representative to OEEC. Lord Coleraine and Sir Evelyn Shuckburgh entertained and briefed the Delegation at NATO, and Monsieur René Sergent, Secretary-General of OEEC, did likewise at the Château de la Muette. Such visits abroad are one of the highlights of the Group and I only wish it were possible for all the Members to take part in them.

We are, however, endeavouring to provide facilities for greater numbers through the Atlantic Community Flights and Ships which we are hoping to arrange for the coming year. The first, carrying a large delegation, is the NATO Flight to Naples, Malta and Izmir (NATO Commands), Athens, Cyprus, Ankara and Istanbul.

Next summer we hope to sail to the Baltic capitals in an Atlantic Community Ship, and perhaps across the Atlantic later next year to Canada and America. It would, I think, be very fitting if we had the privilege of sailing up the great new St. Lawrence waterway, afterwards visiting Boston and New York. Such journeys would certainly promote greater knowledge and understanding of each others' countries and problems than anything else we can do within the Atlantic Community.

JOINT MEETINGS WITH ASSOCIATED ORGANIZATIONS:

I am happy to say that we have had more of these than ever before this last year, principally with the United Kingdom Council of the European Movement, the British Atlantic Committee and with the Atlantic Treaty Association. I hope we shall have even more in the coming year, as I think everyone agrees that such Joint Meetings do much to knit our Organizations more closely together.

OFFICERS OF THE GROUP:

As I have now held the offices of President and Chairman for 5 years, and since I have recently had to undertake certain other commitments, I feel I must relieve myself of some of the executive work of the Group. I am, therefore, glad to be able to inform members that your Council and Committee have unanimously agreed that Sir Alfred Bossom should be invited to take on the Chairmanship of the Group while I remain President for the time being. Sir Alfred has intimated his willingness to serve, and I am very glad to be able to make this announcement at this Annual General Meeting. Sir Alfred's work on behalf of various societies is well known. As an architect with an international practice, he went to the United States in 1903 and was responsible for several of the earliest skyscrapers. He has been Chairman of the American-Mid-European Association, President of the Anglo-Baltic Society, and is still, of course, a member of Parliament. He is Chairman of the Anglo-Belgian Union, the Anglo-Luxembourg Society, the Anglo-Iranian Section of the Inter-Parliamentary Union and the newly-formed Anglo-Turkish Parliamentary Group, and President of the Royal Society of Arts and of the Anglo-Texan Society. He is the holder of numerous foreign decorations including the French Legion of Honour and Belgian and Italian orders. His hospitality to members of the European-Atlantic Group will have been appreciated by many of you. It is clear that we are most fortunate in obtaining his services.

I should like to pay a special tribute here to the wonderful work which the Group's Officers have done during the past year, particularly in organizing the NATO Banquet which was a supreme feat. In this I must single out our indefatigable Honorary Director, Mrs. Elma Dangerfield, on whom most of the burden fell, as well as our Joint Honorary Treasurer, Lord Abinger, Major Anthony Carr, the other voluntary helpers, and the working staff of the Group, for their unsparing energy and devotion.

ATLANTIC CONGRESS:

Finally, I would add that the Atlantic Congress — in which the Group had half-a-dozen Alternate Delegates as well as myself — pointed the way to the ever-widening interest of the Atlantic Community, particularly as regards the rest of the free and uncommitted world.

This, I feel, should be the keynote of our policy for the ensuing year, together with an outward-looking attitude to the proposed economic association of the "Outer Seven" countries, and the whole conception of an eventual multi-lateral Free Trade Area. Indeed, I would go so far as to suggest that the Group might well explore the possibilities of a potential Atlantic Free Trade Area, which might become a pattern for other Regional Groupings.

These and similar questions will no doubt be studied thoroughly in the Atlantic Committee for Economic Development which we propose to set up, and whose findings no doubt we should discuss at further Meetings of the Group as a whole. I think I am voicing the feelings of most of the Members, when I say that the Group has now grown to such dimensions that we should divide ourselves from time to time into smaller Sub-Committees and Sections to discuss, more thoroughly, and to make more adequate recommendations for the development and implementation of the ideals of the Atlantic Community.

I attach to this report a revised list of the officers of the Group, a list of Corporate Members, and of the Meetings we have held during the past year, as well as the year's accounts.

B.

17 July, 1959

Printed by the Victor Printing Co. Ltd., 172, York Way, London, N.1.

Brochure For Nato Banquet 2009

Guest List – Page 203–210

Picture Gallery – Page 218

THE
EUROPEAN-ATLANTIC
GROUP

Request the pleasure of your company at

THE 60TH NATO ANNIVERSARY CELEBRATION DINNER

In the presence of

HIS ROYAL HIGHNESS THE DUKE OF YORK KG

At

ST JAMES'S PALACE

MONDAY 9TH NOVEMBER 2009
6:45 PM FOR 7 PM

MESS DRESS – BLACK TIE – DECORATIONS
RSVP on reply card or to E-AG, 4 St Pauls Way, N3 2PP, or to info@eag.org.uk, +44 20 8612 9213.

CARRIAGES: 10.30l
This card does not secure admittan

THE EUROPEAN-ATLANTIC GROUP

THE 60TH NATO ANNIVERSARY CELEBRATION DINNER

In the presence of
HIS ROYAL HIGHNESS THE DUKE OF YORK KG

St. James's Palace   Monday 9th November 2009

HIS ROYAL HIGHNESS THE DUKE OF YORK KG

PROGRAMME

INTRODUCTORY REMARKS BY THE CHAIRMAN
The Rt. Hon. Baroness Symons of Vernam Dean

A tape recording of the late *Earl of Bessborough*
H.E. Mr Georg Boomgaarden
Princess Zohra of Afghanistan

GRACE
The Reverend Wendy Izod

THE LOYAL TOAST
The Lord Dykes

SPEAKERS
The Rt. Hon. Lord Hamilton of Epsom
Mr Martin Howard
H.R.H. The Duke of York

H.R.H. THE DUKE OF YORK KG

THE RT. HON. LORD HAMILTON OF EPSOM

The Rt. Hon. Lord Hamilton of Epsom, the Chairman of the European-Atlantic Group, was the Member of Parliament for Epsom and Ewell from 1978 to 2001, becoming Parliamentary Under-Secretary of State for Defence Procurement from 1986 to 1987. He was the Parliamentary Private Secretary to the Prime Minister in 1987 and 1988. Lord Hamilton was Minister of State for the Armed Forces from 1988 to 1993.

MARTIN HOWARD

Martin Howard is NATO Assistant Secretary-General for Operations and the senior British Representative at NATO.

THE REVEREND MISTRESS WENDY IZOD

Wendy is a Human Resources Consultant specialising in the financial services sector having been in Human Resources for 40 years. She was ordained as a minister in 2001 and is the Curate of St. Peter's Church, Hever, Kent. Wendy is married to the Clerk and Adjutant of the Company of Pikemen and Musketeers, HAC.

H.R.H. THE DUKE OF YORK KG

THE RT. HON. LORD HAMILTON OF EPSOM

The Rt. Hon. Lord Hamilton of Epsom, the Chairman of the European-Atlantic Group, was the Member of Parliament for Epsom and Ewell from 1978 to 2001, becoming Parliamentary Under-Secretary of State for Defence Procurement from 1986 to 1987. He was the Parliamentary Private Secretary to the Prime Minister in 1987 and 1988. Lord Hamilton was Minister of State for the Armed Forces from 1988 to 1993.

MARTIN HOWARD

Martin Howard is NATO Assistant Secretary-General for Operations and the senior British Representative at NATO.

THE REVEREND MISTRESS WENDY IZOD

Wendy is a Human Resources Consultant specialising in the financial services sector having been in Human Resources for 40 years. She was ordained as a minister in 2001 and is the Curate of St. Peter's Church, Hever, Kent. Wendy is married to the Clerk and Adjutant of the Company of Pikemen and Musketeers, HAC.

NATO'S 60TH ANNIVERSARY:
PEACE AND SECURITY CANNOT BE TAKEN FOR GRANTED

A UNIQUE ALLIANCE

This year, the North Atlantic Treaty Organization is celebrating the 60th anniversary of the signing of the North Atlantic Treaty. It is well and proper that this long and eventful history should be honoured, but the moment to live within old achievements has long since passed. The world has changed, and NATO is changing with it.

Globalization entails a redistribution of geopolitical as well as economic power, and neither North America nor Europe acting alone can shape the 21st century world in a way that corresponds to the fundamental values that we share: a commitment to democracy, individual freedom, the rule of law, open and transparent governance, the market economy, and the peaceful settlement of disputes.

A multipolar world is here. This must be a world where challenges are handled together, and where common rules and strong relationships prevent new conflicts. This new and unstable world needs an efficient NATO that can work together with Partners and international organisations to address potential threats and challenges.

The twenty-eight NATO nations' security cannot be based upon a return to a 19th-century balance-of-power system. In the 20th century, that paradigm's bankruptcy led twice to global cataclysms. It must not be allowed to do so again.

THE MORE THINGS CHANGE

Since the fall of the Berlin Wall a generation ago, Allies have successfully carried out operations that have helped to end crises and stabilise fragile regions. These operations have included a peace implementation force in Bosnia-Herzegovina, a stabilization mission in Kosovo, and a humanitarian deployment to help Pakistan recover from a terrible earthquake. Ongoing operations include a naval task force to deter piracy in the Gulf of Aden, a maritime operation to prevent terrorist activity in the Mediterranean known as Operation Active Endeavour, and, last but not least, the International Security Assistance Force,

NATO'S 60TH ANNIVERSARY:
PEACE AND SECURITY CANNOT BE TAKEN FOR GRANTED

A UNIQUE ALLIANCE

This year, the North Atlantic Treaty Organization is celebrating the 60th anniversary of the signing of the North Atlantic Treaty. It is well and proper that this long and eventful history should be honoured, but the moment to live within old achievements has long since passed. The world has changed, and NATO is changing with it.

Globalization entails a redistribution of geopolitical as well as economic power, and neither North America nor Europe acting alone can shape the 21st century world in a way that corresponds to the fundamental values that we share: a commitment to democracy, individual freedom, the rule of law, open and transparent governance, the market economy, and the peaceful settlement of disputes.

A multipolar world is here. This must be a world where challenges are handled together, and where common rules and strong relationships prevent new conflicts. This new and unstable world needs an efficient NATO that can work together with Partners and international organisations to address potential threats and challenges.

The twenty-eight NATO nations' security cannot be based upon a return to a 19th-century balance-of-power system. In the 20th century, that paradigm's bankruptcy led twice to global cataclysms. It must not be allowed to do so again.

THE MORE THINGS CHANGE

Since the fall of the Berlin Wall a generation ago, Allies have successfully carried out operations that have helped to end crises and stabilise fragile regions. These operations have included a peace implementation force in Bosnia-Herzegovina, a stabilization mission in Kosovo, and a humanitarian deployment to help Pakistan recover from a terrible earthquake. Ongoing operations include a naval task force to deter piracy in the Gulf of Aden, a maritime operation to prevent terrorist activity in the Mediterranean known as Operation Active Endeavour, and, last but not least, the International Security Assistance Force, or ISAF, in Afghanistan. During the Cold War, NATO was an organization of "being" as its mere existence was enough to deter the Soviet threat. Now, NATO is an organization of "being" and "doing".

To safeguard Allied security, NATO has to operate beyond its borders, defending the interests of its members where threats arise, and contributing to a more secure international order. The increasing complexity, number, and tempo of NATO operations make defence transformation an ongoing imperative. All the same, while transformation is a requirement for the Alliance, a few enduring principles remain.

- NATO's fundamental task is the common defence of its member states.
- NATO's decisions are made by consensus.
- All Allies can use NATO to consult on any threats to their security.
- NATO's door will remain open to those countries that share NATO's values and that are willing and able to meet the responsibilities of membership.

A joint vision for a transformed defence planning process will be a core element of NATO's military transformation. The Allies will accordingly make efforts to invest their defence budgets in usable, deployable and sustainable forces.

AFGHANISTAN: A LASTING EFFORT

NATO is committed, under a UN mandate, to fostering peace and security in Afghanistan. This is vital not only for peace and freedom within the country, but also for the security of citizens in NATO countries and the stability of the region as a whole. Above all, Afghanistan can no longer be the launching pad for terrorist attacks against the rest of the world. Towards this end, NATO is also building closer cooperation with Afghanistan's neighbours, in particular the countries of Central Asia and Pakistan.

The Alliance's operation is particularly challenging because of the need to protect civilians and to fight insurgents at the same time. Furthermore, the country needs development, good governance, well-trained and equipped security forces, community reconciliation, and good relations with its neighbours. An efficient International Stability and Assistance Force, where more than 40 countries share the same risks, is the foundation of a self-sustaining Afghanistan that is able to provide for its own security, and the Alliance is helping to train and equip the Afghan security forces to take over ISAF's core stabilisation tasks. All the same, the conflict's complexity means that NATO

or ISAF, in Afghanistan. During the Cold War, NATO was an organization of "being" as its mere existence was enough to deter the Soviet threat. Now, NATO is an organization of "being" and "doing".

To safeguard Allied security, NATO has to operate beyond its borders, defending the interests of its members where threats arise, and contributing to a more secure international order. The increasing complexity, number, and tempo of NATO operations make defence transformation an ongoing imperative. All the same, while transformation is a requirement for the Alliance, a few enduring principles remain.

- NATO's fundamental task is the common defence of its member states.
- NATO's decisions are made by consensus.
- All Allies can use NATO to consult on any threats to their security.
- NATO's door will remain open to those countries that share NATO's values and that are willing and able to meet the responsibilities of membership.

A joint vision for a transformed defence planning process will be a core element of NATO's military transformation. The Allies will accordingly make efforts to invest their defence budgets in usable, deployable and sustainable forces.

AFGHANISTAN: A LASTING EFFORT

NATO is committed, under a UN mandate, to fostering peace and security in Afghanistan. This is vital not only for peace and freedom within the country, but also for the security of citizens in NATO countries and the stability of the region as a whole. Above all, Afghanistan can no longer be the launching pad for terrorist attacks against the rest of the world. Towards this end, NATO is also building closer cooperation with Afghanistan's neighbours, in particular the countries of Central Asia and Pakistan.

The Alliance's operation is particularly challenging because of the need to protect civilians and to fight insurgents at the same time. Furthermore, the country needs development, good governance, well-trained and equipped security forces, community reconciliation, and good relations with its neighbours. An efficient International Stability and Assistance Force, where more than 40 countries share the same risks, is the foundation of a self-sustaining Afghanistan that is able to provide for its own security, and the Alliance is helping to train and equip the Afghan security forces to take over ISAF's core stabilisation tasks. All the same, the conflict's complexity means that NATO and the international community more generally cannot achieve progress in Afghanistan through military means alone.

THE COMPREHENSIVE APPROACH

NATO is not a civilian reconstruction agency. The Alliance does not have a mandate in areas such as institution building, governance, development, and judiciary reform that are the prerequisites for success in integrated civilian-military operations. For that reason, NATO cooperates with other international organisations – primarily the United Nations but also with the European Union, the Organization for Security and Cooperation in Europe, and the World Bank – as part of the Comprehensive Approach.

This Approach complements NATO's efforts to deal with 21st century security challenges such as the proliferation of weapons of mass destruction, energy security, maritime awareness, and cyber attacks. For example, the UN-NATO Declaration, signed in September 2008, will strengthen dialogue and cooperation in key areas, including NATO assistance to UN operations and UN efforts to prevent terrorism.

The Alliance also works with Partners and other troop-contributing countries in its operations. Non-NATO countries bring valuable resources and skills to NATO-led operations while distributing cost burdens across the wider international community.

In this respect, the Euro-Atlantic Partnership Council, the Mediterranean Dialogue, and the Istanbul Cooperation Initiative have proved to be useful frameworks to promote a collective and comprehensive approach to security challenges. These Partnerships bridge dividing lines while helping nations to develop capacities to better manage their security challenges. The NATO-Ukraine and NATO-Georgia Commissions also assist these countries with reforms and their preparations for Alliance membership.

NATO will continue to reach out to the Russian Federation while striving to intensify cooperation based on common interests in areas such as terrorism, counter-piracy, and stability in Afghanistan. The Alliance may disagree with Russia. The conflict in Georgia is a case in point. That said, a viable Euro-Atlantic security architecture must include Russia. NATO is ready for a constructive dialogue, including, whenever possible, cooperation in areas such as operations, disarmament and arms control. The Allies take Russia's legitimate security interests into account, but will oppose any attempt to establish European spheres of influence or to prevent European countries from exercising their right to decide for themselves whether or not to belong to any organization.

NATO AND THE EUROPEAN UNION

Twenty-one NATO members are also EU members. So, the Alliance attaches great importance to its relationship with the European Union. The European Security and Defence Policy will benefit the Allies while fostering a more equitable transatlantic security partnership. NATO seeks stronger NATO-EU cooperation not only on the ground in such places as Kosovo and Afghanistan, where both NATO and the EU have deployed complementary assets, but also in their dialogue at the political level in Brussels. While developing this relationship, NATO and EU members must avoid unnecessary duplication.

THE INDISPENSABLE ALLIANCE

The 21st century has seen the rise of a new set of risks and challenges to peace and security that are no less urgent or potentially dangerous than 20th century threats. Coping with these challenges will not only necessitate active Allied involvement in resource commitment, but also NATO's transformation to develop its efficiency and to improve cooperation with outside Partners and organisations.

At 60, NATO is and will remain the unique forum where North America and Europe consult on common challenges to peace and security, decide on common actions, and share risks and responsibilities. The Allies' shared values, their culture of free and open debate, and even their occasional disagreements are sources of the democratic legitimacy that will always be NATO's most lasting strength.

In an age of unpredictable threats, NATO must monitor the strategic environment, using its political and military resources in cooperation with others to defuse potential conflicts. The generation born after the Cold War's end has already experienced the benefits of NATO's role. Our commitment must ensure that future generations can also live in stability and freedom, as peace and security can never be taken for granted.

JEAN-FRANÇOIS BUREAU
Assistant Secretary-General for Public Diplomacy, NATO HQ

THE EUROPEAN-ATLANTIC GROUP

THE EUROPEAN-ATLANTIC GROUP, a non-aligned, all party, registered charity founded in 1954, is renowned as one of the foremost platforms for high level interaction in the field of international relations.

European-Atlantic Group (E-AG) dinner and luncheon debates are a fixture in the London social scene. The intractability of some issues has been no bar to civilised and perceptive discussions in surroundings such as the Palace of Westminster, premier London clubs and, on occasion, with banquets at Guildhall and the Banqueting House.

There is a variety of fayre on offer for a group whose thousand members include diplomats, parliamentarians, captains of industry and the informed and interested public. Few matters of moment in Europe or America can remain untouched by the wider world of politics and countries such as Afghanistan, Burma, China and Nigeria have lately been the subjects of far reaching group debate and analysis. The list of E-AG speakers recently has been graced by senior royalty, the former presidents of Lithuania and Zambia, all successive ambassadors of America, China and Russia, ministers of state, shadow ministers, the head of MI5, and the heads of our armed forces... At one event, twenty former members of Congress spoke in Parliament to the E-AG. Sir Christopher Gent of Vodafone fame and Hugo Dixon of Breakingviews.com, which has articles heavily syndicated throughout Europe, were forthright on the economy and signposted how the UK economy should recover even before the words 'credit' and 'crunch' were linked in un-heavenly embrace. John Lloyd spoke at a conference on Freedom of expression and the media. Events are held almost monthly.

A focus of the E-AG is on advocating solutions to global problems, where this falls within its reach, and not just in their exposition. These can be reflected in E-AG discussions, the E-AG journal or in E-AG papers. Texts of speeches – and debates when 'on-the-record' – on the website are a valuable tool for practitioners and students. Delegations have represented the group in Brussels and Washington. An annual book prize in the name of the late Hon Director, Elma

Dangerfield CBE, has provided useful footnotes to recent history, as does our affiliate publishing arm, New European Publications. The newsletter furthers a sense of community and continuity in the group.

The E-AG was the brainchild of Mrs Dangerfield, a lady so redoubtable that her obituary in The Times in 2003 could describe her as taking 'No' for an answer only when it issued from her own lips! Many have been the personalities who forged the group in the mould it enjoys today. The founders, including The Rt Hon Lord Abinger and The Lord Layton CH CBE, saw in it a means of facilitating contacts between Congressmen and Senators visiting the UK and the Council of Europe.

The roster of E-AG Presidents have included The Lord Layton CH CBE, The Rt Hon Earl of Listowel, Sir Geoffrey de Freitas KCMG MP and, since the 1990s, The Earl of Bessborough DL, Sir Frank Roberts GCMG GCVO, The Rt Hon Lord Rippon of Hexham QC, The Lord Dahrendorf, Lord Judd, The Earl of Limerick KBE, The Viscount Montgomery of Alamein CMG CBE, Sir Michael Burton KCVO CMG, The Baroness Hooper CMG, Lord Dykes and the Rt Hon Baroness Symons of Vernam Dean.

The future might be our oyster but such pearls as may be nurtured depend on the support of those who actively care – perspectives can vary – about issues such as sustainable development and ecology or Europe or our relationship with America, and the plethora of challenges confronting all of us. The E-AG is 'broad church' but some members may feel it more important that the interested public has a say in the conduct of political affairs rather than the uninterested public having a vote. The speaking of truth to power would be one of the ultimate hopes of the E-AG.

EUROPEAN-ATLANTIC GROUP
4 St Pauls Way
London N3 2PP
Tel: +44 20 8632 9253
Fax: +44 20 8343 3532
Email: info@eag.org.uk
Web: www.eag.org.uk

THE PILGRIM COUSINS

*"Sorry to loose you all.
Come and see us when things are a bit straighter."*

(Punch 16th January 1955)

THE PILGRIMS

THE PILGRIMS OF GREAT BRITAIN came into being at the end of July 1902 under the stewardship of Sir Harry Brittain, with the object of promoting Anglo-American good-fellowship and mutual understanding. The first suggestion as to its formation was made by an American, Lindsay Russell, who was then over in this country. The American Pilgrims were established in January 1903.

Over the 107 years of its existence the British Pilgrims have played host to a remarkable range of guest speakers from Mark Twain to John Major. The British Pilgrims were responsible for oganising the Appeal and construction of the Roosevelt Memorial in Grosvenor Square, dedicated to the Memory of Franklin Delano Roosevelt (unveiled in 1948).

There is a tradition whereby the incoming American Ambassador to the Court of St James's does not speak in public until he has addressed the Pilgrims at a formal dinner given in his honour. The British Ambassador to the United States speaks first before the American Pilgrims.

Since 2002 The Pilgrims' President has been Field Marshal the Right Hon Lord Inge KG GCB DL, former Chief of the Defence Staff and the Chairman since 1993 is Sir Robert Worcester KBE DL. The Annual General Meeting of the Pilgrims is held at the American Embassy in September each year and features the Sir Harry Britain Memorial Lecture. This year's lecture was by Sir Gus O'Donnell KCB, Secretary of the Cabinet and Head of the Home Civil Service.

THE PILGRIMS
Allington Castle
Maidstone, Kent, ME16 0NB
Tel: 01622 606404
Fax: 01622 606402
Email: sec@pilgrimsociety.org

ST. JAMES'S PALACE STATE APARTMENTS
A BRIEF HISTORY

ST JAMES'S PALACE was built by Henry VIII in 1532. The ground plan of the Tudor Palace largely remains, although today has been integrated with four courtyards - Colour, Ambassador's, Engine, and Friary Court. The surviving Tudor elements are the use of red brick, the Chapel Royal, and the Clock Tower, where Henry VIII's cypher 'HR' can be seen above the arches on either side of the Great Gates.

Fundamental architectural change occurred during the reign of Queen Anne at the beginning of the 18th Century when Sir Christopher Wren, followed by his pupils John Vanbrugh and Nicolas Hawksmoor, was commissioned to redesign the Grand Staircase and State A partments. The interiors were reworked by William Kent. A fire in 1809 caused extensive damage, but today the resplendent interiors evoke the late Baroque style of the rooms designed for Queen Anne.

St James's Palace has many historical associations. In 1588, Queen Elizabeth I used St James's Palace as her headquarters to direct the English fleet against the Spanish Armada, and King Charles I spent his last moments here before being executed in 1649.

Queen Victoria was married in the Chapel Royal, St James's Palace in 1840, and Princess Alexandra's wedding reception was held here in 1963.

The Queen's Chapel was the resting place of Lord Louis Mountbatten in 1979. Princess Beatrice was christened here in 1988. The Chapel Royal was the resting place for Diana, Princess of Wales, in 1997 as visitors signed the Books of Condolence in the Lower Corridor.

The Palace is today used as a residence for, The Princess Royal and Princess Alexandra, the Hon. Lady Ogilvy. The Prince of Wales and The Duchess of Cornwall reside in Clarence House. The State Apartments are reserved for receptions, concerts, and functions in aid of those charities supported by members of The Royal Family.

COMPANY OF PIKEMEN & MUSKETEERS
HONOURABLE ARTILLERY COMPANY

THE COMPANY OF PIKEMEN & MUSKETEERS, Honourable Artillery Company, on parade in The State Apartments tonight, is drawn from Veteran Members of the HAC, all of whom have given many years of service to this Territorial Army Regiment, the oldest regiment in the British Army; NATO and indeed, the world!

The Company parades as a Company of Pikemen at the time of King Charles I and its drill is based on a contemporary drill manual written by Col Wm Barriffe, a member of the Artillery Company in the 1600s.

The Company's status was confirmed by the Granting of a Royal Warrant in 1955 by Her Majesty The Queen. The Warrant restricts the Company to a maximum of 63 all ranks who may parade at any one time, but confers the privilege of its members being permitted to wear their service decorations, including parachute and pilot wings! The Warrant further requires that the Company must obtain a Warrant to Parade on every occasion outside its headquarters, signed by either the Rt Hon the Lord Mayor of London or the General Officer Commanding, London District (on this occasion the GOC).

The Honourable Artillery Company has a long and illustrious history including its service in the South African Campaign 1900-02 and in both WWI and WWII and readers wishing to know more can enquire of www.hac.org.uk

What is the relevance of the Company of Pikemen & Musketeers parading at St.James's Palace tonight?

Much greater than you may think! The HAC Regiment forms part of NATO's Allied Rapid Reaction Corps and has supplied soldiers to Bosnia, Iraq and currently Afghanistan. Members of the Company of Pikemen have, during their TA and Regular service spent many arduous times defending the borders of NATO during the Cold War! One recent Pikeman recruit commanded his Hussar Regiment in Bosnia and another Musketeer is currently due to depart for Afghanistan in his capacity as a Reserve Major.

The Company paraded at Guildhall in the City of London for both the 40th and 50th Anniversaries of NATO. The Clerk & Adjutant of the Company, on parade tonight, actually commanded the NATO detachment on the Lord Mayor's Show in 1970 for the occasion of its 21st Anniversary!

The Company parades on occasions of State and semi State in both the City of London and on other military events in the London District and has travelled extensively abroad including America and Europe, especially parading with the Pontifical Swiss Guard in the Vatican in 2006 and with the Grenadier Guards in Bruges to celebrate their 500th and 350th anniversaries respectively.

The motto of the Honourable Artillery Company is ARMA PACIS FULCRA – Arms are the Fulcrum of Peace or Armed Strength is the Key to Peace (used for the best part of 400 years) - a sentiment that could so easily be applied to NATO!

THE HONOURABLE ARTILLERY COMPANY

IN 1537 HENRY VIII FORMED the Honourable Artillery Company (HAC) by Letters Patent, charging it to attend to the 'Better Defence of the Realm' and encouraging it to exercise in handling bows and hand-guns. From the 16th to the 18th Century the Company trained all the officers of the Trained Bands of the City. The Company's other main task was the maintenance of law and order in London on behalf of the City Corporation.

The Company first trained in its practice ground in Spitalfields before moving to its current home in 1641. Armoury House, the HQ, was built in 1735 and has been developed ever since with the latest enhancement of its drill hall being opened by the Queen in May 2007.

The HAC Regiment has a long and distinguished record in the annals of the British Army. Although members of the Company fought in various wars as individuals, the first formed body that deployed on operations was in 1900 in the South African War as part of the City Imperial Volunteers. The HAC's Military Unit became part of the Territorial Army when it was formed at the beginning of 1909.

Two infantry battalions and five batteries of the HAC fought in the First World War. The 1st Battalion served in France and Flanders while the 2nd Battalion saw active service in France and in Italy. Two batteries went to the Middle East while two Reserve batteries and a siege battery fought in France.

At the outset of the Second World War the Infantry Battalion of the HAC became an Officer Cadet Training Unit. The 11th and 12th HAC Regiments of Royal Horse Artillery served in North Africa and in Italy while the 13th HAC Regiment of Royal Horse Artillery fought in Normandy and Holland and across the Rhine into Germany. The Company also provided a Heavy Anti-Aircraft Regiment and two Heavy Anti-Aircraft Batteries. The Artillery Division of the HAC was granted the privilege of firing Royal Salutes at the Tower of London in 1924 and continues to do so. The Regiment also provides Guards of Honour in the City for visiting Heads of State.

Today, the Company has 2,400 members of whom 400 are serving in the Regiment. All the rest have military experience as an essential qualification for membership. The Military Unit has a challenging role as part of NATO's Rapid Reaction Corps with the task of providing small patrols in the forward battle area to acquire intelligence and control long range weapons. Officers and soldiers of the Regiment have been mobilised for service in the Balkans, Iraq and Afghanistan with some 140 members having been deployed on operations since 2003.

Those leaving the Regiment may become Veteran Members and remain within the fraternity of the Company, which they then serve in a variety of ways. One such way is in joining the Company of Pikemen and Musketeers. This Company was formed in 1925 and provides the Lord Mayor's Bodyguard contributing greatly to the ceremonial life of the City. They are on duty at Kensington Palace tonight. In 1979, the Court agreed to reconstitute the Light Cavalry for ceremonial tasks and for keeping alive the skills of military equitation.

A Division of HAC Metropolitan Special Constables was formed in 1919. This Division was disbanded during the Second World War but was reconstituted as a Detachment in 1947. In 2005 the Detachment transferred to the City of London Police.

The HAC is proud of its current role within NATO and delighted that one of its Ceremonial Units, whose members have all served within NATO in one form or other, is associated with the 60th Anniversary Dinner.

WINES & SPIRITS

*Justerini & Brooks 250th Anniversary Cuvée
Extra Dry Champagne, NV*

******

*Sauvignon Blanc 2008
Santa Carolina - Central Valley, Chile*

******

*Malbec 2007
Finca La Florencia, Familia Cassone,
Mendoza. Argentina*

******

*Justerini & Brooks, Directors Tawny Port
Hennessy Grande Champagne Cognac 1982
Talisker 12 Year Old Single Malt Whisky*

BANQUET MENU

CHARGRILLED MONKFISH & SHRIMP BROCHETTE

Tomato & Basil Mousseline
Slow Roasted Vine Tomatoes
Green Herb Salsa

TOURNEDOS OF HIGHLAND VENISON

Spiced Pear & Redcurrant
Rich Game Jus
Pan Haggerty Potato Cakes
Runner Beans, Petits Pois & Savoy Cabbage

CITRUS SYMPHONY

Orange Boodle in Mini Brandy Snap Baskets
Grapefruit & Lime Sorbet
Mandarin Profiteroles

SELECTION OF CHEESES

Celery, Quince Jelly & Cheese Biscuits

CONTINENTAL BLEND COFFEE

Chocolate Truffles, Homemade Fudge & Turkish Delight

GUEST LIST

HRH The Duke of York

The Lord Dykes
 Immediate Past President, E-AG
The Baroness Symons of Vernam Dean
 President, E-AG
Mr Geoffrey Clifton Brown MP
 Vice Chairman, E-AG
The Rt. Hon. The Lord Hamilton of Epsom
 Chairman, E-AG
The Lady Hamilton of Epsom
Sir Robert Worcester, KBE, DL
 Chairman, The Pilgrims; Vice President, EAG;
Lady Margaret Worcester
 Pilgrims
Mr Justin Glass
 Director, E-AG
Lieutenant General David Bill CB
 Military Representative of the United Kingdom to NATO and EU
Mrs Gabrielle Bill
The Rt Hon Lord Carrington KG, CH, GCMG, MC
 Formerly Secretary-General, NATO; Vice President, E-AG
Mr Martin Howard
 Assistant Secretary-General, NATO
Sir Peter Ricketts, KCMG
 Permanent Under-Secretary of State, Foreign and Commonwealth Office and Head of the Diplomatic Service
The Rt Hon Michael Ancram QC MP
Mr Philip Abbott
 Honourable Artillery Company
Mrs Emma Abbott
Mr David Abrahams
 E-AG
Mr Peter Adams
 Honourable Artillery Company
Mr William Adlington
 E-AG
The Rt Hon Bob Ainsworth MP
 Secretary of State for Defence
Captain E.T.C. Album
 Honourable Artillery Company; E. J. C. Album, Solicitors
Mrs E. Album
Ms Sarah Allder
 Guest of Lord Dykes; Institute of Education, London University
Mr Paul Vincent Allen
 Guest of Mr Cahill

Mr Emilie Amory
Mr Boris Andonov
 Finance Officer, E-AG
Mr Christopher Arkell
 Trustee, E-AG
Mrs Val Arnold
 Editor, Court and Social, The Telegraph
Mr Andrew Ashton
 Guest of Mr Matthew Rose
Mr Nicholas Aspinall
 Honourable Artillery Company
Ms Pamela Assiter
 Baxterbear Ltd
Mrs Sonia Ayres
 E-AG; Chair, Hitchin and Harpenden constituency Labour Party
H.E. Mr Giorgi Badridze
 Ambassador of Georgia
L/Sgt A. J. Bailey
 Honourable Artillery Company
H.E. Mr Anthony Bailey OBE GCSS
 E-AG Eligo International
Ms Chelsea Baker
 Baxterbear Ltd
Mr Robert Barker
 Honourable Artillery Company
Mr Malcom Basing
 Honourable Artillery Company; Primus Guaranty UK Ltd.
Ms Sandi Baxter
 Baxterbear Ltd
Mr Peter Beaumont
 Project Director, E-AG
Mr Ian Beesley
 Pilgrims
Mrs Edna Beesley CBE
 Pilgrims
Dr Sheilah Bell
 E-AG
Mr Mark Bicknell
 E-AG
Ms Nicola Blackwell
 Honourable Artillery Company Guest of Mr Wint
Colonel Jean-Michel Boehm
 French Reserve Forces; Guest of Captain Wynterbee-Robey
Mrs S. Bones
 Guest of Mr Price
H.E. Mr Georg Boomgaarden
 Ambassador of Germany

Mr Richard C Borchand
  Guest of Mr Nathan
Mrs Borchand
  Guest of Mr Nathan
Dr Anton Borg
  E-AG
Mrs Sarah Borg
  E-AG
The Hon. Sir Clive Bossom Bt
  E-AG; Vice-President, Anglo-Netherlands Society
Mrs Jan Delia Boulting
  E-AG
Ms Carmen Bouverat
  E-AG
Mr Martyn Bowden
Mrs Lena Bowen
Mr Jonathan Bradley
  E-AG; Dean, University of West of England
Mrs Harriet Bradley
Lt. Col. Tim Bradshaw
  Honourable Artillery Company; O2 2 Troop
Mrs Francesca Bradshaw
Ms Marika Brennan
  Guest of Mrs Phillips
Mr Michael Brent
  E-AG
Sir David Brewer
  Lord Lieutenant for Greater London;
  Guest of Mr Rigden
Mrs E. Broadbridge
  E-AG
Mr Robert Brock
  Guest of Michael Mc Gough
Mr Randle Brooks
  Guest of Mr Cavenagh-Mainwaring
Mrs Juliet Brooks
  Guest of Mr Cavenagh-Mainwaring
Mr Michael Brown
  Pilgrims; Solicitor; Chairman,
  Pooh Properties Trust
Mrs Valetta Brown
Dr James Brown
  E-AG
Mr Antony Browne
Admiral Sir James Burnell-Nugent KCB CBE
  Formerly Commander-in-Chief, Fleet;
  International Strategic Advisor to Shell
  on Maritime Security
Mr David Burt
  Pilgrims; ESU
Mrs David Burt
Mr Michael Burt
  CEO, World Medical Fund
H.E. Dr. Dragisa Burzan
  Ambassador of Montenegro
Prince Grandmaster Emeritus Adrian Busietta
  The Knights of Malta
The Lady Butterworth
Mr Kevin Cahill
  E-AG; Bureau Chief, Global and Western News
  Bureau; Author; journalist; Council, RSA

Mrs Kat Callo
  E-AG; Rosietta Consulting Ltd.
Mr Alexander Campbell
  Honourable Artillery Company
Mrs Sophy Campbell
Mr Neil Capon
  Honourable Artillery Company
Mr Robert Carr
  Association of Former Congressmen; Democrat
H. E. Ms Ana Maria Teles Carreira
  Ambassador of Angola
Dame Marie Angelique Caruana
  The Knights of Malta
Dame Tamara Caruana
  The Knights of Malta
Dame Marisa Caruana
  The Knights of Malta
Mr Pierre-Gilles Caumon
  E-AG
Mrs Melaine Caumon
  E-AG
Mr Charles Cavenagh-Mainwarning
  E-AG; Board Member, Atlantic Council of UK
Mrs Carolyn Wendy Chamberlain
  E-AG
Mr Derek Richard Chandler
  Honourable Artillery Company
Mrs Frances Suzanne Chandler
  Guest of Ms Kat Callo
Ms Lana Chechina
  E-AG
Mr David Childs
  E-AG; United International Pictures
Mr Bhabani Shankar Chouduary
  E-AG BBC; Senior Lecturer, University of Lincoln
Mr Stephen Clarke
  E-AG; Deputy Chief Executive, VTB Bank Europe Ltd
Mr Anthony Coats
  Honourable Artillery Company; Formerly, sabre
  commander in 1 Squadron
Colonel Christopher Coats CBE
Lady Cocks of Hartcliffe
Mr David Coke-Steel
  Guest of Mr Cavenagh-Mainwaring
Mrs Jane Coke-Steel
  Guest of Mr Cavenagh-Mainwaring
Major James Colby
  Baxterbear Ltd; Coldstream Guards
Mrs Sarah Colby
  Baxterbear Ltd
Mr Jonathan Washburn Cole
  Pilgrims
Ms Madge Cole
  The Royal Hospital, Chelsea
Mr John Coleman
  E-AG; Editor, European-Atlantic Journal;
  Author and Publisher, New European Publications
Lord Colgrain
  Guest of Mr Basing
Mr Neil Colledge
  E-AG; Musician

Mr Troy Tarkan Coody
Guest of Ms Eren
Mr Leon Cook
The European Azerbaijan Society
Mr Frank Cook MP
Committee, E-AG
Mr Francis Corbett
Mrs Corbett
Ms Chris Cordrey
Honourable Artillery Company; Guest of Mr Wint
Mrs Julia Couchman
E-AG
Ms Helen Couchman
E-AG; Authoress; Artist; Photographer
Professor James Coveney
E-AG; Former Member of NATO Secretariat; Emeritus Professor of French and European Studies, University of Bath
Mrs Paticia Coveney
Sir Michael Craig-Cooper CBE TD
Vice Lord Lieutenant of Greater London
Dr Julian Critchlow
E-AG; Fenwick Elliott
Major General Andrew Cumming CBE
Soldiers, Sailors, Airmen and Families Association
Mr Richard C Curtin
Honourable Artillery Company
H. E. Mrs Borbala Czako
The Hungarian Ambassador
Mr Marcus Dale
Honourable Artillery Company
Mrs Ann Dale
Mr Clifford Dammers
E-AG; Formely Secretary-General, International Primary Markets Association
Mr Robin Dammers
Professor Philip John Davies
E-AG; Association of Former Congressmen; Director, Eccles Centre for American Studies, The British Library
Sir Alan Dawtry
E-AG
Lady Dawtry
E-AG
Rear Admiral Charles-Edouard de Coriolis
French Embassy
Mrs de Coriolis
Prince Anton Esterhazy De Galatha
The Knights of Malta
Mrs Nora De Gara
British-Hungarian Society
General Sir Peter de la Billière KCB KBE DSO MC & Bar
Lady de la Billière,
Baron Jean-Yves De La Sabliere
E-AG
Mr Carlos De Rodriguez
BP; Guest of Ms Ferrero
Mrs Carmen De Rodriguez
Guest of Ms Ferrero
Sir Desmond de Silva QC
Guest of Ms Hodson-Pressinger

Ms Marisol Deluna
Pilgrims
Bo Aung Din
Chairman, PDP party, Burma
Mr Colin Dixon
E-AG
Mr Emin Dokushi
Mr Grainne Downes
Guest of Mr Cahill
Sir Gordon Downey KCB
Pilgrims
Lady Downey
Pilgrims
H. E. Marija Efremova
Ambassador of Macedonia
Mrs Jane Enright
E-AG; Office of Lord Kinnock, House of Lords
Ms Jacqueline Enright
Guest of Ms Enright
Ms Hameyet Eren
E-AG
Ms Cigdem Erkdem
Guest of Ms Erin
Sir Geoffrey Errington Bt OBE
Pilgrims; E-AG
Lady Errington
Pilgrims; E-AG
Miss Nicole Escue
Pilgrims
Countess Ilona Esterhazy
E-AG Secretary, The British Hungarian Society
Mrs Olga Evans
E-AG
Mr Ali Evsen
Mr William John Faragher
E-AG
Ms Carolina Ferrero
Guest of Mr Glass
Ms Marlain Fielding
E-AG
A representative of Firmin & Sons
A representative of Firmin & Sons
Mr Jim Firth
Gala Group; Guest of Ms Prendiville
The Hon. Ms Agnieszka Fitzclarence
E-AG
The Hon Alexandra Foley
Guest of Sir Desmond de Silva
Mrs M. A. Foster
Pilgrims
Mr Anthony Foyle
Guest of Ms Hodson-Pressinger
Mrs Rose Foyle
Guest of Ms Hodson-Pressinger
Mrs Joyce Fuller
E-AG
Dr Darius Furmonavicius
E-AG; Lithuanian Research centre (UK)
Dr Ruta Furmonaviciene
E-AG
Mrs Marivere Furneaux
E-AG; Barrister; Managing Director, Crown Yard Properties Ltd; Commission Liaison Officer, E.U.W.

H.E. Dr Vahe Gabrielyan
Ambassador of Armenia
Mr Andre Gailini
Dr Agnieszka Gajewska-Jedwabny
Independent Infrastructure Transport Infrastructure Financier, Central and Eastern Europe
Mr Raymond George
E-AG
Ms Andrea Geser
Ms J. A. Gibbins
E-AG
Mr Ram Gidoomal CBE
E-AG
Mr Paul Gladstone-Reid OBE
E-AG
Mrs Catherine Glass
E-AG
Mr Nigel Goddard
Honourable Artillery Company;
Guest of Richard C. Curtin
Mrs Marion Godfrey
E-AG
Ms Anja Gohde
E-AG Director of Finance, Film Producer, New Film Productions (NFP), Berlin
Sir Philip Goodhart
Trustee, E-AG
Mr Nick Goodson
Third Bar Films
Ms Valerie Gordon-Walker
E-AG Vice President, Human Resources, BP
Mrs Barbara Gorna
E-AG; Blackberry Films
Mr John Gouriet
E-AG
Mrs Gouriet
Lord Grantchester
E-AG
Betty, Lady Grantchester
E-AG
Ms Lydia Greer
E-AG; Byron Society
Mrs Rutka Griffiths
E-AG; Formerly Director, British Atlantic Committee
Ms Jane Gully
E-AG; FANY -The Princess Royal's Volunteer Corps
H.E. Mr Antonio Gumende
High Commissioner for Mozambique
H.E. Mr Fakhraddin Gurbanov
The Ambassador of Azerbaijan
Ms Maria Gussago
E-AG
Colonel Tom Hall CVO OBE
Honourable Artillery Company
Mr Michael Handscomb
E-AG
Mrs Jean Handscomb
E-AG
Ms Judith Hanratty
Pilgrims

Mr Jeppe Hansen
Guest of Mr Kahrl
Mr Ian Harrison
E-AG; Barthlomews Tutorial college
H. E. Mr Wajid Shamsul Hasan
High Commissioner for Pakistan
Ms Kate Hawthorn
Mr Robin Hay
Recorder; Husband of Lady Olga Maitland
Mrs A. E. Heard
E-AG Naval and Military Club
Dr Edward Henderson
E-AG N.H.S.
Dr Sally Henderson
E-AG
Mr Edward Hendin
Honourable Artillery Company
Mr Kevin Henry
Guest of Frank Cook MP
Mr Tale Heydarou
The European Azerbaijan Society
His Honour Judge David Higgins
Pilgrims
Lady Hill
E-AG
Ms Anne Hodson-Pressinger
Vice-President, E-AG
Mr Jonathan Horne
Honourable Artillery Company;
Chief Executive, Sampson & Horne Antiques
Mrs Jasmine Horowitz
Guest of Ms Hodson-Pressinger
Mr Jean Pierre Houri
Husband of Ms Maes
Guest of Mr Martin Howard
Mr Alan Howell
Guest of Mrs Boulting
Mrs Maureen Howell
Guest of Mrs Boulting
Mr Zenel Hoxha
President, British Chamber of Commerce and Industry of Albania - ABCCI
Mrs Pauline Hyde
Pilgrims
Guest of Mrs Hyde
Mr Roland Hysa
Mrs Ermira Hysa
Mr Ferdinand Ibrahimi
Mrs Olimbi Ibrahimi
Mr Jonuz Ismailaj
Miss Jona Ismailaj
Mr David Issacs
E-AG; Solicitor
Ensign Andrew Izod
Clerk and Adjutant, Company of Pikemen and Musketeers, Honourable Artillery Company
The Reverend Mrs Wendy Izod
General Sir Mike Jackson GCB CBE DSO ADC
Mr Graham Jarvis
E-AG; Editor, Chartered Institute of Marketing Technology Group
Mrs Elizabeth Haldane Jarvis

H.E. Justice Nihal Jayasinghe
High Commissioner of Sri Lanka
Mr Nicolas Jeffrey
*E-AG; Managing Director,
Tampopo Group of Companies*
Ms Katerina Jeffrey
E-AG
H.E. Dr Ion Jinga
Ambassador of Romania
General Sir Gary Johnson KCB OBE MC
Mr Gregory Jones
E-AG Barrister, Chambers of Robin Purchas QC
Air Vice-Marshal Grahame Jones CBE
Secretary-General, Royal Air Forces Association
Mr Lewis Jones
Guest of Ms Maliderou
Mr Jerome Joseph
Guest of Mr Newman
Mr Paul Joyal
*Managing Director,
Publich Sfety and Homeland Security, USA*
The Lord Judd
E-AG; Past Presient, E-AG
Mr Tom Kahrl
E-AG; Director, Ikonica Ltd
Dr Martin Kazuka
*Sloan Fellow; London Business School;
Adviser to H.E. Dr Kenneth Kaunda*
Mrs Victoria Kernahan
Ashley Wilson, Solicitors
Chief Ajmal Khan Zazai of Afghanistan
Sheikh Nezam Khazal
E-AG
Sheikha Shenda Khazal-Amery
E-AG; Vice-President, E-AG; Sculptress
The Rt. Hon. Lord Kilclooney of Amagh
E-AG
Jacqueline, Lady Killearn
E-AG
Dame Cherry Kirkwood-Martin OBE
Guest of Dr Commander Bryan Olive
Mr Dermot Knox
Baha'i Community of UK
Mr Daniel Dayananda Kumar
E-AG; Jardine Lloyd Thompson
Ms Anne Kurn
Honourable Artillery Company; Guest of Mr Wint
Minister Sumio Kusaka
Minister and Consul-General, Japanese Embassy
Mrs Kusaka
H.E. Mr Lyubomir Kyuchukov
Ambassador of Bulgaria
H. E. Mr Jaakko Laajava
Ambassador of Finland
Ms Annalisa Laeger
Guest of Ms Hodson-Pressinger
Lord Laird of Artigarvan
Guest of Mr Cahill
Mr Ralph Land CBE
E-AG
Mr Tim Lattimore & Guest

Mrs Pauli Laumon
E-AG
Lord Lee of Trafford
Defence Spokesman, Lib Dem
Mr Joe Lennox
The Royal Hospital, Chelsea
Mr Seraphim Leonidas
E-AG; IT Adviser to E-AG
Professor Peter Lewis-Crown OBE
Guest of Professor and Mrs Lutz
Mr Bernard Lind
E-AG
Mrs Sonja Lind
Mr Paul Littlewood
Mrs Susan Lloyd
E-AG
Doreen, Marshioness of Londonderry
Mr Jeffrey Long
E-AG
Mrs Gladys A. Longhurst
E-AG
Mr Alastair Lowe
E-AG
Professor Wolfgang Lutz
E-AG
Mrs Helen Lutz
E-AG
Mrs Hilary MacEwen
Guest of Mr Cahill
Ms Miriam Maes
Chief Executive Officer, Foresee
Princess Zohra Mahmoud Ghazi
Lady Olga Maitland
E-AG; President, Defence and Security Forum
Ms Maria Maliderou
Guest of Mr Glass
Sir Nicholas Mander Bt
Guest of Mr Cavenagh-Mainwaring
Lady Mander
Guest of Mr Cavenagh-Mainwaring
Mrs Helen Mango
E-AG
Commander P.M. Marcell RN
E-AG Director, Reinsurance Company
H.E. Mr Rafael Mareno
*Ambassador of Chile; Permanent Representative of
Chile on the International Maritime Organisation*
Mr Derek Marshall
Director Policy, Defense Industry Council; ADS
Mrs Gloria Martin
E-AG
Guest of Mrs Martin
Mrs Masekgoa Masire-Mwamba
Deputy Secretary-General, Commonwealth Secretariat
Mr Michael Maslinsky
E-AG
Mrs Margaret Maslinsky
M. Philippe Masson
E-AG
Professor Sydney L. Mayer
E-AG

Mr John Mayo
E-AG
Mr Michael Mc Gough
E-AG; The Freedom Association
Mr Neil McCarthy
Guest of Mr Kahrl
Admiral Sir Tim McClement KCB OBE
Mr David McCloud
E-AG
Mrs Jane McGill
Mrs Dulcibel McKenzie
E-AG; Barrister; Author
Ms Amy McKeown
E-AG; Xanthis
Mr Patrick McNally
E-AG; Peace 2000
Mr Alan Mendoza
Director, Henry Jackson Society;
Guest of Yvonne Sherrrington
The Lord Mereworth
E-AG
Mr Chris Minas
Guest of Mr Kahrl
Miss Nadia Minors
Guest of Dr Kazuba; Accountant
H.E. Mr Iztok Mirosic
Ambassador of Slovenia
Mr David Montagu-Corry
E-AG
The Viscount Montgomery of Alamein CMG CBE
Past President, E-AG
Ms Connie Morella
Republic; Association of Former Congressmen
Mr William Morris
Next Century Foundation
Mrs Morris
Next Century Foundation
Mrs Gill Morrison
E-AG
Mrs Sylvia Moynihan
Guest of Thelma L'Estrange (not present)
Mr Amour Mtungo
E-AG
Mr Jonathan Mueller
E-AG; Formerly United States,
Legislative Assistant to Hon Dick Cheney
Mr Andy Munro
E-AG; Guest of Mrs Gordon-Walker
Halina, Countess of Munster
E-AG; UCLH Trust
Ms Eileen Murphy
Guest of Mr Cahill
Mr Shahin Namati-Nasab
The European Azerbaijan Society
Mr Clemens Nathan
E-AG; Clemens Nathan Research Foundation;
Author, For the Sake of Humanity
Mrs Nathan
E-AG
Mr Michael Nathanson
Consultant, Thring Townsend Lee & Pembertons

Mrs Nathanson
Major Graham Neil TD
Honourable Artillery Company
Mr Isuf Neli
Adviser to Prince Leka Zogu II
Mr Philip Newman
Hon Treasurer, E-AG
Mr Charles Noel
Guest of Ms Hodson-Pressinger
Mrs Diane Noel
Mr Douglas Nordlinger
Skadden, Arps, Slate,
Meagher & Flom (UK) LLP
Guest of Mr Douglas Nordlinger
Ms Margaret M. O'Sullivan
E-AG
Mr Peter Oakden
Honourable Artillery Company
Mr James O'Brien
Dr Commander Bryan R. Olive
Honourable Artillery Company;
Commander of Royal Navy
Lieutenant Gavin Oram
Honourable Artillery Company
H.E. Mrs Inaam Osseiran
Ambassador of the Lebanon
MS Marina Elizabeth O'Sullivan
E-AG; Embassy of Ireland
Ms Victoria Page
E-AG
Lieutenant Colonel Philip L. Pearce
Battlefield Tours
Sir Michael Peat KCVO
Principal Private Secretary to The Prince of Wales
and the Duchess of Cornwall
Lady Peat
Mr John Penycate
Pilgrims; Formerly BBC correspondent
Mrs Maria-Rita Phillips
E-AG
Sgt. Julian Phillips
Special Protection Office to HRH the Duke of York
Ms Charmian Porteous
E-AG
Ms Melanie Prendiville
E-AG; Director, Westminster Mortgages
Mr Terence Price
E-AG Formerly MOD
Mr Dr. Firoz Rafique
Guest of Baron de la Sabliere
Mr Nicolae Ratiu
E-AG; Chairman, Ratiu Foundation
Mrs Ratiu
Professor James Raven
Pilgrims Governor, ESU
Mr Clive Rigden
E-AG; Ecosolids
Mrs Jenny Ringo
E-AG
Mr Tim Ringo
E-AG

Ms Anabel Ripin
Guest of Mr Dixon
Mr Andrew Robathan MP
Deputy Opposition Chief Whip
Mrs Philippe Ronald
Mr Lance Roncalli
Senior Vice President of the L-1 Corporation; Guest of Mr Joyal
Mr Matthew Rose
E-AG UBS (Equities)
Lady Henrietta Rous
E-AG
The Hon Mrs John Rous
E-AG
Mrs Elizabeth Rutherford
Guest of Sir Philip Goodhart
Mr Ian Charles Sadler
Honourable Artillery Company
Ms Susan Sandoutia
Compass Rose International
Major Narindar Saroop CBE
Mr Urs Schmid
Deputy Head of Mission, Swiss Embassy
Lt Col. François Philip Schofield MBE
E-AG
Mrs P. F. Schofield
Ms Yasmin Schulte
E-AG
Ms Olita Sciur
Guest of Mr Arkell
Mr Beach Seakin
E-AG
Mr Michael Sefi FRPSL
Keeper of the Royal Philatelic Collection; Guest of Mr Cavenagh-Mainwaring
Mrs Harriet Sefi
Guest of Mr Cavenagh-Mainwaring
Mr David Selves
E-AG; SHIELD
Mr Louis Selwyn
E-AG; Commissioning Editor and Chief Co-ordinator, Publishing and Online division, Clinical Support Services
Mr Ylli Seriani
L/Cpl James Shaw
Honourable Artillery Company; Guest of Mr Ian Sadler
Mr Adrian Shehu
Ms Yvonne Sherrington
Guest of Ms Hodson-Pressinger
Mrs Lilly Sigall
E-AG
Mr Radislaw Sikorski
The Foreign Minister of Poland (to be confirmed)
Mr Chris Simpkins
Director-General, Royal British Legion
Mrs Margaret Simpson
E-AG
Mr Keith Simpson
Shadow Minister for Foreign Affairs
Mr Harry Singer
E-AG

Mrs Hannah Singer
E-AG
Mr Geoffrey Smith
E-AG
Mr Michael Smith
Honourable Artillery Company
Ms Giovanna Solari
E-AG
H. E. Ms Natalia S Solcan
Ambassador of the Republic of Moldova
Princess Somsangouane
E-AG
Mr William Spurgin
Guest of Mrs Morrison
Ms Fiona Stephens
Guest of Geoffrey Clifton Brown MP
Mr Douglas Stephens
E-AG; Formerly Royal Navy
Lady Stewart
E-AG
Mr Hugh Barrington Stewart
E-AG
Mr Christopher Stoner
Mrs Stoner
Mr Peter Strong
E-AG
Mr Ben Symes
Honourable Artillery Company; Guest of Mr Hendin
Mrs Beata Szitasi-Sieha
British-Hungarian Society
Ms Jennabeth Taliaferro
E-AG
Dr Julian Tallon
Guest of Baron Jean-Yves De La Sabliere
Mrs Elizabeth Tallon
Guest of Baron Jean-Yves De La Sabliere
Mr Stephen Tanner
E-AG
Mr Robin Tatam
Guest of Mr Cahill
Sir Cyril Taylor
E-AG; American Institute for Foreign Study
Mr Peter Thomas
Guest of Mrs Foster
Mr P. M. Todd
Honourable Artillery Company
Mr John Tolan
Guest of Baron Jean-Yves De La Sabliere
Mrs Margaret Tolan
Guest of Baron Jean-Yves De La Sabliere
Count Istvan Toronyi-Lalic
British-Hungarian Society
Countess Sonja Toronyi-Lalic
British-Hungarian Society
Mrs A. Torrents Del Prats
Miss Assitan Traore
E-AG
The Rt Hon Lord Trefgarne
Sir Neville Trotter
Committee, E-AG

H.E. Ms Barbara Tuge-Erecińska
Ambassador of Poland
Mr Emir Turkmen
Guest of Ms Erin
Mr Edmund McMahon Turner
Honourable Artillery Company
Commodore P. J. Tyrrell OBE
Honourable Artillery Company
Captain Debra Tyrell
Mr Mark Upton
Baxterbear Ltd
Mr John Varden-Quick
E-AG
Mr Ed Vasey
Foreign Affairs Spokesman, Lib Dem
Dame Phyllis Vassallo
The Knights of Malta
Chevalier Romeo Vassallo
The Knights of Malta
Ms Karen Vaughan
Guest of Mr Cahill
Mr Richard Vaughan
HSH Princess Marie-Therese von Hohenberg
(Mrs Anthony Bailey)
Mr Christopher von Thelen
E-AG; Majesty Capital Ltd
Mr Gerry Wade
Pilgrims
Mr Michael Wade
E-AG
Ms Grazyna Walek
E-AG; Founder, Gustav Mahler Society, UK
Sir Harold Walker KCMG
President, British Society for Middle Eastern Studies
Lady Walker
Mr John Wallace
Pilgrims
Guest of Mr Wallace
Mr Ross Ward
CEO, ADS group and Secretary of the Defense Industries Council (DIC)
Mr Miles Warren
Radrisk
Mr Brian Watkins CMG O.St.J
E-AG
Mrs Elizabeth Watkins
Mr Alastair Watson
Office of HRH the Duke of York
Ms Francesca Wellman
Mr Peter West
Honourable Artillery Company
Mr Anthony Westnedge OBE
E-AG; Committee, E-AG; Governor, English Speaking Union; Formerly Chairman, Canning House; Honourable Artillery Company
Major T. F. Wharton
Guest of Capt. E.T.C. Album
Mrs K. Wharton
Guest of Capt. E.T.C. Album
Mrs Vivien Whitney
E-AG; Guest of Mr Cavenagh-Mainwaring

Colonel Mike W. Whyman TD DL
Honourable Artillery Company
Dr Tim R. Wiggin
Medical Adviser, World Medical Fund
Colonel R. M. Wilkinson TD
Honourable Artillery Company
Professor Alan Lee Williams OBE
E-AG; Vice President, E-AG; Chairman Mid Atlantic Club, Former President, Atlantic Treaty Organisation
Captain Peter Williams OBE
Mrs Doreen Willis-Bailey
E-AG
Colonel Raymond L. Windmill
E-AG
Trooper Andre Wint
Honourable Artillery Company; Invesco UK
Mr Kevin Wood
Honourable Artillery Company; Guest of Mr Wint
Mrs Joan Woodman
Mr Laurence Woods
Guest of Michael and Valetta Brown
Mrs Sally Woods
Guest of Michael and Valetta Brown
The Rt. Hon. Lord Woolfe
Formerly Lord Chief Justice
H. E. Mr Jim Wright
High Commissioner of Canada
Mrs Daphne Wyke
E-AG; European Union of Women
Captain Christopher Wynterbee-Robey
Honourable Artillery Company
Mrs Wynterbee-Robey
Mrs Silvana Xhaferi
British Chamber of Commerce and Industry of Albania-ABCCI
Mr John Zanjani
E-AG
Dr Parastoo Zanjani
E-AG
Prince Leka II Zogu of Albania
Miss Kate Hawthorn
H.E. Mr Michael Zantovsky,
Ambassador of the Czech Republic

Guest List includes E-AG helpers and Waiting List as at date of printing.

THE EUROPEAN AZERBAIJAN SOCIETY

THE EUROPEAN AZERBAIJAN SOCIETY (TEAS) is a not-for-profit independent NGO dedicated to promoting Azerbaijan to an international audience whilst creating a sense of community for expatriate Azeris. TEAS operates as a networking forum, focusing on such areas as business development, diplomatic relations, culture and education to promote greater understanding and co-operation between Europe and Azerbaijan. TEAS is committed to:

- The promotion of Azerbaijan as a modern, progressive, secular democracy.
- Raising awareness of Azerbaijan's enormous oil and gas reserves, and its ability to provide Western Europe with enhanced energy supply security
- Emphasising the speed of the country's economic development – Azerbaijan has been the fastest-growing economy in the world for the last three years.
- Underlining the value of Azerbaijan as an ally of the west – with troops being stationed in Iraq and Afghanistan to assist NATO forces.
- Pushing the issue of the Nagorno Karabakh conflict up the political agenda. TEAS calls for the international community to ensure enforcement of the four outstanding UN Security Council resolutions, which would restore Azerbaijan territorial integrity and sovereignty.

THE EUROPEAN AZERBAIJAN SOCIETY
Tale Heydarov or Leon Cook
Tel: 44 (0) 207 104 2220
E-mail: teas@teas.eu

THE HAMPDEN STRING QUARTET

FORMED AT THE ROYAL ACADEMY OF MUSIC IN 2006, the Hampde String Quartet takes its name from the village of Great Hampden i Buckinghamshire where they gave their first concert. Since then they hav given a wide range of recitals, including at the Amersham Festival in Bucl inghamshire and the Dean and Chadlington Festival in Oxfordshire as we as a series of performances for Coutts Bank and the National Youth Orchestra of Great Britain. All four members of the Quartet have won chamber music prizes at the Royal Academy of Music, including the Sir John Barbirolli Prize and the Max Pirani Award. They have also received quartet tuition from eminent musicians such as Hartmut Rohde, Thomas Brandis, Aleksander Pavlovic, Marianne Thorsen and Martin Outram.

CONTACT: c.reid@ram.ac.uk

THE ALBANIAN BRITISH CHAMBER OF COMMERCE AND INDUSTRY
PARTNERS FOR SUCCESS

THE ALBANIAN BRITISH CHAMBER OF COMMERCE AND INDUSTRY (ABCCI) was established in 2002 to promote and support Industrial and commercial developments in Albania and to encourage British and Foreign Investment in the country. It serves, protects and advances the interest of independent businesses especially in the sectors represented by its members.

The ABCCI can supply information and services supporting trade with the Albania. We can assist you with:

- Marketing information for foreign companies who wish to establish business in Albania
- Information about Albania trade delegation to foreign countries
- Facilitation of meetings with trade missions and foreign business people visiting Albania
- Import/Export procedures, control requirements and related activities

Other key activities include:

- Provision of management training programs designed to improve business efficiency.
- English language training
- Recruitment assistance
- Management consultancy, organisational and its and financial advice
- Infrastructure development
- Arbitration in legal disputes

The ABCCI has the resources, the commitment and the expertise to help businesses make the most of the wealth of rewarding opportunities in Albania and Britain.

THE ALBANIAN BRITISH CHAMBER OF COMMERCE AND INDUSTRY
Mr Zenel Hoxha, President
E-mail: info@abcci.com
Web: www.abcci.com   Tel: +355 4234 10 20

PADDY MAYNE
THE FINAL BATTLE IS IN THE SOUL

THIRD BAR FILMS LTD is due to commence filming in Northern Ireland in 2010 on a feature film to tell the true life-story of the wartime exploits of Lt Colonel Blair 'Paddy' Mayne. In 1939, at the beginning of the Second World War, a big powerful shy solicitor from Northern Ireland joined the Territorial Army, hoping in some way to 'do his bit'. Six years later Lt Colonel Blair was the Commanding Officer of the 1st SAS (Special Air Services) Regiment, the most decorated allied soldier of the Second World War and a legend in his own lifetime. However, returning home after the War proved difficult. Doing his best to fit into a world he barely remembered, Mayne's life was eventually tragically cut short in 1955 when his car collided with an unlit lorry on a dark December evening. Today, half a century after his death, he is regarded as the man who shaped the ethos of the modern SAS.

Third Bar Films is honoured to be associated with the prestigious 60th Anniversary celebrations of NATO, in the presence of some of the most acclaimed representatives of both the UK and Allied Armed Forces.

NICK GOODSON
Tel: 44 (0) 207 198 8004
E-mail: info@thirdbarfilms.com

THANKS & ACKNOWLEDGEMENTS

THE E-AG EXPRESSES GRATITUDE TO: Jamie Shea at NATO and Lucia Eeckelaers in the Public Diplomacy Division of NATO, The Office of the Superintendent of the State Apartments St. James's Palace, The Hampden Quartet, Messrs Punch for donating to the E-AG the cartoons from 1949 and 1955 in this brochure, Tim Cramp of Party Ingredients – caterers, Anne Hodson-Pressinger for the table decorations, Mr George Bodnar (www.gbimages.com and www.gbevents.org.uk) for the official photography, Mr Michael Thwaites – the toastmaster, Justerni & Brooks, Talisker Distillery, Carboast, Isle of Sky, and Diageo PLC, and Tatlers for donating their special 300th anniversary editions.

DONATIONS

The E-AG is grateful to the following guests who have made donations:

Mr William Adlington
Mr Capt. E.T.C. Album
Mr Nicholas Aspinall
Mr Malcom Basing
Mr Alexander Campbell
Mrs Carolyn Wendy Chamberlain
Mr Derek Richard Chandler
Mr David Childs
Mr William John Faragher
Ms J. A. Gibbins
Ms Jane Gully
Ms Judith Hanratty
Dr Commander Bryan R. Olive

Lieutenant Gavin Oram
Mr Terence Price
Clive Rigden
Mr Louis Selwyn
Ms Yvonne Sherrington
Mrs Judith Spooner
Mr P. M. Todd
John Varnden-Quick

DESIGN & TYPESETTING:
Tim Lattimore – tim.lattimore@gmail.com

THE CHILD AND THE TREE

(Punch 21st. December 1949)

A Preamble from Catherine Glass

When I married Justin Glass, I did not realise fully that he was already married. The name of my rival was 'European-Atlantic Group'. At its head, at the beginning of our marital life, was the formidable Elma Dangerfield. We discovered many years later that she was connected with the Secret Service during WW2, and much besides, about which she breathed not a word to Justin during the 20-odd years he worked daily and socialised with her.

Justin was working, as he used to say, round the clock, seven days a week. There were no office hours and people were calling after midnight and on bank holidays, even Christmas. I accepted it because entering into this world of glamour, diplomacy and high intellectual level has been for me the most fascinating experience of my life – not only as a spectator but also quite often as an actor. Life when I was in London was a constant show. I was proud to have met many high-level people, ambassadors and figures of such calibre as Shimon Peres, Prince Andrew and President Kaunda and to have had the opportunity to talk to them.

I remember the first time I met Elma before our marriage in the wonderful Hurlingham Club. These beautiful surroundings – which I could just imagine when I was reading English novels *(Catherine is French)* and dreaming of this world – to which was added to the presence of this eccentric, small and powerful lady, concentrating and talking to me. It made me feel that the novel had taken the shape of a true story that one day I was to help make happen. It was with great satisfaction that I heard Mrs Dangerfield saying to me 'Your cousin, my dear, is a particularly brilliant young man.' Now with the hindsight of 30 years, I realise that the Group would not have survived Elma with its 1000 high quality members and diversify its activities as it did under his management. It produced magazines, created a publishing arm for the group with interesting books in different areas, Bulgaria and WW2 for instance, and focussed on specific diplomatic activity and governmental politics, including in Washington.

How a man working almost alone with three interns was able to realise what the Group did in those times seems to me a miracle. I am honoured to have been present and given where I could my little contribution.

PICTURE GALLERY

of

NATO BANQUET

9th NOVEMBER 2009

at

ST JAMES'S PLACE

NB See also pictures of the occasion in the aforegoing History

Pikemen guard the entrance to the banquet

Top: The Hampden Quartet
*Bottom: The Throne Room with **Lord Hamilton** at the rostrum*

E-AG Presentation Speakers from top: **Lord Hamilton: Lady Symons** *(with John and Harriet Bradley seated immediately in front of rostrum);* **Lord Dykes**

Speakers of Honour, Top: **HRH The Duke of York**
From Left clockwise: **Michael Howard** (Senior British representative at NATO)**, Lady Symons, Princess Zohra of Afghanistan** (NATO's key area of engagement at the time); **The German Ambassador** (the event taking place 20 years to the day that the Berlin Wall fell)

***HRH Prince Andrew** with **Christopher Arkell** (an E-AG Trustee)*
In background: Chief Ajmal Khan Zazai of Afghanistan

***HRH Prince Andrew** with **Jan Boulting** (an E-AG Sponsor)*
In background: General Sir Mike Jackson with Lord Montgomery

HRH Prince Andrew and *Lady Symons* with *Lt-General David Bill, CB,* the senior British military representative at NATO HQ

HRH Prince Andrew with *The Hon. Sir Clive Bossom, Bt*

Clockwise from top: **HRH Prince Andrew** with **Justin Glass** *(The E-AG Director);* **Doreen Willis Bailey** and **Sheikha Shenda Amery-Khazal** *(The E-AG Ladies Committee);* **Anne Hodson-Pressinger** *(An E-AG vice-President)* with **Lana Chehinya**; **Dr Julian Critchlow** *(The Elma Dangerfield Trust)*

HRH Prince Andrew with **Kevin Cahill**

Princess Zohra of Afghanistan (centre) with **Jonnie Varnden-Quick** and **Maria Gussago**

*British Royalty meeting Albanian Royalty in the person of **King Leka Zogu***

Prince Andrew** with **Christopher Arkell** (centre) **and Paul Joyal

A Banqueting Scene

Mr and *Mrs Justin Glass*

*Christopher Arkell (centre) with Tribal Elder **Ajmal Khan Zazai***

*Prince Andrew with **Mr and Mrs John Gouriet***

SAMPLE GUEST LIST

Including

Debating Conventions – Page 236

Tribal Notices – Page 237

Obituary of Mrs Dangerfield – Page 238

THE EUROPEAN-ATLANTIC GROUP

President
Baroness Hooper CMG
Chairman
Lord Dykes
Vice-Chairmen
Geoffrey Clifton Brown MP
Paul Keetch MP
The Rt. Hon. The Lord Radice

Honorary Treasurers
The Lord Layton
Geoffrey Smith FCCA
Harold W. Sands

Directors
Mrs Elma Dangerfield CBE
Justin Glass
Financial Director
Boris Andonov
Address: 6, Gertrude Stree
Chelsea, London SW10 0JN
Tel: 020-7352-1226
Fax: 020-7900-6660

Monday 30 January 2006
7.15pm for 8pm till 10.30pm

Reception and Dinner-Debate

At the **Jolly Group St. Ermin's Hotel**, CAXTON STREET, SW1,

Mr David Blunkett, MP

On

'Are Democracy and Counter-terrorism compatible in the 21st Century?'

Chairman of Dinner-Debate: BARONESS HOOPER CMG

Vote of Thanks: LORD DYKES

Seat Place
Number

LIST OF DELEGATES

A 9	Mr DAVID BLUNKETT, MP	Guest of Honour
A 10	THE BARONESS HOOPER, CMG	President, E-AG
A 8	THE LORD DYKES	Chairman, E-AG

DIPLOMATS

A 11	H.E. Mr JAAKKO LAAJAV	Ambassador of Finland
A 7	H.E. Dr MICHAEL REFALO	High Commissioner for Malta
A 5	H.E. Miss TANYA MILOŠINOVIĆ	Ambassador of Bosnia and Herzegovina
A 14	H.E. Mr VLADIMIRO P. VILLATA	Ambassador of El Salvador
C 1	Ms LIVIA CATALANO	Welfare Officer, Consulate of Italy
F 1	M. DIEGO COLAS	Second Secretary, French Embassy
D 20	Mr DAVID FROUS	Political Section, Embassy of the Czech Republic
C 18	Ms MYRIAN JAUDENES	Attaché, Spanish Embassy
D 1	Mr ZAHID NASRULLAH KHAN	Counsellor (Political); High Commission for the Islamic Republic of Pakistan
E 4	Mr PAUL MORRIS	First Secretary (Police liaison), Australian High Commission
D 19	Mr VADIM V. POPOV	Russian Embassy
E 2	Mr GUY SAINT-JACQUES	Deputy High Commissioner, Canadian High Commission
F 21	Mr PAUL SIMMONDS	Minister (Investment), New Zealand High Commission
	Mr PIETRO STRADA	Spanish Embassy
D 2	Mr SCOTT SYKES	Federal Police Department, Australian High Commission
E 17	Mr OLAPH TERRIBLE	Deputy High Commissioner, Malta High Commission

Seat Place Number:

COMMITTEES

A 13	Mrs MEG ALLEN	Trustee, E-AG; **Dramla SA**
D 16	Mr BORIS ANDONOV	Executive Committee
D 18	Mrs TATIANA ANDONOVA	Guest of Mr Andonov
E 1	LADY ARMSTRONG OF ILMINSTER	Chairman, Ladies Committee
B 11	Mr COLIN BAKER	Finance Officer, E-AG
A 15	Mr GRAHAM COLE, CBE	Executive Committee; Formerly Government Relations Department, **GKN**
–	PRINCESS HELENA GAGARIN-MOUTAFIAN, MBE	Trustee, E-AG; Patron, Commonwealth Countries League
–	Mr JUSTIN GLASS	Director, E-AG
F 2	Mrs CATHERINE GLASS	Member of E-AG
A 4	SIR PHILIP GOODHART	Trustee, E-AG; Formerly Government Minister
D 3	Ms ANNE HODSON-PRESSINGER	Vice-Chairman, Ladies Committee
–	Mrs KATERINA JEFFREY	Ladies Committee
–	SHEIKH NEZAM KHAZAL	Member of E-AG
–	SHEIKHA SHENDA KHAZAL-AMERY	Ladies Committee; Sculptress
E 18	JACQUELINE, LADY KILLEARN	Vice-President, Ladies Committee
A 2	Dr UWE KITZINGER, CBE	Executive Committee, First President, Templeton College, Oxford
A 6	PROFESSOR ALAN LEE WILLIAMS, OBE	Executive Committee; Director, Atlantic Council of the UK
E 16	SIR JOHN OSBORN	Executive Committee, E-AG; Formerly UK Delegation to WEU
A 12	SIR NEVILLE TROTTER, DL	Executive Committee, E-AG; President, Northern Defence Industries; Chairman, British-American N.E. Chamber of Commerce
–	Mrs DOREEN WILLIS-BAILEY	Ladies Committee; Formerly American Embassy

MEMBERS and GUESTS

E 12	Mr DAVID ABRAHAMS	Member of E-AG; Political Consultant, Middle East Strategy
E 8	Ms MARIA ANDIPA	Member of E-AG; Maria Andipa Gallery
F 5	Mr N. H. G. ARMSTRONG-FLEMMING	Member of E-AG; Farmer; Businessman; Formerly: Director, Central Bank of Zambia; Consultant to IMF, World Bank, EU
G 16	Mr GEORGE O. BAILEY, Jr	Member of E-AG; Formerly Carnegie Council on Ethics and International Affairs, Washington DC
G 9	Mrs YVONNE BAILEY	Member of E-AG
G 17	Mr ROGER BARNES	Member of E-AG
E 3	SIR STEPHEN BARRETT, KCMG	Formerly HM Ambassador to Czechoslovakia and Poland; Formerly, Head British Interests Section, Iran
G 14	Mrs SUSIE BEHRMANN	Guest of Mr and Mrs Boulting
H 10	Miss ELIZABETH BIERI	Assistant to E-AG; CAPA intern
B 10	Mrs DIANA BLOTT	Member of E-AG
G 13	Mr PETER BOULTING	Member of E-AG
G 15	Mrs JAN BOULTING	Member of E-AG

2

Seat Place
Number

B 9	Mr PETER BRENT	Member of E-AG
B 6	Dr GORDON BROOKS	Member of E-AG; Head, EMIS Knowledge Based Systems
B 7	Ms LUCIA BUGITTI	Member of E-AG; Ente Nazionale Acli Istruzione Professionale - Christian Association of Italian Workers
E 15	Ms SYLVIE CAMERON	Guest of Mr Saint-Jacques
B 8	Dr WILLIAM CAREY	Member of E-AG; Doctor
C 2	Mr ROBERTO CARSI	Guest of Ms Jaudenes
B 19	Ms ROSEMARIE COCKAYNE	Member of E-AG; Artist
G 8	Mr DINU COLTOFEANU	Financial Services; Guest of Ms Prendeville
G 10	Mr RUTH COLTOFEANU	Head of Probation Service, Surrey; Guest of Ms Prendeville
-	Mrs JULIA COUCHMAN	Assistant to E-AG
F 19	Dr JULIAN CRITCHLOW	Member of E-AG; Solicitor, Fenwick Elliott
F 16	Mr BRIAN CROZIER	Member of E-AG; Author
F 6	Mrs JACQUELINE CROZIER	Member of E-AG
H 12	Miss JOANA DANINI	Assistant to E-AG; CAPA intern
B 2	Mr GARRY DE LA POMERAI	Member of E-AG
H 3	BARON DAVID DE PIRO	Member of E-AG Teacher
C 14	Mrs NORAH DENNEHY	BBC; Guest of Mrs Gordon-Walker
D 6	Mr DAVID DODD	Member of E-AG; Consultant, communications industry; formerly Chief Executive, Multinational Communications Group, Mergers and Acquisitions
F 3	Mr JACQUES MINETTE D'OULHAYE	Member of E-AG; Formerly Merrill Lynch
D 9	Mr FRANK EDWARDS, CBE	Member of E-AG; Formerly: Deputy Chairman and Chief Executive, Humphrews & Glasgow Ltd; Vice-President, China-Britain Trade Group
C 6	Ms SONIA ELDER	Member of E-AG; Committee, NATO Forum on Energy and Security
E 5	Dr HAROLD ELLOTSON	Director, The New Security Programme, Centre for Defence and International Security Studies
B 14	Mr PATRICK EMEK	Member of E-AG; Publisher; Teacher; Author 'The Philippines: A Different Reality'
C 8	Ms LINDA ETCHART	Commonwealth Secretariat; Lecturer, Anglia-Ruskin College, Cambridge; Guest of Mr Thackara
C 5	LIEUTENANT PETER EVANS, RN	Guest of Lt Polly McCowen
D 17	Mrs OLGA EVANS	Member of E-AG; Russian teacher
A 19	Mr HUGH FRASER	Son-in-law of the late Elma Dangerfield
A 18	Mrs GAY FRASER	Daughter of the late Elma Dangerfield
D 7	Mrs MARIVERE W. FURNEAUX	Member of E-AG; Barrister; Managing Director, Crown Yard Properties Ltd; Commission Liaison Officer, E.U.W.
H 13	Mr RAYMOND GEORGE	Assistant to E-AG; Interior decorator
C 16	Mrs VALERIE GORDON-WALKER	Member of E-AG; Formerly Executive Director, Head of Human Resources, WestLB
E 10	Dr G. P. GRETTON-WATSON	Member of E-AG; IEEE Computer Society
	Mrs CHARMIAN GRIFFITHS	Linguist; Travel Guide
D 8	Miss JANE GULLY	Member of E-AG; F.A.N.Y. (The Princess Royal's Volunteer Corps)
C 15	Mr MARK HALSEY	Member of E-AG; Barrister

233

Seat Place Number:		
A 16	GILL, DUCHESS OF HAMILTON	Guest of Dr Keet
C 13	MAJOR CARL HARRIS, RM	Guest of Lt Polly McCowen
H 4	Mr BRETT HAYWOOD	Guest of Mrs Griffiths
G 2	Mr JOHN HOLMAN	Military Commentators Circle
B 15	Ms LOUISA HUTCHINSON	Member of E-AG; Property Developer; Artist
F 8	Mrs PATRICIA IJAZ-UL-HAQUE	Member of E-AG
D 13	Mr DAVID ISAACS	Member of E-AG; Solicitor
D 5	Ms LUCY IVIMY	Conservative counsellor; Barrister; Formerly Stock Broker; Guest of Dr Critchlow
G 18	Mr MANS JACOBSEN	Member of E-AG; International Oil Pollution Compensation Fund
G 7	Mrs MARGARETA JACOBSEN	Member of E-AG
H 9	Mr GRAHAM JARVIS	Member of E-AG; Editor, Chartered Institute of Marketing's Technology Group; Media Services Consultant
C 7	Mr NICHOLAS JEFFREY	Member of E-AG; Company Director
A 17	Dr JOHN KEET	Mrs Dangerfield's doctor; Guest of Mr Glass
D 4	Mr PETER KENT, CMG	Member of E-AG; Chairman, Taiwan Action Committee; Vice Chairman, Asia Pacific Advisory Group; Adviser, Trade Partners, Asia-Pacific Advisers, Trade Consultants to Government; Chairman, Government Advisory Board for Taiwan
D 21	PRINCE MOHSIN ALI KHAN OF HYDERABAD	
D 15	Mr JACK LEE	Paradigm Redshift Limited; Guest of Mr Andonov
D 14	Ms RITA LEEK	Member of E-AG; Barrister
F 13	Ms SUSAN LLOYD	Member of E-AG
E 11	Mr JAMES LLOYD-DAVIES, OBE	Member of E-AG; Formerly R.A.F.
B 3	Mrs GLENYS LONGHURST	Member of E-AG
F 7	Mr CHARLES MACFARLANE	Member of E-AG; Formerly Executive Director, Alliances Licensing & Acquisitions, Proctor & Gamble Healthcare Global
F 14	Mrs JEAN MACFARLANE	Member of E-AG
F 18	Mr MALCOLM MACKINTOSH, CMG	Member of E-AG; Formerly, F.C.O. Senior Adviser, BZW
G 3	Mr SIEGI MANDELBAUM	Member of E-AG
G 19	Mr ROGER MANN	Member of E-AG; Emirates Bank International
G 20	Ms GLORIA JANE MARTIN	Member of E-AG; European Foundation; Heritage Foundation, Washington DC
G 21	Mr SYDNEY L. MAYER	Member of E-AG; Guest of Mr Mandelbaum
H 11	Mr DAVID McCLEOD	Threshers, purveyors of wine this evening
C 3	LIEUTENANT POLLY McCOWEN, RN	Member of E-AG
H 2	Ms MAGGIE McDOUGALL	Member of E-AG; Copy Editor
F 17	Mrs DULCIBEL McKENZIE	Member of E-AG; Barrister; Author; Artist
E 14	THE LORD MEREWORTH	Member of E-AG
B 1	Mrs A. MOLAVI	Member of E-AG
B 4	Mr AMOUR MTUNGO	Member of E-AG; Guest of Mrs Longhurst
E 9	Mr PHILIP NEWMAN	Member of E-AG; Accountant
G 4	Ms MAUREEN O'SULLIVAN	Member of E-AG

Seat Place Number		
E 6	Mr STEVEN PHILIPPSOHN	Member of E-AG; Partner, **Philippsohn Crawfords Berwald**, Solicitors to the E-AG
E 13	Mrs CHARLOTTE PHILIPPSOHN	Member of E-AG
B 12	Mr ADAM R. PITMAN	Graduate in International Relations
G 12	Ms MELANIE PRENDIVILLE	Member of E-G; Westminster Mortgages 2000
D 11	Mr MARK PREVEZER	Corporate Member of E-AG, **Marshall Ross and Prevezer**
G 6	Mr ALASTAIR RATTRAY	Member of E-AG; Guest of Mr Richardson
C 10	MICHÈLE, LADY RENOUF	Member of E-AG
G 5	Mr STEPHEN RICHARDSON	Member of E-AG; Director, SMAART People Ltd; Fellow, Institute of Chartered Accountants
G 11	Mr PAUL ROCHE	Member of E-AG; Solicitor
F 4	Mr ROY DELVILLE ROEBUCK	Member of E-AG; Barrister; Formerly MP, Journalist
B 13	Mr MATTHEW ROSE	Member of E-AG; Spacesearch Ltd
A 3	Mrs ELIZABETH RUTHERFORD	Member of E-AG; Guest of Sir Philip Goodhart
H 8	Mr STEPHEN SCHICK	Member of E-AG; London Europe Society
H 1	SECURITY OFFICER for DAVID BLUNKETT	
B 18	Mr DAVID SELVES	Member of E-AG; Novelist; Treasurer, London Press Association; S.H.I.E.L.D.
F 11	Ms TERRY SHEEN	Member of E-AG; CAPA Educational Programmes Abroad
F 10	Mr MICHAEL SHILLABEER, RVM	Member of E-AG; Royal Protection Officer
B 20	Mr DEREK SHRUBB	Formerly Shell senior Executive; Guest of Mrs McGrath *(not present)*
B 17	Mrs MONICA SHRUBB	Guest of Mrs McGrath *(not present)*
A 1	Mrs ANNE SIEVE	Chairman, Poole United Nations Association; Guest of Dr Kitzinger
E 7	Mr RAY SNOW	Member of E-AG; Law Lecturer
C 9	Mr TIMOTHY SPANGLER	Member of E-AG; Chair, Republicans Abroad (UK); Trustee, Richmond University; Partner, Investment Funds Group
C 12	Mrs SPANGLER	Member of E-AG
G 22	Mrs PAT SPEIGHT	Member of E-AG; Military Commentators Circle
C 11	Mr PIETRO STRADA	Guest of Mr Jeffrey
F 12	Mr HUGH STEWART	Member of E-AG; Managing Director, Joseph Miller & Sons
C 4	Mr JAMES THACKARA	Member of E-AG; Author of *America's Children* and *The Book of Kings*
F 9	Ms SHAHNAZ TIDY	Member of E-AG; Conservative Middle East Cultural Group
D 10	Mr BRIAN TOMES	Managing Director, Chanadon Publications
D 12	Ms CLAIRE TURNER	Member of E-AG
B 5	Mrs MEGAN WARNE	Member of E-AG; European Movement; Atlantic Council; Teacher - specialist area: Citizenship
B 16	Mr GWILYM WARNE	Guest of Mrs Warne
F 15	Mr L. COLIN WEBBER	Member of E-AG; Vice-President, The Victoria League
F 20	Mrs PATRICIA WHEATLEY-BURT	Member of E-AG; Principal Consultant, Trainer and Coach; Trafalgar - The People Business Limited
H 5	Mrs JOYCE WISCHOFF	Member of E-AG; Ironique Ltd; Journalist

5

Seat Place Number:

C 17 CAPTAIN DALE WORTHINGTON, RFA Royal Fleet Auxiliary; Guest of Lady Armstrong

G 1 Mrs V WRAY Member of E-AG

The DINNER SEATING PLANS CAN BE FOUND AT THE BACK OF THIS DELEGATE LIST

A Curriculum Vitae of DAVID BLUNKETT MP can be found on Page 11

*****

FOR YOUR DIARY
Winter/Spring 2006 - Confirmed events

Tuesday, 21 February 2006	GENERAL SIR GARRY JOHNSON, KCB, OBE, MC
	On: 'Security Challenges posed by the Russian Near-Abroad'
	Dinner-Debate: St Ermin's Hotel
Monday 27 March	GEORGE OSBORNE, MP
	Shadow Chancellor of the Exchequer
	On: 'What fillip is needed for the Economy?'
	(provisional title)
	Dinner-Debate: St Ermin's Hotel
Friday 12 May	BARONESS PARK OF MONMOUTH
	On: 'What next for Zimbabwe?'
	Luncheon-Debate: A leading London Club

E-AG Debating Conventions

After dinner and when the Guest Speaker has finished, the Chairman will invite Members and their guests to contribute to a general discussion.

The Chairman will choose the contributors in turn from among those with their hands up.

Contributors are expected to speak with civility and toleration and without causing gratuitous offence either to the Speaker or to the company in general.

They should not make statements but pose questions relevant to the subject under discussion.

They should address their questions to the Chairman, not to the Speaker, and should be concise.

Normally no contributor may speak twice.

MY FLYING CIRCUS, an advance copy of the memoirs of Richard Leven the World War Two bomber pilot who flew a record number of daylight missions. This book is to be published by Messrs Chanadon Publications, which has an affiliation with the E-AG. Brian Tomes of Chanadon, who is here this evening, can answer questions.

THE FEVER OF DISCOVERY by Lady Body is the story of Matthew Flinders, who gave Australia her name. This book in paperback form will be also distributed by Chanadon.

****

THE NATO FORUM ON ENERGY SECURITY at the Marriott Hotel in Prague from the 22-24 of February will bring businesses together with political leaders, NATO Officials and technical experts to discuss emerging threats and the use and development of new Energy solutions. Registration forms are available tonight.

Dr Harold Ellotson, Director of The New Security Programme, hosts the NATO Forum on Energy Security Is present this evening. Questions concerning this forum can also be put to Sonja Kane. Her contact details are: New Security Program, Tel: +44 207 431 8751,mobile: +44(07984 692230).www.energy-security.org, email: skane@sentinelprogrammes.

Among the speakers who have confirmed their involvement are: Prime Minister, Jiri Paroubek, Prime Minister of the Czech Republic; Prime Minister Yuriy Yekhanurov, new Prime Minister of Ukraine; Javier Solana, Head of Common and Foreign Security Policy, EU; General James Jones, Supreme Allied Commander Europe; James Woolsey, former Director, US Central Intelligence Agency; Richard Pearle, Resident Fellow, American Enterprise Institute.; Dr. Wilfred Czernie, Executive Vice President, EON Ruhrgas; Dr. Chris Donnelly, Advisor to the UK Secretary of Defence; Ibrahim Khazar , Leading Officer of Security Affairs, Ministry of Foreign Affairs Azerbaijan; and Karen Harbert, US Assistant Secretary of Energy for Policy and International Affairs among many others.

E-AG GIFTWARE

TIES (£10.50), PENS (Price £2.50) CALCULATORS (£3.00)

THE INTERNET

Visit the Group on www . eag . org . uk.
For IT advice, contact **Graham Jarvis**.

JOLLY HOTEL
ST ERMIN'S

St. Ermin was a 6th century Welshman, who settled in Brittany, France and founded two monasteries. When Henry V11, who was also Welsh, was nearly shipwrecked off that coast, he became convinced that it was only the intervention of the Saint that had named him. He gave thanks by building a chapel on the site of the present hotel in 1496. There was also a nunnery in the Chapel. In the basement of the hotel can still be seen the tiny cells where the nuns lived and prayed. It became a hotel at the turn of the Twentieth century.

JOLLY HOTELS – The leading Italian Hotel chain has 47 hotels throughout the world. A reduction in the room charges for those wishing to stay is on offer to E-AG delegates. For details, contact the Banqueting Department of the hotel on Tel No. 020-7222-7898

ON THE MENU TONIGHT:

Red mullet fillet with green pea, pomme parisienne and champagne sauce Crème caramel

ELMA DANGERFIELD CBE
October 11 1907 - January 22 2006

Elma Dangerfield was a daughter of Empire, both as to her background and her social attitudes. She often could seem like a force of nature. Pertinacious, single-minded, formidable, she would take 'No' for an answer only when it was a declamation issuing from her own lips. Into her ninth decade, she made a point of going out on the town every single night. To those permitted to enter her inner sanctum, she was generosity itself, not so much in a financial sense - material matters were rarely uppermost in her mind - but with advice and help. As a Founder and Hon. Director for 51 years of the European-Atlantic Group and for 32 years of the Byron Society, Elma Dangerfield cut a great dash in the influential political and academic circles she so admired.

Born in Liverpool, much of Elma's childhood was spent in the Far East. She spoke fondly of her *Amar*, or Nanny, in Manila. Her father was connected with the Insurance firm of Jardines and a doyen of the Hong Kong Stock Exchange. It was said that when a financial crisis threatened the savings of investors, he all but bankrupted himself in honouring obligations that were not strictly speaking his. In early adulthood, Elma stayed with her Uncle, Sir Thomas Birkett, one of whose family seats was at 'Beldornie', a vast mansion in the village of Glass, Scotland. A cousin was the Lord Birkett of legal lore; Elma described an episode in which she saw him bring a coffin into court and lie down in it, his forensic point backed up by a showmanship that was much to her taste.

The societal whirl into which Elma plunged - her husband, Captain Edward Dangerfield, complained that he needed to get back to his desk at the Admiralty for a rest, after a weekend with Elma - was far from gadfly. 'Ted' was a personal friend and fellow officer on *HMS Hawking* of the Duke of Kent, who once told Dangerfield not to believe a word appearing in print about the Royals. Edward Dangerfield died of phlebitis in 1941, a tragedy for Elma and her only daughter, Gay, aged 12 years, and damaging for the war effort: he had been in the process of commissioning *HMS Dido*.

Elma always moved in the smartest of sets, though rarely stooped to gossip about celebrities of the day. She did once characterise the Duchess of Argyll by her way of never passing a mirror without stopping. Elma herself, tiny in stature, captivating - to judge by her numerous male admirers, so often either Polish, or famous - would not give a thought to her appearance after having daubed on make-up. In wartime, she had a liaison job at the Admiralty, and with MI9 (a branch of the Intelligence Services), and the Ministry of Information. She was involved behind the scenes with delegations from Eastern Europe. Her researches and contacts led her write '*Beyond the Urals*', with a preface by Rebecca West, a chilling insight into of what befell deportees and dissidents in the hands of the Communists. Her articles in *The Nineteenth Century and After* were among the first articles that alerted a wider public to the extermination by the Nazis of the gypsies and the Jews.

9

Elma's friendship with Sir Edward Hulton resulted in contributions to *Picture Post*; her editorship later of *Whitehall News* and then *European-Atlantic Review* with the Earl of Bessborough, Sir Edward Beddington-Behrens and Lord Leyton among others drew her to subjects so diverse that, in one article, she even explored the unconscionable way that the flower of British maidenhood was inclined to fall headlong into the matrimonial embrace of foreigners. Behind suchlike preoccupations was a concern for the future of Europe and in particular the need to endorse the power of the Council of Europe.

Elma stood for Parliament as a Liberal on two occasions but it was behind the scenes in which she found her metier. Her view was that Europe and America needed more institutions in place as amicable meeting grounds for Parliamentarians and opinion-shapers from both sides of the Atlantic. This led her to form with her colleagues, in 1954, the European-Atlantic Group. Lord Layton had been instrumental in inviting American and Canadian Senators and Congressmen to debate with European Members of Parliament in Strasburg, and suggested to Elma that she should start a group in London with leading Representatives of all the Anglo-European and Anglo-American and Canadian Societies in London. She had been assisting him over Human Rights issues in Strasburg, and on returning to London, Elma approached Lord Abinger and other Peers, MPs, Academics, Economists and Journalists. The Group was founded in London at Abinger's London House, with the first Meetings held at the Anglo-Belgian Club in Belgrave Square. Elma was a Director of the E-AG to the end of her life but was also a co-founding member of other Groups with comparable objectives, whose influence is still felt today *viz* the British-Atlantic Group (forerunner to the Atlantic Council of the UK) and the Mid-Atlantic Group.

Elma's literary pursuits were as dear to her as those of her political career. Her first book was *'A Diary of the Forty-Five'* but thereafter she graduated to more literary themes in *'Byron and the Romantics in Switzerland'* (1978) and her play *'Mad Shelley'*. Elma re-founded the Byron Society in 1972 together with Dennis Walwyn Jones MC, and they remained partners until his death. The Society under her helm has been and still is an eclectic mix of 'Blue bloods' and notable academics. Its programme, devoted to every aspect of Byron's poetry and life, is a tribute both to Elma Dangerfield's interests. She was for many years editor of the *Byron Journal* and its reputation as a serious publication assisted in the rehabilitation of the poet's reputation.

The powerhouse that was the HQ of both societies, and the human dynamo that was Mrs Dangerfield, has been recorded under light disguise by Muriel Spark. A recital of the Presidents and Ministers and notables that have addressed the European-Atlantic Group over the years does scant justice to the pertinacity with which Elma so often secured their attendance. Sheikh Yamani, in the early 1970's when his oil cartel held the Western World to ransom over petrol prices, wished to bow out of his engagement as a Speaker. "If you do not come, it will be an INSULT to this country!" he was informed, before he capitulated to the grimmest Dangerfield *coup de grace*, delivered in a quiet, deadly tone: "…And the PALACE will have to be told!"

Elma Dangerfield was appointed OBE after the Group mounted the 10th anniversary celebration of the founding of NATO at Guildhall; the Duke of Edinburgh, who attended as a Guest of Honour again at the 30th anniversary, replied to the question, "What do you need to do to have a place in the roped-off enclosure?" by saying: "You have to know Mrs Dangerfield!" Elma was elevated to CBE when in her nineties for Services to International Relations. In 2000, she was given a *European Woman of the Year* award.

Many are those who feel that their lives are immeasurably enriched by knowing her.

Justin Glass

DAVID BLUNKETT MP

Born in Sheffield, South Yorkshire, he grew up in poverty after his father was killed following an industrial accident when Blunkett was twelve years old. (The elder Blunkett, a foreman, fell into a vat of boiling water on the job at the East Midlands Gas Board and died a month later. The company refused to pay compensation for two years because he was working past retirement age.) Blind since birth, and educated at schools for the blind in Sheffield and Shrewsbury, Blunkett's chances in life seemed limited. Following his father's death, he was sent on assessment to the School for the Blind in Worcester, West Midlands - where he failed to gain entry. His failed assessment is said to be partly deliberate, due to his rebellious nature and dislike of public schools. However, he later attended the Royal National College for the Blind in Hereford. Indeed, he was apparently told at school that one of his few options in life was to become a lathe operator. Nevertheless, he won a place at the University of Sheffield, where one of his lecturers was Bernard Crick, and went on to enter local politics immediately on graduation. He worked as a clerk typist between 1967 and 1969, and as a lecturer and tutor in industrial relations and politics between 1973 and 1981.

Blunkett became the youngest-ever councillor on Sheffield City Council being elected in 1970 at the age of 22, whilst pursuing a career as a teacher. He served on Sheffield City Council from 1970 to 1988, being Leader of the Council from 1980 to 1987, and on South Yorkshire County Council from 1973 to 1977. He became well-known as a figure on the soft left of the party whilst serving for seven years as the council's leader during the 1980s, and was elected to the Labour Party's National Executive Committee.

At the 1987 general election he was elected MP for Sheffield Brightside. He became a party spokesman on local government, joined the shadow cabinet in 1992 as Shadow Health Secretary, and became Shadow Education Secretary in 1994. Combining reforming zeal with social conservatism, he became a favourite of new party leader Tony Blair.

As Education Secretary

After Labour's landslide victory in the 1997 general election, he became the UK's first blind cabinet minister as Secretary of State for Education and Employment. The role of Education Secretary was a vital one in a government whose Prime Minister had in 1996 described his priorities as "education, education, education", and which had made reductions in school class sizes a key pledge. In the event it was higher education that proved to be the most controversial issue for Blunkett, as he moved towards the imposition of tuition fees at public universities which had previously been free.

As Home Secretary

At the start of the Labour government's second term in 2001, Blunkett was promoted to become Home Secretary, a long-term ambition of his. Observers saw him as a leading rival to Chancellor of the Exchequer Gordon Brown's hopes to succeed Blair as the next Labour party leader and potential Prime Minister.[1]

Appearing to be tough on immigration and asylum was a central issue for Blunkett during his time at the Home Office. In December 2001, he controversially called for immigrants to develop a greater "sense of belonging" to Britain. In April 2002, he proposed new powers which he claimed would curb illegal immigration and unfounded claims for political asylum.

The European Atlantic Group Brochure

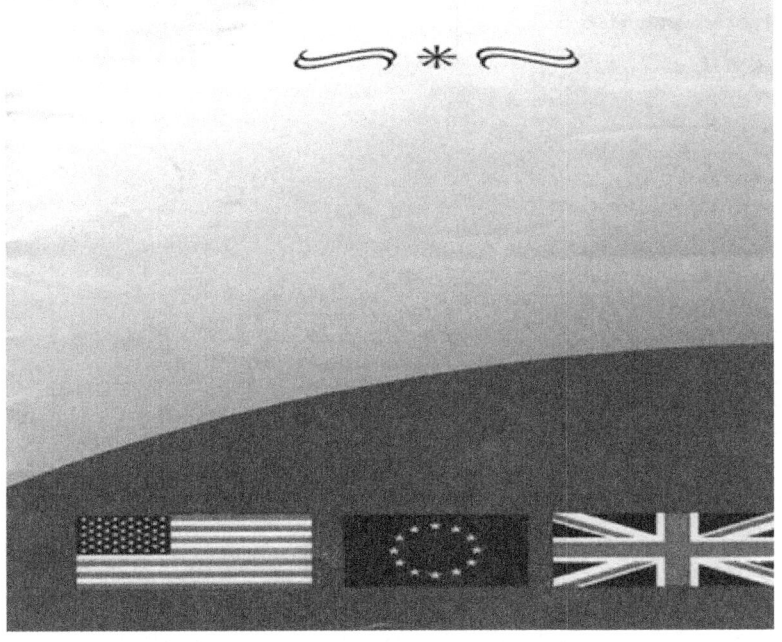

Lord Dykes, President of the E-AG from 2007 to 2009, chairing the E-AG at the Naval and Military Club.

The EUROPEAN-ATLANTIC GROUP, a non-aligned, all party, registered charity founded in 1954, is renowned as one of the foremost platforms for high level interaction in the field of international relations.

European-Atlantic Group (E-AG) dinner- and luncheon-debates are a fixture in the London social scene. The intractability of some issues has been no bar to civilised and perceptive discussions in surroundings such as the Palace of Westminster, premier London clubs and, on occasion, with banquets at Guildhall and the Banqueting House.

There is a variety of fayre on offer for a group whose thousand members include diplomats, parliamentarians, captains of industry and the informed and interested public. Few matters of moment in Europe or America can remain untouched by the wider world of politics and countries such as Afghanistan, Burma, China and Nigeria have lately been the subjects of far reaching group debate and analysis. The list of E-AG speakers recently has been graced by senior royalty, the former presidents of Lithuania and Zambia, all successive ambassadors of America, China and Russia, ministers of state, shadow ministers, the head of MI5, and the heads of our armed forces… At one event, twenty

Lady Symons awarding the Elma Dangerfield Prize to John Spencer in the Savile Club for his seminal work *Hitler and the King*

former members of Congress spoke in Parliament to the E-AG. Sir Christopher Gent of Vodafone fame and Hugo Dixon of Breakingviews.com, which has articles heavily syndicated throughout Europe, were forthright on the economy and signposted how the UK economy should recover even before the words 'credit' and 'crunch' were linked in un-heavenly embrace. John Lloyd spoke at a conference on *Freedom of expression and the media*. Events are held almost monthly.

H.E. Dr Kenneth Kaunda President of Zambia for 27 years, with E-AG Vice-Chairman, Geoffrey Clifton Brown MP.

A focus of the E-AG is on advocating solutions to global problems, where this falls within its reach, and not just in their exposition. These can be reflected in E-AG discussions, the E-AG journal or in E-AG papers. Texts of speeches – and debates when 'on-the-record' – on the website are a valuable tool for practitioners and students. Delegations have represented the group in Brussels and Washington. An annual book prize in the

President Vytautas Landsbergis of Lithuania with Julia Couchman at the Oxford and Cambridge Club.

name of the late Hon Director, Elma Dangerfield CBE, has provided useful footnotes to recent history, as does our affiliate publishing arm, New European Publications. The newsletter furthers a sense of community and continuity in the group.

The E-AG was the brainchild of Mrs Dangerfield, a lady so redoubtable that her obituary in The Times in 2003 could describe her as taking 'No' for an answer only when it issued from her own lips! Many have been the personalities who forged the group in the mould it enjoys today. The founders, including The Rt Hon Lord Abinger and The Lord Layton CH CBE, saw in it a means of facilitating contacts between Congressmen and Senators visiting the UK and the Council of Europe.

The roster of E-AG Presidents have included The Lord Layton CH CBE, The Rt Hon Earl of Listowel, Sir Geoffrey de Freitas KCMG MP and, since the 1990s, The Earl of Bessborough DL, Sir Frank Roberts GCMG GCVO, The Rt Hon Lord Rippon of Hexham QC, The Lord Dahrendorf, Lord Judd, The Earl of Limerick KBE, The Viscount Montgomery of Alamein CMG CBE, Sir Michael Burton KCVO CMG, The Baroness Hooper CMG, Lord Dykes and the Rt Hon Baroness Symons of Vernam Dean.

The future might be our oyster but such pearls as may be nurtured depend on the support of those who actively care – perspectives can vary – about issues such as sustainable development and ecology or Europe or our relationship with America, and the plethora of challenges confronting all of us. The E-AG is 'broad church' but some members may feel it more important that the interested public has a say in the conduct of political affairs rather than the uninterested public having a vote. The *speaking of truth to power* would be one of the ultimate hopes of the E-AG.

The Rt Hon Margaret Beckett addressing the E-AG at the Caledonian Club, with Lord Dykes.

We welcome – more than welcome – everyone who can contribute to and help with our work. For further details, please contact:

The Director
European-Atlantic Group
4 St Pauls Way
London N3 2PP

Tel: +44 20 8632 9253
Fax: +44 20 8343 3532

info@eag.org.uk
www.eag.org.uk

Index

Abinger, James the Rt. Hon. Lord, 131, 135, 138, 148, 170, 176
Allen, Meg, 13, 87
Ambassador of the Philippines and Thailand, the, 175
American Ambassador to NATO, the, 176
Amery-Khazal, Sheikha Shenda, 30, 96, 99, 225
Andonov, Boris, 91
Andrew, HRH Prince, 60, 61, 62, 216, 223, 224, 225, 226, 227, 229
Anyaoko, Chief, 48
Argyll, Duchess of, 36, 169
Arkell, Christopher, 62, 94, 223, 227, 229
Ashdown, Paddy Sir, 66
Astor, Nancy, 21
Atholl, Duchess of, 136, 161
Aung Din, Bo, 24
Ayres, Sonia, 106
Aza Arias, Alberto H.E.Don, 56
Baker, Colin, 87
Bangeman, Martin, 46
Bardens, Dennis, 100, 114
Baxter, Sandi, 87
Beckett, Margaret the Rt. Hon., 69
Beddington-Behrens, Edward Sir, 159, 170
Ben, George, 57
Bennett, Frederick Sir, 70

Bernard, Daniel, 43, 47
Bernstorff, Count, 58
Bessborough, Lord, 57, 90, 107, 108, 119, 132, 134, 138, 146, 151, 152, 154, 170
Bevan, Ernest, 71
Bill, David Lt-Gen CB, 224
Birdwood, Lord, 138, 152, 175
Birkett, Elma, 168
Birkett, Henry, 160, 165, 171
Birkett, Lord, 169
Birkett, Thomas Sir, 168
Blunkett, David, 40, 65
Bolting, Jan, 59
Bonham Carter, Violet Lady, 149, 175
Boothby, Robert Sir KBE MP, 143
Boothroyd, Betty the Rt. Hon. MP, 99
Boris, King of Bulgaria, 26
Bossom, Alfred Sir, 61, 176
Bossom, Clive the Hon. Sir, 61, 103, 105, 224
Bourgan, Luc, 23
Bouverat, Carmen, 82
Bradley, Harriet, 221
Bradley, John, 62, 221
Brammall, Lord, 95
Brittan, Leon the Rt. Hon. Sir PC QC, 46, 51
Browne, Dominick the Hon., 93
Browne, Terence, 156
Buck, Anthony Sir, 29, 72

Buck, Bienvenida, 72
Bullock, Alan, 119
Burger, William, 25
Burke, Edmund, 7
Burton, Lady, 62
Burton, Michael Sir, GCMG, GCVO, 14, 61, 94, 95
Bush, President, 73
Byron, Lord, 98, 106, 107, 173
Caesar, Augustus, 113
Cahen, Alfred, 120
Cahill, Kevin, 54, 226
Campora, Mario, H.E. Dr, 12
Carr, Anthony Major, 176
Carrington, the Rt. Hon. KG CH KCMG MC, 53, 60, 96
Carter, Jimmy President, 143
Cartledge, Bryan Sir KCMG, 47
Caruana, Peter the Hon. P, 74
Carver, Michael, 119
Chalfont, the Rt. Hon. Lord OBE MC PC, 51, 88, 119, 150
Chalker, Lady, 161
Chamberlain, Carolyn, 46
Chamberlain, Neville Sir, 70
Chehinya, Lana, 225
Churchill, Randolph, 37
Churchill, Winston, 26, 30, 62, 67, 119, 120
Clarke, Kenneth, 40
Clarke, Wesley, 49
Clifton Brown, Geoffrey Sir MP, 6, 14, 20, 21, 94
Cobbold, Hermione, 109
Cobbold, Lord, 109
Cohen, Ronald Sir, 40
Colcraine, Lord, 176
Cole, Graham, 87
Coleman, John, 113, 114

College, Neil, 23
Colyton, Lord, 155
Commissioners of the United Kingdom, the, 176
Commonwealth High Commissioners, the, 176
Constable, John, 48
Cook, Frank MP, 15
Cook, William Sir, 176
Couchman, Julia, 17, 21, 30, 69, 80, 82, 95, 142, 157
Crawley, James Lt-Colonel OBE, 11, 12
Critchlow, Julian Dr, 63, 94, 97, 225
Curtin, Tom, 16
D'Erlanger, Leo, 159
Dahrendorf, Ralph, Lord KBE FBA, 20, 73, 92, 119
Dali Lama, the, 71
Dangerfield, Edward Lt. Cdr., 136, 140, 169
Dangerfield, Elma CBE, 5, 35, 81, 85, 107, 132, 158, 165, 168, 216, 230
David, Simon, 89
de Bessenyey, Countess, 90
de Cuellar, Mr, 31
de Freitas, Geoffrey Sir, 24, 150, 176
de Gaulle, President, 150
de L'Isle, the Rt. Hon Viscount, 143
de la Billiere, Peter General Sir, 97
De La Morena, Felipe H.E. Don, 28
de Marenches, Count, 119
Dilks, David Prof., 28

Dodds-Parker, Douglas Sir MP, 150
Domingo, Placido, 104
Dorril, Stephen, 36
Downing, Barry, 165
Dreyfuss, Christopher, 58
Duchêne, François, 119
Duchene, Pierre, 73
Duke of York, HRH the, 59, 61, 163, 222
Dunkel, Arthur, 24, 25
Duroselle, Jean-Baptise, 119
Dutt, Krishan LRPS, 17
Dykes, Lord, 48, 63, 221
Eban, Abba, 15, 47
Edelman, Maurice MP, 154
Eden, PM, 64
Edwards, John MP, 175
Eisenhower, President, 64
Elliott, Baroness, 161
Ellis, Hugh Sir, 176
Emek, Patrick, 12, 93
Fielding, Fenella, 104
Fokine, Yuri H.E. Mr, 65
Fookes, Jane MP, 161
Foot, Michael the Rt. Hon., 37, 107, 119, 173
Forrest-Miquel, Olivia, 37
Foyle, Christina, 161
Fraser, Gay, 173
Frey, Lou the Hon., 14
Frith, Royce, the Hon. QC, 17, 56
Fry, Elizabeth, 100
Fu Ying, H.E. Mrs, 71
Furmanovicious, Darius, 106
Gagarin-Moutafian, Helena Princess, 99, 162
Gale, Richard General Sir, 150, 176

Galloway, George MP, 59
Galvin, John General, 52, 56
Genscher, Herr, 74
George VI, King, 46
George, HRH Prince, Duke of Kent KG KT GCMG GCVO, 137, 139, 140, 144
George, Raymond, 93
Gibb, Claud Sir, 159, 176
Gilbert, Martin, 119, 120
Gladstone, David, 58
Glass, Catherine, 37, 46, 93, 98, 216, 228
Glass, Justin, 5, 9, 13, 39, 54, 83, 85, 107, 216, 228
Goering, Herman, 26
Goodall, David Sir GCMG, 71
Goodhart, Phillip Sir, 17, 63
Goold-Adams, Richard, 176
Gorbachev, President, 22
Gore-Booth, David Sir, 28
Gore-Booth, Paul Sir, 67
Gottlieb, Mili, 66
Goulden, John Sir, 23
Gouriet, John, 68, 229
Graham, Katherine, 161
Grantchester, the Lord, 156
Griffiths, David, 72, 147, 148
Griffiths, Eldon Sir MP, 12, 17, 24
Grove, Dr, 137
Gruenther, Alfred General, 145
Guise, George, 69
Gussago, Maria Guissipina, 4, 108, 226
Guthrie, Charles Sir, later Lord, 51, 59
Hahn, Kurt, 26
Hall-Spencer, John, 26, 27
Hallstein, Walter Prof, 153

Hamilton of Epsom, the Rt. Hon. Lord, 17, 95, 97, 220, 221
Haseler, Stephen Prof., 64
Hassan, HRH Prince, 22, 29, 30
Hayek, Friedrich, 53
Heath, Edward the Rt. Hon. MP, 17, 145, 149
Henty, G.A., 49
Heraclites, 56
Heseltine, Michael, 120
Hibbert, Reginald (Reggy) Sir, 92, 119
High Commissionaire of Pakistan, the, 175
Hitler, Adolf, 26, 27, 70, 140
Hodson-Pressinger, Anne, 90, 225
Hoffman, Everett, 21, 95
Hooper, Baroness CMG, 29
Hooper, Lady, 94
Hope, Peter, 175
Horne, Alistair, 119
Horrabin, Ian Sir MP, 176
Howard, Michael, 222
Hulton, Edward Sir, 170
Hurd, Douglas the Rt. Hon. CBE MP, 7, 51
Hussein, King, 22
Hussein, Saddam, 14, 30
Hutchinson, James Sir, 154
Hutchinson, Louisa, 70
Indian Commissioner-General for Economic Affairs, the, 175
Iranian Charge d'Affaires, the, 175
Ireland, Cliff, 90
Irvine, Lord, 75
Ismay, Lord, 145
Jackson, Mark Captain, 49, 50

Jackson, Mark General Sir GCB CBE DSO ADC, 48
Jackson, Mike General Sir GCB CBE DSO ADC, 48, 91, 97, 223
Japanese First Secretary, the, 175
Jarvis, Graham, 93
Jeffrey, Katerina, 62
Johnson, Russell Lord, 142
Johnston, Eric, 175
Johnstone, Russell, 24
Jones, Aubrey the Rt. Hon. MP, 154
Joyal, Paul, 62, 227
Judd, Lord, 38, 94, 95, 97, 98
Judith, Countess of Listowel, 119
Jure, Jorge Luis H.E., 103
Kaunda, Kenneth Dr, 18, 20, 21, 22, 46, 88, 110, 216
Kazuba, Richard, 165
Kazuka, Martin Dr, 20
Keeble, Curtis Sir GCMG, 43, 44, 119
Kelly, David Sir, 145, 159, 176
Kelly, Lady, 176
Kelly, Sue, 11
Khan, Ajmal Chief, 24, 51, 66, 68, 223, 229
Khayyam, Omar, 97
Khomeini, Ayatollah, 69
Khrushchev, 44
Killearn, Jacqueline, Lady, 21, 38, 89, 99, 100, 108
Kimberlee, 82
King-Hall, Stephen Cdr Sir, 138
Kinnock, Neil, 11, 12, 18
Kitchen, Geoffrey, 154
Kitchener, Lord, 100

Komorowski, Stanislaw H.E., 44
Lada-Grodzicka, Clarissa, 78
Lamb, Caroline Lady, 107
Landsbergis, Vytautas, 22, 23
Layton, Lord, 148
Layton, Lord CH CBE, 24, 131, 132, 135, 138, 148, 149, 150, 155, 170
Ledochowska, Elizabeth Countess, 105
Lee, Jennie Miss MP, 143
Leith, Barnaby the Hon., 163
Leno, Dan, 80
Leonidas, Seris, 81
Leven, Richard, 26
Lidderdale, Lady, 161
Limerick, Lord, 14, 71, 75, 76, 78, 94, 95, 111
Listowel, the Rt. Hon. Earl of, 148, 155, 159
Liverpool, Archbishop of, 143
London, Lady Mayoress of, 175
London, Lord of, 175
Londonderry, Lady, 58
Long, Jeffrey, 90
Longdon, Gilbert MP, 152
Lownie, Andrew, 26
Lowry, Mike Lt-Colonel MBE MC, 12
Luns, J.M.A.H., 52
Macauley, Rose, 136
Macdonald, Ramsay, 136
Macmillan, Dorothy Lady, 138
Macmillan, Harold, 145
MacRae, John Dr, 15
Maitland, Olga Lady, 58
Major, John, 46
Martin, Glora, 65
Marx, Karl, 15
Mathathir, Tan President, 53, 54
Maude, Francis the Rt. Hon Sir, 94
Maudling, Reginald the Rt. Hon. MP, 154
Maxwell, Robert, 28, 83
Mayhew, Patrick Sir, 43
Melville, James Sir MP, 136
Melville, Lady, 136
Melville, Mary, 40, 88, 136
Mereworth, Lord, 74, 163
Michael, Princess, 72
Monnet, Jean, 73, 119
Montagu Corry, David, 58
Montgomery of Alamein, Viscount CMG CBE, 17, 60, 107
Montgomery, David, 119
Montgomery, Lord, 33, 56, 92, 94, 223
Morris, Richard Sir, 16
Mosley, Max, 105
Mugabe, Robert, 22
Munster, Countess of, 44
Myrdal, Karl Gunnar, 53
Nagy, Imre, 120, 144
Napoleon, 52
Nasser, President, 64
Netherlands, HRH the Prince of the, 146, 175
Newman, Cardinal, 45
Nezam, Sheikh, 96
Nichols, Beverley, 134
Norstad, Lauris General, 176
Nureyev, 165
O'Connor, Murphy Cardinal, 41
O'Conor Donelan, Joseph, 140
O'Conor Donelan, Mrs, 140
Ogilvy, Angus the Hon., 136

Ogun, Dele, 24
Olorenshaw, Daphne, 78, 79
Onslow, Lord, 40, 58
Oppenheimer, Peter, 35
Orwell, George, 136
Osborn, John Sir, 94
Oswald, Julian Admiral Sir GCB, 46, 75, 92, 94, 97, 98
Oswald, Roni Lady, 98
Page, Jane, 78
Pakenham, Lord, 159
Pankin, Boris H.E. Mr, 99, 100
Papworth, John Rev, 59
Pattie, Geoffrey Sir, 67, 90
Peres, Shimon the Hon. MK, 47, 48, 216
Philippsohn, Steven, 87
Philliip, H.R.H. the Prince Duke of Edinburgh, 38, 42, 146, 172, 175
Pilsudski, Rowmund, 136
Pomian, Jas, 45
Portillo, Michael the Rt. Hon., 45
Prendergast, Kieran Sir, 106
President of the Carnegie Endowment for International Peace, the, 176
Quinlan, Michael Sir GCB, 70
Radice, Lord, 41
Radulovitch, Monty, 171
Raeburn, Christopher, 104
Raikes, Victor Sir, 136
Ralston, Joseph General, 68
Rathbone, Eleanor, 136
Retinger, Joseph, 45
Richards, David General Lord, 51, 66
Rifkind, Malcolm the Rt. Hon. Sir QC MP, 73

Rippon, Geoffrey the Rt. Hon. Lord of Hexham QC PC, 17, 20, 74, 87, 148
Roberts, Frank Sir GCMG GCVO, 43, 44, 70, 119, 120, 144, 148, 150, 176
Robson, Christopher, 120
Rogers, John Sir Bt, 148
Rosemary, 38, 81, 84
Rothenstein, John Sir, 154
Rous, Zeenat Hon Mrs, 62
Rumsfelt, Donald, 68
Runcie, Lord the Archbishop of Canterbury, 69, 70
Sahlgren, Klaus, 53
Sands, Harold Winthrop, 156
Sarasin, Pote, 175
Sassoon, Phillip Sir, 131
Schumann, Maurice, 150
Scott, Derek, 64
Scott, JB, 154
Segell, Glen Dr, 31
Seitz, Raymond H.E. the Hon., 55
Selves, David, 6
Sergant, Rene, 176
Seton Watson, Hugh Prof, 152
Sforza, Count, 65
Shaker, Mohammed H.E. Mr, 73
Shakespeare, William, 165
Sheen, Terry, 110
Shelley, 140
Sherfield, Lord, 17
Sherrin, Ned, 104
Shrimpton, Michael, 15
Shuckbergh, Evelyn Sir, 176
Sigall, Lilly, 103, 104, 106
Sigmon, Robert, 155
Simeon, King, 26

Slessor, John Sir, 175
Smith, Alan, 155, 156
Smith, Geoffrey, 156
Smith, Ian, 21
Smithers, Peter, 148
Snow, Lady, 15
Somerset, Duke of, 58
Spaak, Paul-Henri, 159
Spark, Muriel, 171
Stalin, Joseph, 71
Stanislavsky, A., 65
Stewart, Hugh, 10, 97
Stewart, Lady, 10
Story, Ronald Sir, 136
Supreme Allied Commander, the, 175
Symons, Lady, 27, 50, 62, 94, 221, 222, 224
Taylor, A.L. Lt., 22
Thatcher, Margaret PM, 18, 36, 67, 69, 71, 143
Thomas, Ivor, 136
Tiarks, Henry, 88, 132, 154
Todd, Vivenne, 112
Torphichen, Lady, 90
Trollope, 28
Trotter, Neville Sir, 94, 95, 99
Trump, Donald President, 52
Turkish Ambassador, the, 175
Tuthill, John, 67
Unwin, Brian Sir, 23
Unwin, Peter CMG, 29, 120

Varnden-Quick, John, 63, 226
Vlieland, Maxine, 78
von Habsberg, Otto, 14
von Richthofen, Herr, 74
Vorster, 21
Wade, Michael, 45, 109
Walker, FM, 165
Wall, Stephen Sir KCMG LVO, 50
Walwin Jones, Dennis MC, 98, 132, 134, 159, 160, 171
Watson, Alastair, 61
Waugh, Evelyn, 79
West, Rebecca Dame, 136, 144, 169
Westland, Augusta, 87
Westnedge, Anthony OBE, 90
Wilibrord of Northumbria, St, 162
Wilkinson, Ellen, 136
Williams, Shirley Lady, 79
Willis Bailey, Doreen, 62, 225
Windsor, Duke of, 140
Wörner, Manfred, 41
Wright, Oliver Sir, 12
Yamani, Ahmed Zaki Sheikh, 37, 172
Young, Oliver, 24
Younger, Kenneth the Rt. Hon. PC MP, 143
Zemyatin, Leonid H.E Mr, 57
Zogu, Leka King, 227
Zohra, Princess, 63, 222, 226